Displaced Person

By John Clellon Holmes

Novels

Go
The Horn
Get Home Free

Poetry

The Bowling Green Poems
Death Drag: Selected Poems
Dire Coasts

Essays & Memoirs

Nothing More to Declare
Visitor
Interior Geographies
Gone in October

Displaced Person

The Travel Essays

Selected Essays by John Clellon Holmes

Volume I

The University of Arkansas Press

Fayetteville   1987

DESIGNER: Chiquita Babb
TYPEFACE: Linotron 202 Granjon
TYPESETTER: G&S Typesetters, Inc.
PRINTER: Thomson-Shore, Inc.
BINDER: John H. Dekker & Sons, Inc.

The paper used in this publication meets the minimum re-
quirements of the American National Standard for Permanence of Paper for Printed Library Materials Z39.48-1984. ∞™

LIBRARY OF CONGRESS CATALOGING-IN-PUBLICATION DATA
Holmes, John Clellon, 1926–
     Displaced person.
     (Selected essays / by John Clellon Holmes ; v. 1)
     1. Holmes, John Clellon, 1926–   —Journeys.
2. Authors, American—20th century—Journeys.   I. Title.
II. Series: Holmes, John Clellon, 1926–   .   Essays.
Selections ; v. 1.
PS3558.03594A6 vol. 1   814'.54 s   87–5558
ISBN 0–938626–91–4   [814'.54]
ISBN 0–938626–92–2 (pbk.)

For Shirley—
Fellow Traveller,
Beloved Companion

.

Acknowledgments

from WALKING AWAY FROM THE WAR:

"Four: London: Games, People, Play," first published as "Exile's London" in *New Letters*, Spring 1978.

"Five: A Wake in the Streets of Paris," published as "An American Requiem in Paris" in *Venture*, April 1970.

"Six: Encounter with Myself in Munich," published as "Encounter in Munich" in *Playboy*, March 1972.

"Seven: Venice About Which Everything Has Been Written," published as "A Mirror of Venice" in *Travel & Camera*, September 1969; and as "Ezra Pound, the Hippies Land the Pigeon of St. Mark's" in *One Hundred Years of Ezra Pound*, The Limberlost Press, No. 16, 1986.

"Eight: Flesh and the Machine," first appeared as "Thanksgiving in Florence" in *Playboy*, November 1971.

"Nine: Awake in Rome," published as "Awake in Rome" in *Quarterly West*, 1978.

"Ten: See Naples and Live," first appeared in *Playboy*, June 1970.

ROCKS IN OUR BEDS published as "Rocks on Our Beds" in *Stony Hills*, Spring 1981. Published as part of the book *Gone in October*, Limberlost Press, 1985.

L.A. IN OUR SOULS published as "In Search of Los Angeles" in *Playboy*, May 1972.

Whenever I find myself growing grim about the mouth; whenever it is a damp, drizzly November in my soul; whenever I find myself involuntarily pausing before coffin warehouses, and bringing up the rear of every funeral I meet— then, I account it high time to get to sea as soon as I can.

—Melville

I have travelled a good deal in Concord; and everywhere, in shops, and offices, and fields, the inhabitants have appeared to me to be doing penance in a thousand remarkable ways.

—Thoreau

Contents

Displaced Person

Prefatory Note

This book—volume one of a proposed three-volume collection of non-fiction—deals with *Places,* and views them through the special lens of what D. H. Lawrence called "the Spirit of Place"—by which he meant not only the data of the senses as evoked by new locales and experiences, but the response of the entire sensibility to the look and feel and "mood" of what it confronts.

The *Places* here are a cultural region (New England) and its influence on some of its present-day writers, eight European cities and one American megalopolis seen in the flux of contemporary history, and a state of mind out of which certain indigenous aspects of our national character are explored.

Volume two will deal with *People,* and volume three with *Ideas.*

—John Clellon Holmes

ROCKS IN OUR BEDS

A Dark Valentine to New England *1981*

My heart is heavy as lead
because the blues have spread
rocks in my bed.
                        —*Duke Ellington*

Elective affinities, correspondences, analogies. Oh, New England, how you curse your scribblers with a double-view! The autumn twilight haunted by burnt August in the wood smoke; skeletal tree-shadows on virgin snow in the piercing clarity of winter-sun; the loosening loam and early budlets of hesitant, pastel spring; the summers, languid and abuzz and brief, tinged with the fore-knowledge of the red and yellow withering to come—in such seasonal places the senses are poised, keen, made avaricious by

3

the imminence of change. The imagination smoulders, flares, dies, only to flare again. And boys in attic rooms in redbrick factory towns, or in the kerosene kitchens of upland farms, or in sight of deep water in the Bostons and New Bedfords of the region, sit up late, alone, and one night start to write. New England, oldest and most homely of American places—it's what's fleeting and elusive in you that demands words! The centuries-old redbrick towns and upland farms remain, but the scribbling boys are stabbed by a premonition of their own mortality. Time, as inevitable as December, drives them on, and all too often away.

I was one of those ruminative boys, Jack Kerouac was another; Charles Olson, Robert Creeley, John Weiners, Larry Eigner—still others. New England's stony fields and twisting streets, which had bred the earliest American literature, bred us too. Later, we would decamp for the New Yorks, Mexico Cities, Friscos, and Londons of the vast and morally ambivalent world beyond, but New England, a mere postage stamp on the immense envelope of modern consciousness, was nevertheless stamped, uncancelled, on our imaginations. To the critics, we were all wanderers—the flotsam of cities, jazz, dope, and psychic anarchy. Actually, we were seeking to align the phantom vision and the factual reality of that double-view, and the taproot in us (what Lawrence called "the spirit of place") wouldn't pull. It had ensnarled itself in the inhospitable soil of Massachusetts, New Hampshire, Maine, and Connecticut. And it held.

On the banks of the flood-choked Pemigewasset River in Plymouth, New Hampshire, in 1937, I stood in muddy shoes, with a paperbagful of doughnuts just tonged out of the grease by our half-Algonquin cook, Dorothy, watching with awe as upwrenched trees sailed seaward, and the pilings of the bridge to Holderness stood stubborn and spanless in the boiling surge, and knew the dawning of a first awareness—this was a world-

4

in-time! Rushing heedlessly around us, into us, through us! And I had no words to deal with the perception, and thereby discovered the reality, and the necessity, of words. I ached to build pilings that would withstand the flood in me.

Downriver a few days later, beyond where the Pemigewasset flowed into the Merrimack, Kerouac watched those same trees quickeningly borne under the Moody Street Bridge in Lowell on their way to that most austere of seas, the North Atlantic, and perhaps first heard the dire *mwee-hee-hee* of Dr. Sax echo in the roar beneath his shoes. We would discover this eerie correspondence in our lives only years later in New York, up way past midnight, the river of traffic in the clashing street below roaring as loud as the converging rivers of our boyhood, and bringing the memory back to both of us in the same instant.

Oddly, though we were associated with New England all our writing-lives, both of us having written novels about it, Kerouac and I were outlanders there. Though we had both been born in Massachusetts (at opposite ends of the state), I had spent much of my childhood in New Jersey, California and Long Island, and Jack was of French Canadian stock, and was always dogged by a dark sense of foreignness. Yet we both felt New England in us, as if it were a mother-place, spectral with *déjà vu*. Through all his peregrinations, his many temporary homes, Jack longed for a cabin in the deep woods of New Hampshire, or for the cozy kitchens of Lowell. It was the one ghost-hope that never left him. For myself, after ten years of city-life had started to corrode my nerves, I instinctively moved to a ramshackle house in Connecticut, took to the saws and hammers, and made a home at last.

Once, during one of his spells of desperate spiritual homesickness, when the cabin-vision was upon him like a claw on his forehead, Jack wrote to me: "Oh, John, Alack, a John, John a dreams, I'll be Thoreau to your Emerson." Elective affinities a-

5

gain. Literature, like a gravestone-rubbing, laid over life until the shadow-image and the substance of the stone were one, words at once approximate to the granite that had endured and the person lying under it who hadn't, except as a name, a scrap of scripture, and the dates. The source of our awareness of time and eternity was in the handsawn clapboards that had withstood a hundred raging Novembers, and in the old bricks behind which all the Dickensian looms had long gone silent, and in the impersonal sea on which no whaler, trawler or merchantman had ever left a mark to indicate that they had set out, and somehow gotten back, and set out again, and one day not returned. We lived with this as we lived with the seasons. All voyages, like all youths, all summers, all vaulting hopes, end in the ambiguity of the Pequod stoven-in as much by Ahab as by Moby Dick.

Kerouac's immodest analogy between the Concord writers and ourselves was natural to the likes of us, though it was somewhat inaccurate. Like Emerson, he had a taste for the arcane and mystical; like Thoreau, I had an equal taste for logic and clarity. He was given to pithily-stated apothegms like Emerson. I tended to see things, Thoreau-like, in terms of irony. Like Emerson, Jack was notorious in his time, a freshet of hints that undammed other men. I sank quickly and quietly into an obscurity not unlike Thoreau's. Both of us, like them, eventually looked to the East. In our different ways, we were Transcendentalists. I beat out my exile in the suffocating cities, and became a countryman—a reasonably good carpenter, electrician and recluse. Jack never made it, and remained psychologically displaced and physically uprooted until it killed him. Both of us had a taste for the local, and for locality, but when we were together in New England, he and I, we never felt the need to speak of the place. We didn't enthuse over quaint houses, mittened winters, waterfront taverns, Scollay Square when it was sordid and exciting, brown doilied parlors, icy nosetips, furnace ashes on the stoops, hard cider with a prickle in it, the primitive content to be found in blazing fireplaces, the smell of damp books in plain stone libraries, April's uprush in the throat—it all just came back, the dust-covers on the furniture of these memories snatched off in an instant, and we knew we need not explain anything to each other about—well, all that.

But it was New England that spoke in *Doctor Sax,* where all the coagulated evil in the world gathers like a cosmic boil, and then bursts into a husk of doves. Equally, it was New England that drove my Old Man Molineaux (in *Get Home Free*) to struggle against his kedge anchor, hungering after wild places, only to collapse at the end, capitulant and secretly relieved, having experienced them all in his imagination anyway. In New England, speculation is no farther away than the woodpile; spiritual bliss comes to the swinger-of-birches.

So we were subtly different from Ginsberg or Burroughs or Corso in our crowd. We wore a sense of the past like a birthmark. Indians skulked our dreams. Guilt, like the evening cry of a loon over a sinister, fir-girt lake, guilt for the truths we had believed in and failed to find, encouraged in us a fatal premonitory sense. Still, I was privately proud of the name of the bad versifier that I bore, and Jack was pursued all his life by a feeling that an unknown heritage was his—but from whom? He never stopped trying to search out his enigmatic lineage. Allen (from New Jersey) and Bill (from St. Louis) and Gregory (from Lower New York) never felt this strong pull backwards, not alone to family, but to place, to continuum, to a tradition of mind constantly in need of freshening. Time was the ghost behind the woodwork for Jack and me, and in our inmost natures we believed, despite rapturous or desperate asseverations to the contrary, that he who fights time can only lose. We were Transcendentalists with hangovers—that was the difference. We had moral rocks in our beds.

We liked the great Russian novelists because of New England. We were no strangers to cramped rooms, cold streets, extremes of introspection. We were at home with Zen Koans and "dark nights of the soul" when they came to us, having read Emily Dickinson and William James. The ambiguities of puritan fervor and pagan fever entered us with Hawthorne, reaching an ultimate pitch in Herman Melville, an outsider in New England himself, in whose work language struggles to at once contain and release the intuitive knowledges that lie buried beneath all intellection.

The bed's a place for dreams, and rest, and love—a private place. But our beds were like New England's stony fields. You had to work hard before you could dream in them, much less hope. You piled the stones into fences, you dug and heaved and dragged at them in all weathers, raging, despairing, intent, all alone at the task, but always brooding on *more* than the task—because you knew the fences would outlast you. Kerouac played phantom baseball games in his upstairs room; I deployed armies of lead soldiers in battles as complex as Waterloo. But as we played them, we mused far beyond these callow games, and early on we both began to write away the psychological bruises of nights spent in those rocky beds. Robert Frost found in the day's toil out of doors the proper stuff for the evening's poems—but what austere and metaphysical bucolics they were! Melville found a fatal image in a fish. Just as Kerouac did in a milltown and its river, baldly deeming his account of it, *Faust Part Three*. And I saw in a reprobate old boozer all our secret hopes for heaven. We were religious men without a creed.

I could always drive a nail straight, and liked the same clean *thwack* in a line of poetry. Olson knew that a poem and a porch stood up for the same reasons. Creeley made poems like the earth makes gems, subjecting rare stuff to great pressure, and waiting a long time. Jack's litmus-paper consciousness recorded

8

the destiny, as well as the immediacy, of all sensations. Even our lyrical effusions, our vernal affirmations, were somehow autumnal too. Prodigality and thrift, excess and asceticism, hope and despair, warred not only in our world, but in our very natures. That was the New England view—commonplace and dooming as Eve's McIntosh, as mysterious as the sweet syrup prisoned in the winter-tree.

The restlessly speculative nature achieves no certainties, no home port. Thoreau moved from Walden Pond, Henry Beston from the Outermost House. Melville ended up on 26th Street in New York as obscure as Kerouac in Florida. For New Englanders handle fame badly. It never corresponds to the sort of spiritual eminence they're after. They look over their shoulders or down at their feet when praised, as if the praiser hadn't glimpsed what might be truly praiseworthy, and cheapens praise by easy praising. Suspicious of groups, movements and messiahs, the New England writer knows that below the fumy brain is the importunate heart, and below that the sap that spring draws up into the loins, and below that the dumb feet planted on rock, and beneath the rock—clay. It is a view that sees the human being as the fragile circuit between heaven and earth, life as a limbo-state, and literature the record of a passage-through—the continual dissolution of forms into other forms, the clearing of a field. I think that those of us, who were from New England and became associated with the so-called Beats, brought this subtly different double view to their concerns. Hindu *fakirs* lie on beds of nails, the spirit conquering matter itself. But we had abstract rocks in our beds, and our nights and our lives were troublous with their haulage. "Go moan for man," Kerouac said, and his work was just such an outcry and a lamentation. Olson's enormous construct, *Maximus,* glimpsed all the world and all of time in Gloucester, just as Thoreau had done in Concord. Creeley, like Emily Dickinson before him, was a miniaturist, a

9

diamond-cutter, but whole psychic worlds circled dangerously in his bitterly compacted prisms. My own work attempted to express a certain edge of fond skepticism about appearances, and a stubborn feeling for the heart that beats beneath our masquerades, which, as I've gotten older, seems the only part of wisdom on which I'll stand.

So, New England, you taught us to find the blessing in the curse you laid on us; you accustomed us to gales and sometimes perishing in them; you gave us a taste for things that are homely and well-made; you fashioned us into a peculiar breed— gloomy, speculative, always wrestling with that urgent poetry that only life-and-death-keyed people feel choking up in them, travelers whose wanderings are only circuitous routes of return.

Beyond the last league of the last sea is New Bedford again. Or the grave. Robert Lowell was heading for Back Bay when his life gave out. Jack's back in Lowell now. We New England writers of this time sold our wooden nutmegs to the world, and some of us have lived to see them prized as artifacts. Who knows? Perhaps that was the intention all along. To see the spirit in the meanest of things. For after the night, is light. Then dark again. But that new dark is *peopled,* and the field less rock-strewn than before.

WALKING AWAY
FROM THE WAR

A Journey   *1968–71*

Prologue

Almost twenty years ago, in the third year of Vietnam, my wife and I went to Europe. I had the bad habit of carrying the world on my shoulders in those days, and for the only time in my life, I think I was considering expatriation.

On the surface, the following account of that trip is an example of the sort of travel book American writers from Washington Irving to Paul Theroux have brought back so often from what used to be called "the essential European experience" that such books constitute a minor but respectable American literary genre. My record has all the travelling novelist's characteristic discoveries—the armchair Marco Polo's eerie sense of *déjà vu* when in places he has inhabited in his imagination for years, the involuntary gawking at pictures and buildings he thought he was too sophisticated to do more than notice, the barely repressed solemnity of literary pilgrimages to the graves and houses of the giants of his youth, his unwilling surrender to senses that seem peculiarly raw to the merest nuance of light and weather and taste; and above all, his helplessness before those wild swings of mood that overcome the stress-heightened sensibility—exultation suddenly doused by melancholy, pleasure turning Janus-like to irritability—in fact, everything that accompanies a journey whose real destination is inward. For most American journeys are Jamesian in their implications, and like it or not, know it or not, I was coping in myself with what James once called "the complex fate" of our nationality, and doing it, as he had done, in foreign places.

The book is also, inevitably, something of an historical memoir as well, and it cannot be separated from those long, stalemated, victory-less years in Southeast Asia, nor from the war-to-stop-the-war that threatened to upheave the streets of American cities with the worst civil strife in a hundred years, and possibly, just possibly, bring down the Republic itself.

All of this—dangerous, premonitory, bewildering—was in the air in 1967, and today I am surprised to see how faithfully this account reflects the reckless over-drinking and over-reacting and over-cerebrating of the period, even as the business of the day (in my case, wandering strange cities, looking for—?) went on. In any case, this is how one American tried to come to terms with his country in Europe, and failed, but came to terms with himself anyway, and came home.

It is not an exhaustive record of what happened on our trip, and the daily journal that I kept as we moved on is half again as long as the book. But we no longer experience contemporary life as narrative, and vivid moments, isolated in the flashbulb of powerful emotions, are all we have to show for a segment of time. This book is a collection of such moments, short "exemplary tales," all written out of a similar mood, in which the techniques of fiction are employed to intensify real events in the hope that what gets onto the page may at least suggest all that doesn't.

Everything in the book is true, and happened more or less as I describe it. Nothing has been altered, except a proper name or two. The title is meant to be understood in the same way we understand what a person means when he says: "I was in an accident, but I managed to walk away from it." Survival, not flight or apathy, is what is implied. It has always been my habit to map unknown cities with my feet, and my personal survival of that bad, mid-war year (not to mention the worse end-of-the-war years to come) began on the "walks"—aimless, indefatigable, and relentlessly introspective—that are recorded here.

ONE

Escape

There was the need to get away. Away from America. It had been coming on for a year or more, one's mood gradually darkening and thickening, like those ugly, swollen thunderheads that stifle summer over tornado country. The war in Vietnam, the war in the streets, the war in the American soul: one hated caring about it so much, one knew one had cared too long, but one couldn't stop. By the strange springless May of 1967, the very air in America had become poisonous. The tension-band across the forehead tightened a notch day by day. The newspapers squeezed the stomach of anxiety. The evening news on TV would only stay down with dollops of bourbon. One was irritable when sober, apocalyptic once drunk. One's sex life suffered a splintering. Even one's small talk became Spenglerian. Portents of insurrection among black people, disaffiliation among the young, and impotence in Congress were everywhere.

During a particularly evil hangover, one made a diagnosis. One was crisis-happy, one was suffering from Fitzgerald's "non-combatant's shell-shock." One had been eyeball-deep in petitions, demonstrations, protests, gathering *worry* over it all for months, and no good had come out of it. One was forty-one, and had paid attention for twenty years. Living on nerves and booze and cigarettes and headlines had ravaged one's insides. One felt like a man trying to swallow a scream. So—guilty, cowardly, a quitter or not—one schemed to get away. "To regain perspective," one announced at noon. "To survive at all," one knew by midnight. But at any rate, away!

Surreptitiously, one put aside an overdue novel, and did money-articles instead. One found oneself adding and subtracting columns of figures on letters from anxious friends. One put the household on a pauper's budget, and signed a contract to teach a year hence, and borrowed on that contract. One nourished the obsession carefully as the summer's fires consumed the cities and the nerves. Aqaba, Newark, the DMZ; Flower Power, draft card burnings, Love-Ins; Washington somnolent in its imperial drowse, New York as airless and threatful as if Kafka were its mayor. Until the necessity burned thin and blue in one's brain: To get away now! To get away from the sight of tragic, mad America breaking its heart! To make it to Europe, and surface out of the nightmare. If only for a few months.

But where first? There were old friends in London . . . but *London*? One ground one's teeth at the very thought of any further "swinging"; of hippies, psychedelics, rock, pot, mod, happenings, marches—all that feverish, faddish napalm that was burning down what was left of the contemporary brain. Paris? Rome? No, not yet. Not at first. Where then?

Reading Yeats' *Meditations in Time of Civil War* for the fourth time in as many months, an idea came: Ireland. Maudlin, lovely, superseded Ireland where all the causes were fueled with nostalgia and poteen. Above all, the *west* of Ireland where immemorially poets had withdrawn, like Horace, when the world was too much with them. Simply rent a car and vanish in the wild, peat-bog counties of the West. Go mend the wound in Yeats country. Only eight hours on an airplane would take one utterly, miraculously *away!* So ran the hope.

One held on through the stupifying dregs of August, living on the promise of sea-fresh winds in Connemara, hoarding the last of the stake. And then, muddled with bon voyage scotches and the hilarity of the friends who bought them, one found oneself aboard Aer Lingus Flight 104 at 9:30 P.M. on Labor Day, as wobbly with tension and relief as a prisoner who has somehow made it over the walls—off to Europe for the first time in ten years. And immediately ahead, before one slept again, elvish places with names one knew from poems that had changed one's life twenty years before. Lahinch in County Clare that very night! Incredible. A wicked joy stole up into one's throat at the anticipation of total irresponsibility.

The plane taxied ponderously to the head of the runway, and gunned its engines to a scream. One's wife, who didn't like to fly, gritted her teeth bravely, tipsily. One urged the huge bird towards the liftoff with the concentrated longings of months, wild with impatience all of a sudden; and felt the earth drop away from the tires, and the massive weight of the machine come to rest, with a final shudder, on a current of dark night air as palpable and reassuring as a long comber. And one knew the

19

keen, unhuman delight of being severed, of leaving the old rad-dled Self behind, of voyaging outward from all the suffocations of the street-pent consciousness. The air, coursing over one's face from the nozzle above, was suddenly pure, cold as iced wine, interstellar. The cabin hummed with settlings-down. The last, remote lights of Long Island swung away in the Atlantic dark below. The stewardesses, in parochial-school blouses and de-mure green skirts, were taking orders for drinks, and one got a double for the wife, and a single for oneself, and grinned as witlessly as Huck Finn on his raft. One had escaped.

TWO

Taking the Wound to Yeats Country

Tailwinds chased us
across the North Atlantic. We gobbled five hours between
drinks. I set my watch on Irish time, and Shirley kept hers on
New York time (the time of our bodies), and managed an hour's
sleep. But I wanted the dawn, I wanted the first sight, I felt sober
and ceremonial. The East eventually paled behind huge ranges
of cloud, and we descended towards the mottled plateau of cumulus over which they towered. I yawned and tried to blink
away fatigue, and then the clouds broke all of a sudden, and

there was Ireland below, starkly green; the sea, washing up on a long, ragged strand, light blue and foaming; the skies along the horizon, under the clouds, all *fierce* pastels—blues and violets and azures, scoured and empty as a morning at sea. All my weariness evaporated in an instant. The immense excitement came, the thrill of going great distances in the wink of an eye towards absolutely new and unknown places, the sheer adventure of it, the essential optimism of moving on, no matter how embitteredly. We put down at Shannon in an overcast at 8:00 A.M.

Passport inspection, customs, renting a car took no more than half an hour. We got a Ford Anglia station wagon, prim and black and deliverable in Dublin a week later. We changed our money. We had tea and toast in the airport restaurant. Everyone was helpful, but we must have appeared stunned and bewildered to them, fumbling with the strange coins, and not talking much. Actually, we were disconcerted by their calm, their generosity, their smiles—the abrupt change of manners fully as shocking as the change of time.

"Keep reminding me to stay left," I said, struggling with the unfamiliar gearshift as we turned out of the airport onto the country road to Lahinch. I wanted to make time against the exhaustion that was gathering. I had been up for twenty hours by then, and the preceding weeks had taken a certain toll, and so we fled down the lush, unkempt roads of late summer Clare under a sullen sky. There were donkey carts with milk drivers sidesaddle on them, and muddy bicycles pedaled by red-cheeked, expressionless women in cotton stockings, and ruminative old men staring off into stony fields, and occasional squalls of cold rain splattering the windscreen as we neared the coast. It was Ireland, we were there, and yet I couldn't grasp it, it wouldn't jell for me.

The country opened and flattened as we approached Lahinch

on its long, wide shingle of beach (people strolling there far out, dogs racing around with gleeful self-importance), and, on a sort of narrow esplanade just above the sands, St. Anthony's Hotel. In its dark, stuffy vestibule, smelling of lunch, we were told by a thin-lipped young man in an enormous, Alastair Sim sweater that they were filled up, due to a golfing competition. He was sorry, there wasn't a bed to be had in the whole town. But if we were going north, why didn't we try Kinvara just over the border in Galway?

It was forty kilometers away through the wild, hilly Burren country, and I was seriously tiring now. But I wanted to find the right place before I let up on myself, superstition about a "bad start" for our trip was in me, so I shifted to that reserve tank of energy we never suspect we possess until it's needed, and we took off through desolate, somehow punished countryside, through raw hills whose upper halves were cobbled with grey rock, through miles of stone walls higher than any in New England, and abandoned houses in ruin on the edges of cropless fields where fat, dingy sheep huddled and munched like prissy ladies imagined by Lewis Carroll. It was strange land, stark and poignant and empty, somehow peopled with the *absence* of the starving cottagers who had emigrated over those cold seas so many decades before.

"It's lovely, isn't it?" I said, unhappy with the word, and muddled a little by the strangeness.

"Yes," said Shirley, "but so sad too. So spent. They've gone away, and here we've come to find them."

Kinvara, on its little crescent of a bay, was neat and compact, the slate-roofed houses painted cheery yellows and blues; and Winkle's Hotel, on one side of the little central square, looked just right to our weary eyes. We got a cozy little room upstairs at the back, with a rusty crucifix over the bed, a blurred photo of Robert Emmett, and two smothering comforters.

23

We had pints of Guinness, and drove a little through the rainy twilight of the empty town, and then came back to chat with the barboy over double shots of Paddy's, yawning and chilly now, and had an indifferent meal of greasy chicken parts and slices of ham (the tourist season was just over, they apologized), and capitulated early.

We slept long and late. I simply pitched over into my exhaustion, and woke only once to hear a tremendous gale rushing at the roof, and rain coming in great, noisy spatters against the panes, the room so cold the bed was as delicious as a nest. The bed I'd gotten out of back in sultry, tense New York (how many hours ago?) had looked as if a fever patient had thrashed on it for days. But now the heat of our bodies under the heavy comforters melted me into a state of blissful languor, and I drowsed for nine hours without moving. I had been chasing sleep desperately for months, with all the red-eyed, fretful obsession of the insomniac, and this first night away it finally caught up with me.

Time is an illusion in which our minds perpetually lag behind our bodies. But the senses make their own adjustments to its dislocations, and I awoke in Ireland. I went out into streets through which a trickle of black-coated women wound their way to Mass. The wind drove hard over Kinvara Bay down by the seawall where a rented caravan, with a green conical top, stood on a patch of grass, horseless between the shafts, its occupants still asleep within. (American students with guitars and no draft cards?) I could smell the horse stabled somewhere nearby, and I itched to be off into such country odors, but reasoned with the itch. I was watching myself like a hospital attendant watches a docile madman at the opera.

All I knew for sure was that I wanted to go to Thoor Ballylee not fifteen miles away (where Yeats had lived in a restored tower during the Irish Civil War), and didn't realize that my mind, rested now, *slowed,* was nevertheless still seeking correspon-

24

dences to the very national dilemma I was fleeing. But Yeats was special to me. I had published awkward, reverent "imitations" of his work years before, and his ability to be, at once, a poet and a public man had always struck me as peculiarly contemporary. He had lived through the "terrible beauty" of our anarchic times with singular integrity, and I wanted his ambiance, as if somehow it might rub off.

The rain-washed pavements of Gort, the market town of the district, milled with skittish sheep and fat-assed cows lumbering about in their own pungent dung. We turned at the sign for Coole, drove four miles through lanes of dripping trees, turned again, and saw the tower rising out of its bedraggled wood, a small, rain-swollen river foaming around its foundations. We parked, and walked across an arched bridge where a rubber-booted boy goaded a few black cows. The tower itself, with its attached cottage, was square, blunt, defensive, one of a series of such towers built centuries before in that part of Ireland, from which the gentry of the time flashed alarums when marauders were in the county. Yeats had come there during the Troubles— famous, aging, plagued by prophetic premonitions about *his* time, to have carven in stone:

> I, the poet William Yeats,
> With old mill boards and sea-green slates,
> And smithy work from the Gort forge,
> Restored this tower for my wife George;
> And may these characters remain
> When all is ruin once again.

Remain they had, and whatever ruin had come was elsewhere. Reading the words, I experienced an odd twinge of embarrassment. Permanence! The embarassment of this bald appeal to *permanence!* No one I knew, no matter what secret dreams about posterity he might have nourished in his cups, would have had pride enough in his vision, or faith enough in the power of his language, to so tempt the future with that challenge. It smacked of a stubborn certitude on which not even the least existential scribbler of my era would have bet his ego. My own house in Connecticut did not even have my name on the mailbox.

Two ladies in the chilly entry got us started, armed with a shoulder-slung tape machine and two ear plugs. The flat, spare, nervous rhythms of the poems reverberated harshly in my ears as we walked through the whitewashed chambers of the cottage, and into the tower proper, and a large, barrel-ceilinged dining hall. Here, at this very table, Yeats had played the poet-Cincinnatus with his illustrious guests, and later written a poem that prayed his daughter might preserve a "radical innocence" in the riderless days that had come. I tried to imagine that white-haired, rather myopic, distracted man peering solemnly through his pince-nez there in the flicker of stubby candles, perplexed by an age that seemed to me, scant decades later, almost Arcadian compared to my own.

When I looked out of the large window that fronted directly on the stream-sized river swirling not four feet below the casement itself, I recognized the literalness of images that had once seemed fabulous with allegory to a twenty-year-old tyro-poet in prosaic New York. For *there* was the "darkening flood," rust-colored, brimming, working its patient demolition on tower and bridge; and *here* was the "chamber arched with stone," but arched to carry the immense weight of masonry above it, rather than the imagery of a poem; and *everywhere* "the haystack- and roof-levelling wind," smelling as wet and grey as the Atlantic not many miles away. Seeing what his eyes had seen grounded what his imagination had made of it as surely as a tree grounds lightning. His dilemmas had been no simpler than my own, his reconciliations no easier.

Up a narrow, window-chinked, circular staircase as treacherous as a ship's ladder (was he never drunk when that wind soughed through the arches of the bridge?), we issued into a gloomy, Gothic bedroom, painted in garish and heraldic blues and greens and blacks; a spooky place for love, it seemed to me—like an amateur fortune teller's lair, or the room of a kid in the throes of astrology. But then Yeats was of Aleister Crowley's generation after all, a generation driven half mad by faithlessness, and so vowing allegiance to the craziest of faiths. And such days had come again. Forty-eight hours before, I'd heard Hindu mantras chanted solemnly in Thompkins Square. Gurus were everywhere once more. Desperate times breed desperate needs, and who was I to mock his seances? I, who (two days ago) had consulted the *I Ching* about our trip?

The "Stranger's Room" above this was more to my taste— whitewashed and spacious, with deep alcoves suggesting stormy afternoons spent over arcane books, and something lofty and mind-broadening about the ceiling; and above all that, the battlemented roof with somber views of land rolling away on all sides—distant houses in their trees, far hills reclaimed from the stone, the sound of rushing water below, all muted by that mood of harsh remoteness that comes over the country when, all at once, tumid summer has become damp autumn. We had cigarettes, and searched for the coast we couldn't see.

, "We were the last romantics," he was saying of himself and his friends as we looked towards Coole from Ballylee, and I understood the simple truth of the line for the first time. Romantics, yes, because they had thought that "traditional sanctity and loveliness" could root the town-bred consciousness, torn by politics and parched by psychologies, back in the fecund dark of the earth again, and thereby restore coherence to our mutilated natures. Romantics, most ironically, because town-bred violence, in the guise of troopers clattering over that very bridge, had appeared in this remote county anyway, and town-bred ambitions, at the last, had drawn Yeats back to the clamourous world again. For like the ideal retreats of all writers seriously bent on the symbolic life (those houses in which weary, worldly men hope to die in bed), the tower had been abandoned after a few brief years, and Yeats had died, absurdly, in the south of France.

Romantics, yes. But not the last. For here I'd come out of the angry streets of my own country's troubles, one more romantic, imagining a settled place in time of war, an Archimedean spot on which to make a stand in an era of general dissolution, a house that might *become* ancestral. I tried to puzzle it all out, but what I really wanted was the exile's comforting bitterness, and a drink. It was too soon for pertinent thoughts.

The tape spun off, the wind keened eerily, the mood started to dissolve, and we went down through the tower again, through its empty chambers, down its torturous stairways, which only a poet, brooding on analogies, could ever have found hospitable, and nothing of Yeats the man was there. Only the poems, only the images of permanence his mind had flung against the "darkening flood," and the dirty weather of his time.

Potent weather, violent weather massed tremendous clouds as big as Matterhorns over Connemara that afternoon as we made for Clifden. Weather gusting up all of a sudden to spatter the windows into a blur of rain. Weather turning the dark, primeval rocks silver and gold when a bit of sun pierced through. Weather that had gathered itself in sheer virtuosity by six that evening (as we sat on a headland on Mannin Bay, chug-a-lugging Irish whiskey out of a fresh bottle) to present us with this awesome spectacle: rain washing the hills across the water with drab browns and bleared greens; mist shrouding the mountains beyond in shifting greys and violets; a bar of sunlight turning the deep, central channel of the bay a sparkling, Bermudan blue, and gilding the old walls of a tumbledown house in a fugitive afterglow; ominous storm-clouds building up black as doom to the east. Weather! All of it at once, *days* of it in a moment, whole dramas of weather unfolding before the startled eye, more of it than a dozen Marins could have gotten onto canvas or paper.

There, at the bottom of a scrubby field, I saw a tipsy-roofed house, rimed green with lichen, whose neglected out-buildings waded to their foundations in the tidal bay. A line of buffeted gulls perched stoically on the roof-ridge; a pair of rubber boots, muddied by a day's tramp, stood empty by the door; the deep-bayed windows glowed golden in the last of the sun, suggesting threadworn armchairs, cold flags, peat hissing in a grate, tea. One tasted vagrant salt in the air.

"What a place to write a *final* book," I thought, for the house seemed not to have been built, so much as rooted in its lonely spot, and it seemed to promise that the speculating mind would become rooted there as well—the bone-keen days scouring the intelligence of all superfluous abstractions, the black, roaring nights making the imagination flare up dangerously. And yet there was something disquieting about it too—a raw, torn beauty that was dwarfing to a man, on that coast demented by extremes; above all, an *abjectness* to the land that made me re-alize that I had come to such a place too late. Certain humilities of mind, certain diminishments, are no longer creatively feasible after forty, and I could never have felt fully at ease in all that inhuman violence of wind and water. Too many streets, and street corners, and street-corner anxieties had come between the hopeful youth, who would have loved it, and the harried man, whom it unnerved. Or so it seemed in the elusive clarity of two straight whiskies under those hugely surging skies.

That night in a big bed in the Glenowen House above Clif-den, we decided to drift north into Mayo, and eventually wash up in Sligo where Yeats had lived as a boy and where he was buried.

"Just to give us a direction," I said, uneasy in the role of literary pilgrim.

"Isn't that where we've been heading all along?" Shirley replied.

We got an early start the next morning, full of breakfast bacon, and drove straight across the austere inner-plain of Connemara, occasionally passing bikes abandoned by the side of the road, their riders off in the bog somewhere cutting peat or fishing, and five-foot-high stacks of the hardening peat in black cairns, and swatches of yellow gorse splashed on the barren slopes of low hills. Leenane, at the head of its fiord, was full of anglers and their cars and tackle. Men smoked and talked by the side of the road, cows stood dumb as postboxes in the middle of it, sheep cropped its weedy edges. Muddy dogs hurried along on urgent business, becapped boys stared and called out, and every other car had its wipers going, as if to jinx showers.

Going through tiny, narrow-walled Foxford, I spied the dim glint of bottles in a dusty window, pulled over to avoid a donkey cart, and dashed into a minute bar, no bigger than a butler's pantry, and bought a half dozen of Phoenix Ale, which we drank later (along with slabs of soda bread, country butter sweet with clover, and tinned corned-beef from Kildare) out at the end of a puddled road near Enishcrone on the coast.

I wanted to get out of the car, I wanted to sit on a rock and watch the big seas piling in on a shingle that was as snaggle-toothed as any in Nova Scotia, but the rain was coming in fierce gusts off the water again, and so I didn't, and felt cheated. But when I turned on my wipers, there, down on the beach, young men collected periwinkles in the downpour, and here, right beside the car, a seventy-year-old man propped his bicycle against a fence and went down into the rocks on some lonely forage of his own, undeterred by the squall. I felt silly, and anxious, and constrained, like a vacationing city-dweller who can't sleep for the crickets. The summer's tensions had spread caution through me like bacilli, and I was reacting to the weather as if it were more bad news against which I had to steel myself; prisoner of a reflex like an iceberg, two-thirds of it invisible.

All the way into Sligo, I concentrated on thinking nothing. I willed willessness, and grew more tense and indecisive and out of sorts. I tried to *penetrate* the countryside through which we drove, to receive it as *Irish* countryside, to experience myself there. But it wouldn't happen, not even when I located myself on a mental map—on this bit of road, with Dublin to the east, and Galway to the south, and all those leagues of water between me and the sick turmoil in the States. It wouldn't happen, and all of a sudden I felt numbed. The grass I looked at (those particular blades of grey-green grass) and the stones around which they grew, would not become Irish grass, or Irish stones, for me; that is, grass and stones uniquely *there* in Ireland. I was emptied of any sense of location, and a feeling of utter hopelessness swept through me, as if the secret, healing power of those new and unknown realities, on which I had banked the last of my nerves, was sealed off from me by some impenetrable plexiglas in my consciousness. I was appalled, disheartened, furious. I had the urge to tear at my forehead to dislodge the obstruction there. That being impossible, I made for Sligo City and a no-nonsense drink. The hell with Ireland, I told myself grimly. The hell with *having* it.

Then, of course, with the rapid alternation of moods characteristic of a pressure-cooker personality taking everything too hard, I felt fine again. The streets of Sligo were narrow, steep, you felt them verging downwards towards the river, which boiled under the bridges, surging around abutments, as dark brown as a river of frothy Guinness. We got a room at the top of an old, bustling, commercial traveller's hotel half-way up the High Street—amazingly, the Bonne Chère! I liked it immediately. I liked the dark-carpeted stairways, and the ponderous, dark wardrobes in the corridors, and the leavings of afternoon teas on the tables of the restaurant below. And I liked the covey of pretty, chattering, black-smocked, raven-haired Mayo girls (with complexions the color of thick cream, and shrewd red lips, and "chick" earrings), who ran the place. We'd heard the restaurant was the best in town.

We walked the streets, dodging into tiny, dim pubs when the showers came. I felt immensely better, and even the new hotel that was going up, cantilevered out over the river, as grotesquely, impersonally *moderne* as a Holiday Inn (our first sign of the get-the-moss-off, progressive Ireland that would so depress us once we got to Dublin), couldn't sour my spirits. The shabby, old-fashioned Yeats Museum in a damp old rectory on Stephen Street, with its yellowing photographs, and 1916 headlines, and mahogany display cases of early editions, was comforting some-how. Countess Markiewicz, like an elegant penguin in her riding habit; the patriots of the town council, posed as stiff as deacons in Edwardian collars; the swords and horse pistols of the local militia reverently behind glass: it all belonged to a vanished world; a world of tail-coat conspiracies, cottage industries, and political manifestoes invoking the hedge-poets; where tears and outrage came easily and made a difference; where some nourishing link to the rural past was still intact; a world where even revolution had been made within the rules of decent men. I liked it. It seemed naïve and anachronistic and *possible*. I left a handful of coins for the building fund.

"You *are* feeling better," Shirley said as we dressed for dinner.

"Does it show that much?"

"*That* shows," she said, indicating the bow tie that I was knotting. And she was right. It was a rainy twilight in Ireland, and suddenly I felt pulled-together, inquisitive, open to everything, *American*. The smell of damp coal-smoke from the chimney pots

32

on the steep-roofed buildings across from our window brought back our ten-year-old London winter with the quick pang of a good memory. People hurried up the narrow sidewalks towards supper. The marquee of the tiny movie theater switched on, advertising a Grade-C English thriller. The sooty blackbirds of Sligo roosted amid their droppings on perilous window ledges. Deep-throated bells tolled six over the rooftops, and I was full of a John Ford, 1930's vision of Ireland: Victor McLaglen brawling, drunk with bewildered guilt, through the alleys of an RKO Dublin; trench-coated Preston Foster, Commandant of an army without banners, under a grimy streetlamp near the docks; Margot Grahame's pale face reflected in a shop window like a soiled lily in the gutter. All that illusory, cinematic Ireland was vivid and safe around me, my imagination decades removed from the realities of Saigon, the bitter, unchangeable truths of my current life temporarily lost in the romance of youth. I suppose the bow tie was a dead giveaway.

Downstairs, we had fresh salmon, and prawns, and vegetables with the soul cooked out of them. We chatted with one another like friends, and splurged on a bottle of fairish Beaujolais, and liked each other (and everything else) immoderately. Afterwards, nothing would do but that we go out, rain or no, and find a warm place for a nightcap. Neither of us wanted to lose the mood, and it seemed so elusive.

We went to the bar of a small inn on the other side of the river. It was empty but for a barmaid, playing the Supremes to amuse herself, who poured us Power's Irish, and informed us that she had spent nine months in Pittsburgh two years before.

"Because there's nothing to do here. No proper dancing hall even," she said, at once guarded and interested. "I go to Dublin on my two-weeks. And I'll go back to the States one day, I suppose."

She had the savvy, gauging eye of Ann Sheridan behind a

33

lunch counter, and she handled the drunk who lurched in, looking for the men's room, with the ease of someone who'd been out into the big world. But I fancy we must have reminded her of some failure of nerve that had brought her back to this small, provincial city, for she said: "Yes, I suppose Sligo's pretty. But it's prettier in Kerry, if you *like* the country." Obviously, she wasn't keen on it. "I've my old mother here, which is why."

But no steady young man, and few prospects of a husband in celibate Ireland, and that air about her of discontent and making-the-best that I felt in the wet, chilly streets an hour later where people milled out of the movie, and dissatisfied voices reverberated between the buildings; where three woeful, mini-skirted girls stood in a doorway because of the drizzle, laughing too loud with a kind of aimless defiance, and then went off disconsolately to bed, for there was no one there to pay attention to them. No Saigons for them, and yet they yearned for the excitement of something, anything—and probably even a national disaster would have done.

The next morning I was out at dawn again, prowling the town before anyone was up, but for the cast-out cats. I was a dawntime walker at home, but there was a special urgency to my early rising that first week out of America. Once awake, I simply couldn't stay in bed. I was trying to experience as soon as possible the shock of being away, I wanted the essence of the new places immediately—the newless streets, the squares where harangue had left no echoes, the radio announcers excitedly reporting race-meets, the placid rhythms of a wholly *local* life without "events." I wanted to encounter a world that did not bear my wound.

Also, during these first walks, I gradually realized that I was scouting the terrain as well. It came as a surprise. I was studying window-boxed houses on quiet back streets, and thinking:

"There? Could we make it *there,* if we had to?" I was casing the pubs, the green-grocers, and the bit of picturesque quayside, convenient for an evening stroll, a block away. I was honestly surprised to discover, now that I was in Europe, that one corner of my mind had been calculating expatriation all along. It was a sign of a graver lack of gut than I had admitted to before. So I turned the day back to Yeats. Might as well visit the grave too. It was only five miles away. I sought refuge in the tourist who lurks, mental-camera poised, even in the refugee.

At last the sun shone. The sky was burnished, buffed to a high gloss, airily blue. Across it, a few stately summits of white cloud moved far up, like schooners dwarfed beneath their spinnakers. There was a pure tang in the air as we started down the long, curving road into Drumcliff Valley. Everything glistened, and one's eyes were new.

We saw the church of St. Columba in its grove of trees there on the plain from some miles away, its four-spired tower rising weightlessly out of the foliage, isolated from the low, whitewashed, thatched farm houses that stood at a respectful distance around it. Beyond, the huge, bare knob of Ben Bulben humped up ponderous and glowering towards Donegal.

St. Columba's was nothing but a modest country church, named after the Irish saint who had battled the followers of Finnian there in the Sixth Century—appropriately enough, over a book. There were a few cars, a few other pilgrims, and the sun was very warm on our faces as we entered the square of shadowy trees around the church. The graveyard was overgrown, neglected, tombstones pitched up out of the earth, wild roses twining them, an unkempt, dense profusion of growth everywhere. The church tower was built of unfaced, grey stone, mottled and pocked with years, severe as a country priest who, despite his need of a shave, has never doubted his own authority. The grave

35

itself was just to the left of the entry, a slab of freshly-hewn, dark, polished stone, conspicuous by its location and condition, the famed epitaph newly chiseled:

> Cast a cold eye
> On life, on death.
> Horseman, pass by!

For some reason, the first thing I thought as I read these words was that the exclamation-point was an error. I couldn't remember whether the poem from which the quote came had ended with one, but knew that it wasn't necessary. It insisted too much, it was somehow overwrought, it vitiated the tone of harsh command. I had never realized so keenly how the perfect words carry their own implicit punctuation.

Suddenly I was aware that it was chilly under those big trees. We were actually shivering. The whole scene was strangely macabre: the sun-bright morning, the immense emphatic clouds moving over the stark hump of the mountain, the deep shadows there in the graveyard (with just a touch of the dank to them) that automatically drew one's gaze out towards the plots and kitchen-gardens beyond, drenched in a rich, Van Gogh light. It was very cold there, cold as a crypt; it felt forever sunless, clammy with death. Shirley registered it too: the unmistakable feeling that we were intruders—we, who had picnicked for years in deserted New England cemeteries, drinking wine in the warm drowse of October afternoons, tracing out centuries-old inscriptions, glad to be away from the plank tables and evil trashcans of public recreation areas where even the elms seem to have been "erected," along with the Chic Sales and barbeque pits. This was a wild, cold, austere place, a place of mysteries in which I did not believe, mysteries made palpable by the presence, there at my feet, of a man and his fulfilled wish.

He had been famous in the world, his literature's greatest

poet, his nation's darling, a man justly honored by that world, and revered by everyone to whom language was a vocation and a faith; a hero in an unheroic age whose great artists, almost alone, carry the burden of a civilization that is murderously beset by its own contradictions. And yet he had sought to complete some secret design by lying here in this remote region of his boyhood, to affirm a last continuity by returning to the very earth in which his symbol-seeking intellect had imagined the only redemption for our steel-and-concrete-smothered century—though, due to a war, it had taken ten years after his death to complete the pilgrimage.

We walked around to keep warm. The church no longer functioned except on Festival days, and the other graves were not particularly old, all of them in need of a weeding. The roses had run riot everywhere—huge, gorged blossoms, myriad thorny creepers. There was something almost malevolent in their tangled, crushing abundance, burying whole plots, and one could not avoid the primitive thought that these flowers had fed on dead flesh. I read the inscription again ("Horseman, pass by!") as cars flashed along the highroad to Lissadel and Bundoran a hundred yards away. The air was thin, vibrating.

And then, all at once, I became aware of the shrill, ugly squawking of blackbirds in the branches of the trees above, an angry caterwauling of invisible, guardian birds. A fight broke out up there, there was a turbulence in the air, obscene wings threshed and flapped among the leaves—black, shiny, ominous. The quarrel grew in pitch, a mad fierceness entered their shrieks, as if they were disturbed by an alien presence (the way birds will sometimes squall out warnings, tree to tree, when they spy a cat hidden somewhere below), and one knew, with a shiver, *whose* was the alien presence there. The hubbub rose to a kind of frenzy, one looked up with an involuntary, almost primordial hunch of shoulder, as if expecting a plummet of wings to swoop out of the obscuring leaves, vicious beaks pecking at one's eyes. One had blundered into a non-human place, a place pulsing with dark, non-human life, life of another dimension than that of our consciousness, bird-life, plant-life, where the awful cycle of growth and decay, from which men shrink back instinctively, sensing their own mortality, goes endlessly on and on.

It was not pleasant, not reverent or sobering, to be standing there. I seemed to be verging on some scary, ultimate reality— the great *bong* that all along had lain at the end of even the poet's tirelessly *created* life. The birds never ceased their ugly squawking, the air was cold as bone, and (to this troubled man) the utter irrelevance of sorrow or reflection was unsettling. We hurried away, back into the sun.

Some places are saturated in the spirit that has striven to transform them with thought, some places are *conquered* like that. But this place was inchoately alive with the mystery of the sentience beneath thought. It suggested the sacred and abominable groves of heathen times, and divination practiced with the entrails of dead things. It stirred up that twinge of primitive awe against which we have tirelessly erected our godless cities and philosophies.

And yet it was the proper place for Yeats somehow. He had known the vanity of joy and anguish alike, and known the folly of *that* knowledge too. But the "cold eye," which he had achieved after all the vanities of fame, responsibility, despair and wisdom had been burned away, was not an embittered eye. He had simply accepted that *this* was where he would come to rest—beyond sanctification, beyond men, *returned*. That final acceptance that turns a mystic back into a man.

My own recent anguish was diminished to nothing in an instant. I was alive. I was alive no matter what cul de sac my world stumbled down in its blindness. For a moment, as we drove away, I felt, as Yeats had once, a strong and irrational desire to bless everything I saw (the trees, the low houses, old Ben Bulben), as if I actually believed I could, so blesséd felt I by it all. I touched my wife impulsively, intimately.

I *knew* where I was.

Blessings or no, some inner shift had occurred, for that night, after one of the black-smocked girls had brought us our coffee in the nearly empty restaurant of the Bonne Chère, Shirley winked at me, and said: "She's taken a fancy to you, you know."

"What do you mean?"

I had been talking steadily for three-quarters of an hour, completely engrossed in finding the true words for my reactions of the day, at ease the way a man is only at ease when he is no longer asking himself whether he is or not, absorbed in everything, flowing with it. The elusive impediment of the last days had simply vanished.

"She thinks you're attractive," Shirley said with a smile. "And you are. She can't keep her eyes off you."

The girl came back with the bill, and, lo, 'twas true. She looked down into my face with a shy, melting awareness, a look that all men understand, a look which only the looker fails to realize is eloquent with the flush of sensual arousal. I chatted with her while counting out the shillings, and flirted with her a little, and she was flustered, her pretty dark eyes trying not to dwell on mine, her bashful mouth trying to form a public smile.

I suppose I seemed voluble, relaxed, and, above all, American to her. I suppose she was bored, her consciousness drowsing in the trance that all routine induces after a while. Certainly our two bottles of wine must have seemed worldly to a young girl not many months off the farm, and my manners are courtly enough when I'm of a mood. But I don't think that she was at all aware of the powerful aura of sex-attraction that came off her, as intangible and unmistakable as perfume. I existed in her

39

eyes, I was alive for a moment in her secret, girlish life. I was immensely flattered, and tipped her generously, and didn't tell her how I loved her for being there to cap my day.

I had been snappish, trigger-happy, distracted, tense, *partial* for longer than I knew. I had been carrying myself like an armful of broken crockery, willing every response, thinking in such terms as "Irish grass," as cowardly as a cat bristling at shadows, believing he is brave. In short, unattractive. Now, nothing was changed, and everything was changed. Part of the horror of America's current travail (I realized) was that it had driven us all murkily inward—for both our genius and our despair are Kantian, and we take everything too hard, too personally. But between them, the nameless girl in Sligo and the famous man in Drumcliff had turned my eye outward again, and I let up on myself for a while, and began to recuperate.

"Tomorrow," I said to Shirley, feeling humor rise in me along with the happiness, "Dublin. But tonight, *America* ... And, if you will," gesturing first at her, and then at myself, "the congress of these states."

THREE

Whispering in the Pubs

                I was ready
for Dublin, or thought I was. The worst of my sense of dislocation had ebbed away as a hangover does by mid-afternoon, and
if I had stopped making instant, brain-numbing calculations
about the *real* worth of the quixotic money, at least I knew
which coins were which. I'd had no trouble with the brogue
because, like the whiskey, there was a hard edge to its flow, and
it left that aftertaste—like biting on a penny at a high altitude—that constitutes the difference between eloquence and

rhetoric. My nerves were detaching themselves from America one by one, and I fancy I was a reasonably good companion for the first time in weeks as I drove across Ireland the next morning, talking about Dublin with not a little charm.

"Dear, dirty Dublin . . . Dublin of the sorrows." These weren't my words, but they cover the Dublin I evoked for Shirley: a wholly imaginary Dublin, at once tough-minded and sentimental-at-heart in the best modern style—that is, shabby, rain-dark, restive, bittersweet, impoverished, by-passed; its mood derived mostly from the old, brick Third-Avenue-under-the-El of my student days, fleshed out by exposure to the likes of Joyce and O'Casey. This fanciful Dublin was a city in which a man who was sick to death of the suicidal, chemic stink of the world's New Yorks might breathe up the richer human odors of back-wardness, clogged drains, stale metaphysics, stout, sad chastity, and verse. As it turned out, I was as absurdly prisoned in my fantasies as the immigrant Irishman of a century ago who probably saw, in the shimmer of the afternoon sun on the rain-washed sidewalks of New York, the promised pavements-of-gold. Like some other cities I had never visited, the Dublin in my imagination had a reality more vivid than the streets through which we walked after delivering the Anglia to the rental agency, and I looked at the real Dublin and registered it as counterfeit.

The city, in that year of its life, was mean enough, but it wasn't the meanness of proud poverty and stubborn isolation from contemporary history, but rather the shoddy, Day-Glo, cheap-goods meanness of the Discount House. Dublin resembled one of those smallish New England cities, ashamed of its red-brick, its dowdiness, its piety, its thrift, and bent on living down its reputation as a backwater. It was plunging into the modern world like a businessman sometimes plunges into a love affair in middle life, and all of its vices were venal.

The hazy, late-summer afternoon along O'Connell Street was odorous with the fry-foul smell of cafeterias. Posters in the windows of department stores advertised a folk-group called the Wolfe Tones. The marquees of the movie palaces flickered on and off with that idiotic, mechanical frenzy (suggesting a stuck-switch and an absent electrician) that depresses you with a premonition of what the world may be like once our species vanishes and only the machines remain. The Liffey, that most elfinly-named of rivers, bringing to mind the soft-focus blur of spring showers, and a source somewhere far up in the greeny dells of fairy Ireland, was found to be mud-befouled and pungent-as-an-armpit at low tide, full of sodden newspapers and the rusty skeletons of bicycles, and about as poetic as the Hackensack in the swelter of a hot September.

"No one knows how to *walk* in this town," Shirley complained as we breasted through the crowds. And it was true. People milled up and down the streets like farmers on a midway. The unconscious reflex of going up a street on the inside and going down it on the outside, which is programmed into the inveterate city-dweller's nerves so deeply that he is unaware of it, had yet to be developed by these Dubliners, and I felt an unhappy identification with the occasional cart-horse that staggered along between the shafts of a vegetable wagon in the snarls of traffic, with all the indentured horror of the work-animal's dawn-to-dusk existence in the noxious exhaust of cruel, beeping machines awful to see in the long strings of saliva hanging from his bruised lips.

Dublin! Where was it? There was just a hint in the man hawking fresh pears from a baby carriage on the far side of the O'Connell Bridge, just a hint—in his harsh singsong cry, his chips-greasy cap, his priest's mouth and toper's nose—of that canny wit that is the gift of streetlife to the poor. But Davy Byrne's on Duke Street had the deep carpet, the restaurant-supply-house fixtures, and the subdued murmurings of ladies over sherry, that characterize a Schrafft's on matinee-Wednesdays, and our double shots of Power's made even the bartender look up at the waiter's order.

My mood was blurring. I wanted to sit back in the smoke-dense, comforting blear of a "local," I wanted to drink a pint and eavesdrop among habitués, I wanted a saloon, and so we went up narrow Grafton Street where the double-decker buses lumbered along like elephants down a cattle-chute, and took the first right, and ducked into Macdaid's. Tiled floor, tall dusty ceilings, an air of cozy shabbiness, pints of Watney's. But Mac-daid's, too, was filled with an intermittent, undersea muffle.

I cocked my ear: "Do you hear it?"

"No," said Shirley. "What? I don't hear anything."

"That's what I mean. Everyone's *whispering*."

Whispering in the pubs! In the next days, we were to go to a clutch of bars and restaurants, and always hear that same muf-fled whispering of a dentist's waiting room. The coffee-girls in the dark-panelled, upstairs room of Bewley's Oriental, which was fragrant with fresh-ground Colombian and warm treacle, were as abashed, and indrawn, and virginally guarded as convent girls serving conventioneers. The uniformed boys in the Shelbourne Lounge, who tonged ice into our whiskies without being asked, as if, of course, they knew that Yanks had a thing about *cold*, nevertheless studied us suspiciously as if we were some new species of Heidelburgher from whom it was best to keep a proper distance. Eventually, I felt as raucous and awkward as a stevedore in a tea-room.

"My God," I said to Shirley, "whatever happened to—well, dammit, the *real* Dublin?"

The real Dublin finally got through to me in the Chopstick, the best of Dublin's mysterious profusion of Chinese restaurants. Perhaps that hushed, somehow slippered, ominously *dimmed* atmosphere that gives Chinese eating places the world over an air of being fronts for some obscure Secret Society appeals to the Irishman's taste for intrigue, exile and the clandestine, but as I repeated my order for the third time to the impenetrable waiter (the Big Mandarin? The Hatchet Man? You always wonder), I realized that Dublin was the only city I knew, the epitome of whose public style seemed to be a Chinese waiter! Rectitude, silence, invisibility—Americans, who expect to feel more immediately at ease in Ireland than, say, England (because of the Kelly or Kennedy down the block back home) are not prepared for the pure Celt when they encounter him. For he is not the boozy, loquacious, sentimental Mick, whose blood runs in so many of our veins, but a certified mystic, a profoundly austere and profoundly abstracted spirit, indifferent to the flesh, bedevilled by images, a martyr to his own moody pride and persecution-mania, and somehow unfocused in his racial identity now that economics are destroying that island-isolation that resisted seven hundred years of war and politics. "My" Dublin, silly as it was, suffered a strategic setback before the austerities of that Chinese waiter, and we walked back along the quays of the Liffey in a twilight that was not poetic but faintly lurid with neon. I grew morose.

"It's certainly not what I expected," Shirley said.

"Well, give it a chance, for Pete's sake!" I shot back out of all reason. "Don't just jump to conclusions that way ... Besides, there's tomorrow—"

But tomorrow I was scheduled to be interviewed by a reporter from the *Irish Times,* and after those first hours in Dublin I wasn't looking forward to it. Like so many Americans, I expected to be asked for my impressions of the country, because that is the first thing we want to know from Europeans visiting the States, as if above everything else we earnestly needed their reassurance that we are friendly, gifted, attractive, civilized, wor-

45

thy; as if we could frame no question more urgent than, "Do you love us?," and, on receiving an affirmative reply, had to reveal the depths of our uncertainty by asking, "Why? For What? How Much?" But I had no perceptive, cut-to-the-bone, Lawrencian insights into Ireland. Mostly I was feeling grumpy and confused, and no writer can afford to be confused when talking to a journalist, who is usually concerned about getting his "lead," and comes to an interview involved with the story he must write once it is over, rather than the story that might develop while it is going on. Whatever impressions I had were so blurred by my expectations that I didn't trust them. After all, how could you tell a Dubliner that Dublin seemed to have all the unique panache of Fall River, Massachusetts? Was it even true?

Fat, dingy seagulls waddled about amid the drifting newspapers on Capel Street at six A.M., and I liked the town a little better without its crowds. Walking the riverside, I watched the sun come up down the Liffey towards the sea, as burnished as a white-gold shilling in the mist. Trim *Gardai,* hands behind their backs like schoolmasters monitoring an exam, paced in twos along Ormond Quay. The air was thick with bog and brine and coal-smoke. I crossed and re-crossed the river, smoking Carroll's No. 1 (tiny filter cigarettes you consume in five puffs), and remembering that series of travel-pieces that ran in Cyril Connolly's magazine, *Horizon,* during and just after the war, that were collectively entitled, *Where Shall John Go?* Teneriffe, Jamaica, Ceylon, New Orleans, the Great Barrier Reef!—these were some of the answers. Anywhere away from the bleakness, the squalor, the austerity, the helplessness of a played-out Europe! Anywhere away from the grubby dustbin of a civilization clearly going out of business. Now the tides of longing ran in the other direction, and Europe, in its turn, was receiving cargoes of the bewildered and the battle-weary. In my own lifetime it had changed and changed back again, and I stood in the center of the Grattan Bridge, looking upriver at the sooty façade of the Four Courts Buildings, and wondering where John could go to escape the debacles going on in the New World if not to Dublin, and just how much of the damage to his optimism and enthusiasm might be permanent.

We were due to meet the reporter for lunch at the Bailey, which was a hangout for newsmen and poets, and was supposed to have certain unclear Joycean associations, like so many places in Dublin. It sounded good enough, for by now I was counting on a drink or two to wing the interview, but the Bailey turned out to be another of those capacious, brand-new lounges, decorated in light woods, Acrilan and leatherette, with coffee-table-high tables in the back where a man's relationship to his glass would be (shall we say) attenuated, and that spurious atmosphere of a smart living room that is precisely what you are fleeing when you go to a bar. "Ye gods," I said to Shirley, "be careful your glass doesn't sweat on the *Realities.*"

At which remark, I heard my name spoken, punctuated by a question mark, and looked up. A slender young woman, in a chic red-and-green-velvet pants suit, stood there, the hand of a little girl clasped in each of hers.

"Judith Brooke," she said.

She was pretty, intense, feline, with the alert expression of a small animal, modishly close-cropped black hair, bright eyes that took your measure openly, and an impatient mouth. I had never seen her before.

"The *Irish Times,*" she said, as I noticed the portable tape-machine slung from her shoulder.

She was American, she was the ex-wife of an Irish painter, and she had been in Ireland for eight years or so. She established

47

all this with that quick, economical directness with which Americans present their credentials to one another—"What do you do?" (a question considered impertinent in Europe); "I do *this,* I'm from *there,* I'm interested in *that*" (everyone in America carrying his identification papers in his mouth, and everyone else authorized to peruse them on demand). She apologized for bringing along her children, who were astonishingly beautiful and grave little girls whom Shirley entertained while their mother fiddled with the dials of the machine and went through her prepared questions.

She wanted to know about the Hippies, drugs, the Black Panthers, Vietnam. She wanted to know, for her Irish readers, where an American writer, who had been associated with youth and dissent for years, thought America was drifting. Her questions were mostly couched in such a way as to elicit usable quotes, but when we broke off for a moment, she said: "Look, if there's something more you want to get in, just tell me what to ask you," and I heard a curiosity that went well beyond the task at hand.

The novelty of the situation took me by surprise, and my answers became at once prolix and full of that impatient verbal shorthand that makes a man sound terrifically insightful to himself, and vaguely illogical to almost everyone else.

Besides, I didn't want to talk about America. Suddenly I wanted to talk about Ireland. I wanted to find out how this young woman had managed her expatriation, and if it really worked for her, and whether one could make it in *this* city. Typical, obsessive, American questions that I was to ask, and be asked, for the next four months.

"Why do you stay on?" I interrupted. "Do you really like Dublin that much?"

"What? No, not really. I mean," switching off the tape, "yes,

I like it. That is, I know it by now, and the girls are settled in
school, and—"

"Because it seems awfully characterless to me. I can't get a
sense of its mood."

She laughed uncertainly, and decided the interview was over,
and began to talk: "Well, I went home a couple of years ago,
just for a visit, and I had the strangest feeling. I was absolutely
thrilled and terribly excited for about three days, and then—"
She lapsed off, as if she had been playing the candid, and-what-
do-*you*-do American for years there in cautious Dublin, but had
gotten out of the habit of being plunged, herself, into the casual
inquisitions that we all take for granted at home. "Then I began
to get nervous."

We talked easily and directly for a few minutes, and I liked
her. She seemed an intelligent, resourceful person who had been
unhappy not too long ago and was intent on getting over it.
Conversation with her was pleasant, because she looked at you
while she spoke and she acknowledged any awareness of herself
that underlay your replies. But the children had finished their
orange squashes, and were getting restive, and Shirley made a
move to extricate us.

"Look," Judith said all at once, "why don't you both come out
for dinner tonight? I promised the girls we'd go to the zoo, but
I could pick you up at, say, the Shelbourne at four. I'm out in
Rathfarnham, but it's not more than twenty minutes away."

Plainly, she was hungering for talk. She didn't want to let it
go. She wanted to get out a bottle of whiskey, and sit around it,
and talk American talk. She hungered for the nervous, excited,
contentious *rush* of conversation with countrymen who could
understand the ambiguities of her expatriation—the sheer relief
of being out of the States, and the nagging suspicion that everywhere else was somehow frivolous; the delight of being in mar-

velous, supportive Europe, and the edge of lonesomeness that comes over Americans at twilight in a foreign place; above all, the troubled knowledge that all *that* was still back there, still feverish, unfinished, fateful, infuriating, still going on without you; still, maddeningly, *home*.

What can we Americans do? Even our exiles result from un-requited love, and we search one another out in the obscurest cities, and sit around and revile the current state of the Republic, congratulating each other on having gotten free of it, staying up all night, and getting drunk, wondering why we feel so keyed-up, and indefatigable, and *happy* all of a sudden, and then real-ize—that tireless American energy is in us again! It was too early in our trip for me to like these thoughts very much, but Judith was there, and I did like her, so I looked at Shirley, and we agreed.

"Marvelous!" Judith exclaimed. "I'll get us a bird."

The afternoon gloomed over. A desultory, light rain fell oc-casionally into the muffled streets as we walked towards Parnell Square and the Municipal Gallery. The pubs were closed for the "holy hour," and we plodded on through drab and empty blocks.

A lank-haired young man, bearing a startling resemblance to Mick Jagger, slouched through the rooms of contemporary Irish painting, his ochre-spattered jeans leaving a trail of rainwater on the creaking parquet, his solemn, damn-your-eyes bohemianism somehow pathetic in the light of those mostly-atrocious pictures, among which he so obviously longed to discover one of his own. What would he have thought had he seen a Rauschenburg, a de Kooning, even a Wyeth? All the dispiriting, stubborn, hopeless hope of the provincial artist, of Sherwood Anderson in Wines-burg, came off him like the smell of mothballs at the opera. The nakedness of his yearning to be in some *center,* not to be demeaned any longer by his irrelevance, to be challenged by work commensurate to his imagination, depressed me, because I was fleeing in disgust from just such a center, from just such pointless relevance.

"Look," Shirley said. "Isn't *that* by Judith's husband?"

It was a medium-sized nude, with dark splashes of color in a rich impasto, the recumbent figure unwillingly assuming a pose that was at once vulnerable and erotic, the eyes full of those anxious questions—"What went wrong?," "What am I to do?," "Do you still love me?"—that cloud so many American eyes now that we are no longer happy innocents in the world's playground, but have assumed our share of its wickedness and complexity. Post-Jamesian eyes. It was a picture of Judith, and it was good. Somehow psychologically sound. It caught the feeling of a relationship between artist and model that was foundering.

"What do you think?" I said.

"I like her. I understand her. But are you sure you're ready for an *American* night this soon?"

"I meant the painting," I snapped back, irritated by her remark because it cut too close to my own thoughts. "Besides, maybe she can give us some clue to this goddamn town."

We drifted back towards the river down puddled alleys onto which the dusty back-windows of junk shops opened, crammed to their tops with water-stained mattresses, religious chromos, mouldering books, brass knickknacks. Scruffy dogs hurried along in the wet. On the Liffey docks, huge steel vats of Guinness waited to be loaded aboard tankers for Liverpool. The rain stopped, the sky broke raggedly, and the prams appeared in St. Stephen's Green out of nowhere.

"I don't know," I said disconsolately. "I can't seem to get the feel of it."

"But what did you expect?"

"My own youth, I suppose. Being broke, and reckless, and hopeful. I guess I expected to feel the way we all felt in the Village just after the war." Having finally said it, I could laugh at it. "What a distance to come to discover *that* banality."

We all squeezed into Judith's tiny car. Shirley had bought a boxful of tarts and eclairs and Napoleons while I was getting a bottle of Power's and another of Medoc. She was piled under all this in the front seat as I took a little girl on each knee in the back. They were full to bursting with the wonders of Phoenix Park Zoo, particularly a mammoth sea lion as awesome as a dreadnaught, who swam on his back and trailed his whiskers in the water like mooring lines. Judith was happy as we drove out through the suburbs. The afternoon had turned fair again, the air was limpid and yellow, and she was feeling voluble with the single Pimm's Cup she'd had at the Shelbourne. And besides, there was the evening ahead. She pointed out the sights with that delighted sense of proprietorship one only feels for adopted places.

She and Shirley were deep into householding talk when all of a sudden, at a spot where the road forked, a bicycle, pedaled furiously by a tow-headed delivery boy who was obviously *late,* appeared out of nowhere and grazed the right fender of the car with a bruising thump.

Judith slammed on the brakes. "Good God, did I hit him!" Out the back window, I could see the boy sprawled in the road among his parcels, the front wheel of his bike knifed-over but undamaged. Shirley stayed in the car with the girls, while Judith and I ran back. The boy was sitting up, rocking back and forth, and trying to wince back tears. Aside from a badly skinned knee and torn trousers, he seemed unhurt to my hands. Ten or twelve people gathered, among them a young doctor on his way home, who confirmed this. The boy was over the worst of his fright, he was chagrined at having run into us, and seemed mostly panicked by what his employer, a chemist, might say about his tardiness. All he wanted was to get away from the solicitous adults, from the doctor, from the *scene* there in the road. But Judith had come unstuck.

"I didn't see him, I really didn't see him," she kept repeating, as she wrote out her address and phone number and license plate for the doctor as well as the boy. "I'll go straight away and report it to the *Gardai*. Do you think I ought to phone his parents?" She looked around into all those Irish faces, pleading her concern, as if seeing the hateful words, "Reckless, drunken Americans!," forming in every mouth, words that were not there at all.

I got her away. "But I'm really *not* tipsy," she insisted with a trembling lip. "But I should have seen him ... Did *you* see him? ... God, the girls will be scared to death."

We reported it at the local police station, and went on, but Judith was miserable. "Mummy was careless," she explained to the elder of her children, who hadn't asked. "Mummy still forgets sometimes about keeping to the lefthand side ... I think that's what it must have been, you know. I probably wasn't staying over far enough," which wasn't true. In any case, this only mystified the girls, who were *Irish,* after all.

We turned up a long avenue of trees with open park on either side, and there, at the end of it, a large estate-house stood, its tall windows glowing with the westering sun, flanked by formal gardens, phalanxes of mossy wall and immense limestone urns.

"We live in the basement," said Janet, the youngest child, "and Maeve and I have our very own room."

The evening was pleasant and troublous. I was somehow moved by Judith and her girls living alone that way in their meandering basement full of books and clutter and unmade beds in that Regency house that had been turned into flats. Moved by the tour of the evening gardens, where the terraces were in need of a weed, and rain-bleared, vaguely Romantic statuary stood in niches in the crumbling walls, and beyond, the placid, green, poignant country rolled away south into Wicklow. Moved when Maeve, the eldest child (and somehow the more fatherless, the more wrenched of the two) showed me the brave little strip of peonies and violets that she had planted outside her window. Moved by Judith's continuing worry about the accident with the delivery boy, which had made her feel abruptly alien there. And moved, finally, by the whiskey to which we all attended a little recklessly.

Judith cooked and talked. No, she loved Ireland, and had lived in the south counties while she was married, a marvelous cottage life. And, yes, Dublin was all right, there was free-lance work here, but the sea lion in the Zoo was "the realest thing in town—the hell with Leda and her bloody swan . . . " She knew everybody, we must go meet Austin Clarke the next evening, and—And unmistakably she was lonely, living pretty much on her wits, and feeling stranded. What did I think would happen in the States? Weren't the reports of spreading civil disaffection exaggerated? She couldn't believe that America was coming apart like that. Was it true?

She stood by the fridge with her New York-sized drink, a slender, modish young woman, glancing into the living room where Shirley was making drawings for the girls, and then looking at me with her husbandlessness plain as day in her eyes. It had been so much fun to be in Ireland, and now it wasn't so much fun anymore. The dark eyes asked: And you? What about you? You drink hard. How does your life go? She let me have that look, and then she said: "But the truth is, I'm afraid to go home. I'm afraid of what I know I'll find. And yet it *is* home. Mine, at least. It doesn't mean anything much to the girls."

A recognition passed between us, an admission of peculiarly intense awareness, which I decided to treat as a man-woman thing, not being able as yet to confront the strange clairvoyance that often marked the relations of Americans abroad that year, as if some dreadful fissure had opened under all our feet, out of which the evil odors of tear-gas, napalm, charred tenements, and burning draft cards had seeped up to foul the natural optimism of the national character. Somehow it all *couldn't* be happening, and yet it was. And no matter how much we hated America, we loved it more, and what could you do with that?

So I flirted with Judith in a harmless way, and she softened, and the evening passed. I discovered that I was still over-compensating, like an ex-lunatic who is continually afraid that he will break into tears, and so laughs too heartily, and in the wrong places. Shirley knew what was happening, she saw the morose, tipsy glint come up into my eyes, and steered the conversation away from such dangerous shoals as the war and the Congress. She encouraged my sallies with Judith, and seconded Judith's proposal that we get together the next day, and we called a taxi at one.

Outside in the soft, wafting darkness of the Irish night, Judith all at once put up her mouth to be kissed, as yearning and as grave as her daughters, eyes lidded with an exhaustion of the nerves, despite her protests that it was still early. "And you really think that chemist's boy's all right?" she whispered in my ear as I drew away. "I'm sure I would have panicked if there hadn't been a man along," her hand small and inert in mine. I tried to reassure her, and we pulled away over the crunching gravel, and down the long drive back to the Dublin road.

"Look," I said to Shirley when we were halfway home, "how about going to Edinburgh for a few days *before* we hit London?"—where we would be staying with American friends.

"That sounds fine. But what made you think of it?"

55

"I have no expectations about Edinburgh," I said. "And we don't know anyone there."

The next morning there was rain again, rain that would have only deepened the green in Galway, but which ran in black streams down Dublin's sooty walls, a cold, drenching downpour that immediately went through my raincoat, and my jacket, and on into the bone. I sloshed over to Aer Lingus on O'Connell Street, and booked us to Edinburgh the next day, and then phoned Judith from a pillar box.

"Listen, something's come up, and we have to leave to-morrow——"

"Oh." She was just awake, or hungover, or embarrassed. "Well, then, we'll go see Austin Clarke this afternoon."

I didn't want to see Austin Clarke, and invented an appointment out in Howth. Also, I said, we were going to the Abbey that evening to see O'Casey's *Red Roses For Me.* Not an invention.

"I'll come in and meet you afterwards then. At the Plough just across the street." She laughed a brave and uncertain little laugh. "Lord, I haven't felt *this* bad for months. It's kind of nice."

I felt that bad too, but it wasn't nice. It was too similar to too many mornings during the past year. "I'll get a baby-sitter," she was saying. "It's just so marvelous seeing someone from home."

I felt like a quitter all of a sudden—for not wanting to see Judith because of those questions in her eyes, for pettishly wanting out of Dublin because it was no longer the Dublin of my fancies. So we arranged it.

Shirley and I moped around that day, dodging showers. In the spacious dark-green rooms of the National Gallery there was a splendid Gainsborough portrait, as cool and pure as unblemished marble, and as remote from my uncentered mood as the rationalism of the eighteenth-century. The brass door-knockers on Merrion Square reflected the large park in its center with nary a Sara Allgood nor a Cyril Cusack in sight. But the twilight came clear and rain-freshened and vaguely rose-tinted on Eden Quay where we had a good steak and a half bottle of Beaujolais upstairs in Daly's, and I clutched at the feeling of spurious excitement that the panelling, and smoke, and pre-theater crowds aroused in me, only to lose it for good in the Abbey—now housed behind one of those new, brick-and-glass façades that pass for theaters but resemble nothing so much as smallish electronics companies in Cambridge—where we saw a respectful, lackluster production of O'Casey's great hymn to the old Dublin, "my" Dublin, performed with the reverence and incomprehension that is the fate of genuine plays once they have become classics, before a respectful, lackluster audience that sipped lukewarm coffee during the intermissions, and murmured about fashions and the weather. While O'Casey keened on about "sorrow like slush up to our ankles," the lady next to me shifted uncomfortably in her seat, as if she was embarassed by the eccentric vernacular and naïve emotions of some country cousin. O'Casey's Dublin, with all its wit, squalor, hope and blarney, was no more relevant to contemporary Ireland than the Book of Kells in the library of Trinity College across the river, and I felt as patronizing as a social worker for regretting it, but I did. It was the dear, old, dirty past I wanted, being already a refugee from that commercial future (so much more *humanly* squalid) that the bulldozers and the discount houses were ushering in. Where in God's name could John go?

To the Plough, a comfortable, well-lit pub across the street; to Judith, looking very "mod" in earrings and eye-liner and brocade, and having a drink with her editor on the *Times*. He was slight, tweedy, with the narrow, ungiving mouth of a sober Trevor Howard, and he didn't say very much. He eyed our bumper

whiskies as he sipped his pint, as if they confirmed some conclusion about reckless America that he had already formed. I tried
to draw him out about Dublin, and he was at once defensive and
apologetic, carefully plumbing every chance remark I made for
those layers of allusion and sophistication that so many residents
of small, provincial cities assume lie behind the trivial conversation of visitors from "the big world." I bought a round or two,
and the talk limped, and Judith became chattery and ill-at-ease.

"Tell me about P. J. Clarke's," she said. "Who's going there
now?" and then turned to her friend. "It's this Irish bar on
Third Avenue."

What could I tell her? Clarke's hadn't been any fun for years.
The tieless afternoons of talk and beer were as dead as Kennedy's Camelot.

"But then you've probably been there, haven't you?" she
added to the editor.

He had, years ago, and he had found it raucous, smoke-
bleared, and counterfeit-Irish. I suddenly glimpsed the image of
the Irishmen that he thought he saw in my eyes—Brendan Be-
han, drunk, and dishevelled, and in song; Barry Fitzgerald as
quaint and sage-folksy as some Finian dreamed-up on 45th
Street; Pat O'Brien, the good-guy priest. But actually it had been
Louis MacNeice, the Ulster poet, who had formed my image of
Ireland:

> For common sense is the vogue
>   And she gives her children neither sense nor money
> Who slouch around the world with a gesture and a
>   brogue
>   And a faggot of useless memories.

The lines came back like a snatch of melody from twenty years
before. But were they any less mistily romantic than the colleens
and leprechauns and shamrocks of popular myth? Those memo-

ries—all secondhand, all "useless"—were *my* problem after all, not his. They embodied *my* fantasy of escape, not the reality in which he had to live and work. Suddenly, the inexorability of modern life, the demon of progress that had Dublin too in thrall, sobered me, and I stopped trying to rebuild the city a little closer to my preconceptions. D. H. Lawrence had once said that all Americans were "escaped slaves," but now, in dread of the future, our sentimental journeys always seemed to take us back to some feverishly-imagined *past,* to some comforting feudalism in the mind that we had dreamed up in our democratic freedom. Only to find that disappointment was turning us into the spoiled-sports of the Western World. Judith seemed to recognize the quiet passing of "my" Dublin in the way I listened to her friend without that impatience to get-to-the-point that is so American, and she made a stab at hilarity.

"My God," I thought, "that's the way we all used to be— eager, impulsive, confident that our energy can overcome everything, including our own dashed hopes!" Would a few scant months of wandering return that eagerness to my eyes? Only if I opened those eyes to what actually lay in front of them. Only if I relented. The "useless memories" had to go, like that excess baggage you jettison to keep the lifeboat from capsizing. All at once, Joyce's "Silence, exile and cunning" seemed the canniest prescription for whatever lay ahead.

They drove us home through dark, dank, empty streets. It was only a little after midnight, but for the most part Dublin was in bed. The Liffey, smelling of diesel oil, reflected the quayside street-lamps as wavery aureoles of green with centers of tarnished copper. The sky was ponderous with rain that would fall later, and our goodbyes were quick and simple. I took Judith's face between my hands from the backseat, and kissed her a soldierly kiss, at which her friend accorded me the same look of tactful disapproval that had greeted our whiskies, and suddenly I wondered whether perhaps he wasn't her lover after all, which in circumspect Dublin would have been more than enough reason for reserve. True or not, I settled on this notion, not wanting to read any more subtle cultural meanings into what might be only a simple matter of discretion.

"Come back sometime," Judith said. "Maeve was so thrilled because you were interested in her garden. She told me that she liked 'that tall American with the glasses,' and she sent a kiss to thank you."

She reached over, and delivered it warmly.

The next morning, in an Irish fog, we flew to Edinburgh without ever seeing the Irish Sea. Nothing much happened in Edinburgh. Except that the sun came out as we drove down Princes Street, and stayed out thereafter. Except that there were flowers in little pots on the dashboards of the taxies, and the women had the quiet chic, and the men the bemused friendliness, that I have always associated with Boston. Except that we walked in that stately, handsome city with its air of intellect honed to a keen edge by the clear highland light, and devoted our few days there to pictures, and delectable meals, and rubbernecking, happy to surrender the role of refugee for that of tourist. At least for a little while. Also, the pubs were noisy.

FOUR

London: Games, People, Play

After the dank twilight of King's Cross Station, where the grimy bulbs are never off and the puddles on the taxi-pavements never dry, there was the blue door of Jay Landesman's house in an Islington backwater with the little park just opposite and the Turf Accountant on the corner; and Jay himself posing in the doorway—John Cassevetes restyled by Carnaby Street—in the starched white middy of a provincial repertory's *Pinafore,* complete with particolored neckerchief, ancient basketball sneakers, and Paul

McCartney's haircut; and, in the living room, Fran in her "eyes," the lower lashes painted on in black, and crescents of silver and green eyeliner on the upper lids. A dusty Klieg light stood in one corner like a Cyclops designed by Giacometti, and Jay slouched in a wooden dentist's chair in which even the embalmed Jeremy Bentham would have looked uncomfortable. Fran brought the tea and booze and ice, and we bridged the fourteen months since the last time in New York with the mad gossiping of old friends.

"You've come just in time," Jay said. "We're going into a very social phase."

We moved into their basement with its dominoed linoleum, whitewashed brick, and Kodiak bearskin rug that felt like greasy brillo to the feet. We slept under a Ralph Ortiz "destruction" on the wall—a disembowelled mattress slashed open to resemble a monstrous vagina furzed with horsehair, out of which the severed ganglia of broken springs protruded.

The three-storey house had been turned into a Landesman-environment—just as cluttered and eccentric and interesting as other domiciles in New York or St. Louis in other years. Fran spent her mornings in the large, womb-like brass bed upstairs that became littered with books, correspondence, and her Emily Dickinson-scribbles as the hours passed. Jay had his rigorous schedules—visiting the pear-man, the herring-man, the bread-man each morning in the Chapel Street Market, pausing to tease the ashen-faced Twiggies in the local boutique, having his elevenses with antique dealers from Camden Passage, putt-putting off to Charing Cross Road on his Suzuki after lunch, dropping by every afternoon to check on a sad and foppish tyro-hippie named Marvin (Jay called him Tony for some reason), whose neighborhood head-shop was floundering, and napping in the

box room off a landing for the hour before twilight. Their life
was a careless mix of Haight-Ashbury and Grub Street as Mi-
cawber might have improvised it. They had quietly dropped out
of public ambitions and interior decoration. They were "at
home."

"What's the project these days," I asked Jay.

"Oh, I'm between projects. But then the whole project-
concept may be only another illusion. I keep busy with my
rounds."

London was in a fine, autumnal flare-up of life that year. A
decade before, it had been *grey*. Grey faces pinched with austerity. Grey clothes making everyone look as anonymous as refugees. Miserly fires in the pubs. Roast beef and roast potatoes
drowned in a glutenous gravy. Green Park grey with coal-
smoke, Whitehall grey with befogged purpose. And in *The En-
tertainer,* John Osborne had portrayed Brittania as no better than
a *Folies*-girl pretending to be Valerie Hobson. It had all been as
depressing as having Christmas dinner in a Lyon's Corner
House, but now England seemed pulled together by a new energy, a new flamboyance, and a new humor. The reason was
simple: at last it had admitted that it was little more than a small
island off the coast of Europe, a geopolitical anachronism, and
so, with the islander's survival-instinct, it had buried Kipling
once and for all (along with his sentimental solemnity), and proceeded to raise the world's hemlines, decorate the Beatles, pay
some attention to the national cuisine, and so become, briefly,
the setter-of-fashions for the Western World. All the girls looked
like other, younger Redgrave sisters no one had been told about,
and even the fledgling barristers, hoisting their pints off Chan-
cery Lane, were facsimiles of Vidal Sassoon. The very air
seemed lighter, and the light airier. You smelled money and cos-

metics and oregano. The Thames sparkled, the parks were as lush as Constables, and at last you could see the newly-scrubbed dome of St. Paul's from miles away.

Dowdy old London had gone bonkers with chic.

* * *

During our first week there, on one of those rainy afternoons that are so cozy in London, with a single luncheon-martini fueling him, Jay tried to build a party out of his address book. Christine Keeler wasn't in; Bill Burroughs couldn't come till Tuesday; Tom O'Horgan was involved in rehearsals for *Futz*; Annie Ross was off to the Midlands on a gig; Peter Cook and Alan Brien and Yoko Ono were otherwise engaged. So we ended up with a bosomy American girl, just back from Afghanistan, who instantly launched into one of those gobbledegook-indictments of "the Giant Universal Computer" that struck the young that year as so incisive as they smoked their hash. There was a nice painter from down the street, and his not-so-nice girl who had a fascinating wart under one dissipated eye. There was novelist Jeremy Brooks (your Jack Hawkins-jawed Englishman), and his wife Eleanor, who had the admirable, non-trendy class of certain English countrywomen. And there was Heather Somebody who arrived with her parrot, George, on her shoulder.

Wine bottles collected like bowling pins on the coffee table. Smoke drifted upwards in undulating layers through three and four o'clock. *The Ballad of Billie Joe* played over and over on the phonograph as Fran snatched naps on the couch. And there was London humor, which, that year, was as irreverent and mocking as the tone that had pervaded midtown drinking circles in New York in the later Fifties—the Lenny Bruce-tone as imitated by Peter Sellers. The haze of wine and pot and nerves insulated the room against the hours, and we discussed the various things that Billie Joe might have thrown off the Tallahatchie Bridge, and I became bemused for ten full minutes with the certainty that only I knew for sure.

The afternoon slipped, without a seam, into evening. People appeared and disappeared. The street lamp outside the window was haloed with yellow mist. Fish and chips, spread out greasy and delectable on a sheet of tabloid, materialized from around the corner. Mild Marvin and his kewpie-doll wife, Deborah, arrived in Edwardian jackets of black velvet, with three acid-heads, all of them totalled on LSD, who sat around, saying not a single word, their heads moving back and forth with the conversation, like so many stoned anthropologists, watching us drink our juice and smoke our grass. Peter Cook called back and still couldn't come. Someone arrived with the news that Cass Elliott had been busted for possession right off the *Queen E.* in Southampton, and Jay spent half an hour on the phone trying to locate her. Jeremy decided on a complicated incest-solution to the *Billie Joe* problem. The acid-heads listened attentively, the way you listen to a language you don't understand. The hallway was heaped with sopping mackintoshes, and most of the wine bottles had become dead soldiers. The American girl, way over her head by now, was fed and gotten off to the theater. Marvin broke his silence and announced the imperativeness of immediate removal to Ischia, and Deborah's stockings were found to be laddered and ill-fitting.

Later, under the large opaque globe that hung over the dining table, Jay said, finishing up the wine: "So much for *Time* Magazine's idea of 'swinging London'—friends getting together to talk about a song . . . We rarely go out anymore."

* * *

Cass Elliott and her "old man" of the moment sat under that globe, having a lunch of chicken livers, tangerines and pot. A hired limosine was parked outside among the street-kids of Islington, the chauffeur lounging with his racing-paper against a mudguard in the blandish sun. Jay and Fran had known Cass long before she became one of *The Mamas & The Papas,* a rock group that had broken up, not happily, a little while before.

Cass let her boyfriend massage the soles of her bare feet as she talked about what had happened. She had the elongated face of a jolly Shetland, with the savvy eyes and busy mouth that usually indicate self-confidence that has been hard come by, and she had turned her fatness and her plainness into a kind of kinky glamor that you had to admire.

"Finally, we just got on each other's nerves . . . They're off on a different trip than I am . . . John kept saying: 'Cass, you're not listening to the Distant Trumpets anymore' . . . Groovy tidbits like that." Her careless laugh revealed an ambitious, fame-hungry girl, who had yearned, years before, for show business and its tinsels, and had lent her talents to the rock-scene only on a temporary basis. She thought for a second: "Well, *shit,*" she concluded philosophically, "We had a kind of symbiotic relationship, trying to become a real *group,* to think alike, but finally our emotional lives got all mixed up with one another—" She took a tangerine and proceeded to peel off the rind with pudgy fingers, and then she sniffed at her own propriety. "Well, I just don't dig people making it with other people's people, if you want to know. It's uncool, it's messy, it's—*décadent.* That's what I mean."

Fran took a turn on the joint, studying Cass' self-absorbed expression: "You mean, you're hung up on monogamy, and all that crap?" she said at last. "God, it's all *that* that's decadent to me. Because people of our age always assume that people of your age live by a new and saner morality, a morality that *we* tried to pioneer, and now—" She shook her head: "That's particularly weird."

A certain gap opened over the table. Cass was a little shocked, and Fran was a little disappointed, and both recognized that an impasse had been reached. As did Jay.

"Speaking of morality," he said. "Here's a story. Sandy Koufax and a buddy went looking for Fran's brother Sam in his bar in Gaslight Square in St. Louis. Only it had turned into a gay joint, and it was jammed with *boys*. Well, Sandy got up to the bar, got himself a drink, and said to his friend—"

"'We had to fight our way in,'" Cass interrupted, "'and we'll have to fuck our way out.' . . . Christ, Jay, *I* told you that story the last time I saw you."

Everyone laughed, like so many Nathanael Wests, like moralists-on-a-merry-go-round, like Americans that year.

Up six flights of a stolidly middle-class building of flats on Goswell Road, Marvin, in his black velvet suit and silver lamé shirt, gave a "wild party" that was probably typical of the pseudo-hippie scene in London then. Four rooms jammed with people shoulder to shoulder. Rock-dancing in one, a light-show in another, talk in yet another, the kitchen an anarchy of drinkers. Lonely boys down from Oxford peeked at "birds" from Camden Passage, and stared away into the middle distance when they were caught. Trippers sprawled on pillows around the walls, giggling or comatose depending on the fix. Somnambulist girls danced with their own bereft shadows.

In the light-show room, twenty people sat on the floor, passing joints around in the darkness as Marvin introduced drops of colored water into the double-lenses of his light-machine, drops that swam upwards on the wall like viruses exploring the vein, or halted midway to form phalluses with swollen, blue heads.

The room tittered when the projector focused and unfocused on vivid spots of magenta, reproducing the tightening and un-tightening of abstract anuses. All these blown minds, supposedly freed of that kind of psycho-sexual association, responded exactly as they would have responded if not stoned. I choked out of a bottle of warm wine, and sweated in the crush of bodies, realizing that even the blown mind seeks meaning, and meaning is grounded in the known world, so where could pot or light shows take us—except farther away from the Garden, deeper into the Expulsion?

Nevertheless, Marvin was nice, harried, thrilled—though his evening was plagued with the kinds of silly accidents that always occur on schedule in the suburbs. The movie-projector for the dirty films wouldn't work. A fuse blew in the kitchen, and he had no replacements. Too many people arrived whom nobody knew. A girl got sick all over the dancers. Everything was confusion and discomfort. He took me into the conversation-room to show me, in all seriousness, the Beardsley illustrations to *Lysistrata,* all carefully, beautifully matted and hung in their sad attempt at naughtiness. He seemed to be torn between a combination of manic anticipation and paranoid worry.

Well he might have been worried. The whole scene was as uncool as teenagers shooting up in a parking lot. The apartment was thronged with strangers. On the way to it, we had passed five couples who had only *heard* about the party. Marvin kept throwing his keys out of the window so dim figures in the street below could let themselves in the downstairs door. You could hear the music four blocks away. A boy was having a bad acid-trip in the bathroom, and the entire place smelled like an Arabian armpit. Any policeman, who was curious and could follow his nose, might have wandered in, taken a toke or two, and busted the whole party.

London's hippies, it seemed to me, were less cogent, less original, and less a judgement on their society than the American brand. Though they had more sartorial style, they didn't seem to be having any more fun, and they hadn't learned the iron law of all counter-lifestyles: *An orgy is only an orgy when it isn't held nightly everywhere by everyone.* If dressing up in hip gear, and sucking the wet end of a badly-rolled bomber, and groping the boy or girl next to you, could blow a mind, what kind of mind was it? I said as much to Shirley as we walked home.

"Oh, you know as well as I do," she said. "Be generous. After all, back home the kids don't even sterilize their needles."

It was true enough. That past summer, Flower Power had begun to wither in a plague of hepatitis, and San Francisco's moral earthquake had proved to be only another bohemian trembler, after all.

One night after dinner, Christine Keeler, at odds for the evening, called Jay, who told her to come right over. The Landesmans had known her for a year or two, and knew I'd be intrigued. What writer, in these parlous times, wouldn't be fascinated by a party-girl who had almost brought down a government?

She was taller than I'd imagined, with a fairly large frame, wearing a plum-colored velvet dress stretched taut over ripe breasts, dark and abundant hair in a tumble on her shoulders, and something alert and ferret-like about her not-unpretty face. A stubborn girl, canny rather than bright; a girl who mistook airs for manners. With her, a friend named Lorraine, a show-girl-type from Australia, with metallic blonde hair and a fleshy figure, with whom she was "pal-ing" at the moment.

A strange evening ensued. Christine went through a curious transformation as she drank—and she drank steadily and well with Shirley and me, as the others turned-on. She changed from an opinionated, defensive, self-dramatizing *gamin,* who seemed to accept the world's conception of her (alluding darkly to powerful government forces that were protecting her in return for silence), into something considerably different. Her speech became quicker, less prim, more insinuative; her eyes studied you with a kind of ironic, smoldering interest; the gap between her tabloid-image and her life-experiences widened before your eyes, and she came into focus. Until, at one moment, amazingly, she was talking directly and cogently out of her dilemma, and saying to me, an absolute stranger:

"I pushed my mother away from me in the jail, you know. 'Don't touch me!' I begged her," her face pensive and interesting as she engaged the memory. "Why did I do that, I wonder? Because, you know, when I look in the mirror, I see just what *they* see, what she must have seen . . . And yet I don't really *feel* like that anymore. Why is that?"

There was no hint of self-pity in her voice, no false histrionics or counterfeit remorse, and I felt that with one single, small push of human feeling, on anyone's part, she might come into a recognition that would reconcile her, and so I leaned towards her encouragingly. She mused on: how she had hated her stepfather for "plaguing" her when she was a girl, for treating her "good" mother so badly, but how, oddly, she had become closer to him than to her mother since "the trouble." And what was she to do with that? It was hilarious, really. She was in a kind of limbo now. She couldn't change addresses without informing *them.* She couldn't leave the country. Her recent marriage had broken up in violence and foolishness. They wanted her to play the Harlow part in Mike McClure's *The Beard,* but had I *read* it? Could "Christine Keeler" say those lines? Her eyebrows arched ironically, and I poured her another drink, and she slipped away—that is, she sheared off from the moment we had reached, and everyone else piled in, not having heard our conversation, and the chance was lost. But I was *with* her from then on, and we continued to drink, and the others rolled more joints, and eventually we were playing the Truth Game, an old ploy of Jay's.

This involved everyone in the room asking a single, outrageous question of everyone else, which had to be answered with an equally outrageous candor, the questions, of course, becoming increasingly blunt and impertinent as the questioner, having been questioned himself, took his turn. A few examples of the questions:

Christine to Lorraine: "When are you going to make it with me?"

Christine to me: "Are you going to fuck your wife tonight?"

Lorraine to me: "Have you ever had a homosexual experience?"

Me to Fran: "Why is it that I always feel that you and I have never really connected with one another?"

Jay to Christine: "Johnnie said today that maybe I was bucking-for-saint, because I don't *do* anything anymore, except things like this. Have you ever thought of *that* as an alternative?"

Me to Christine: "Why don't you just decide to love yourself?"

The various answers have no place here, but it can be said that that night the Truth Game, which I had seen shrivel egos and pulverize relationships in the past, brought certain honesties out into that room, everyone there having drunk enough, or smoked enough, or lost enough, to lay it down, whatever it was, the way it seemed to them.

Still, Christine, when she left, had re-achieved the sardonic, offhand mask without which, perhaps, her London might have become Blake's *London,* and when I took her small, rather soft little hand, she glanced at me, and said indifferently: "Anyway,

71

it doesn't matter much, any of it, does it? . . . Have you had a
good stay in England?"

His projector finally fixed, we went to Marvin's to see his dirty
movie, Jay having beguiled him for the last few days with the
notion of making one themselves. Another evening among the
Zombies. A fat boy sat in a shadowy corner, behind a crescent
of scraggly beard, sniffling through the end of a coke-high. Sullen Mick Jagger look-alikes arrived in sickle boots and silk shirts
to stare at everything with watery, dead eyes. Tall, leggy girls, in
vinyl minis, sat on the parquet, showing their crotches to no one
in particular. Marvin looked like a tousle-headed dormouse at
the Mad Hatter's tea-party, and Deborah's black-net stockings
bagged sadly at the knee. More of those fat, sloppy English
bombers were rolled—the kind that come apart in the mouth as
they circle the room—and everyone proceeded to turn-on in
preparation for the film.

The lights were doused, the murmurs quenched, and the ten-
minute movie was shown. It turned out to be a French film
about Father Christmas, made in the Thirties, which had had a
small reputation among pornography-buffs of twenty years before, but which had been superseded, in quality and explicitness,
long ago. Grainy images of diligent and inept lust flickered on
the wall: a lonely, dark-haired girl idly playing with herself; a
flashback to a lesbian-foray with a governess; disjointed shots of
thrashing limbs, desperately exploring hands, avid mouths.
Then a jump-cut to a sort of Rube Goldberg fucking-ma-
chine—all coils and pistons and fan-belts—onto which the
young brunette awkwardly climbed, massaging her breasts as if
she had a terminal itch, and writhing with embarrassed approxi-
mations of pleasure. Father Christmas sat watching all this with
wet-lipped delight, only to be confronted by a naked angel, with

72

cardboard wings, who proceeded to mount *him*. With a fey little grimace, he wickedly removed her wings as she settled down. The brunette rode the machine, the angel rode Santa, and the fifteen-odd people in the room watched them watching each other. The last shot—when Santa, *in extremis ejaculatio,* whipped off his Santa-mask and plopped it over the rump of the brunette—brought only a few nervous titters.

Lights, coughing, a sudden eruption of offhand remarks: "You never see *blonde* pubic hair in these films," a blonde girl said. "But the details always fascinate me," hazarded a young man. "I mean, the decor. That room was right out of Max Ophuls."

Jay took over, the imp of irony in his eye, and described his notion of the film they should make. There would be parts for everyone. His friend, the American novelist, would work out the details of the story line. A girl-painter that he knew would design the costumes and sets. The basic idea was marvelously simple: a young couple is trapped in Madame Tussaud's overnight. The eerie atmosphere arouses their appetites, and they proceed to commit the Conjugal Act on the floor. Animated by this discharge of sexual energy, the waxworks come to life and an orgy ensues, during which the young couple are initiated into every known variation of Erotic Congress. Jay reeled off ten or twelve, with enthusiastic explicitness, looking from face to face with the mandarin-smile of Walt Disney winging a story-idea for his associates.

Everyone began suggesting scenes, cloaking their excitement in an impenetrable cool. One girl thought there should be a sequence of Marie Antoinette being sodomized by De Gaulle, but a purist with a historical turn of mind felt it should be Robespierre instead. The fat boy mumbled something about Eisenhower and Khrushchev, obviously seeing himself in the latter role. Marvin felt that it would be better if the film was kept

73

rigidly a-political, but that a poetic segment involving Jack the Ripper and the Brontë sisters might be "kicky." I suddenly had an urgent desire to laugh—the pot had reached me—because here were all of Marvin's waxworks people, talking quite seriously about appearing in a movie as waxworks come to life, and doing all the things before a camera that they somehow felt they couldn't do at that moment, in that room, where, presumably, they were free to do anything they liked.

Before I could stop myself, I heard a voice describing a movie about people planning to make a dirty movie—a voice with a hint of raillery down in it somewhere—my own voice. "Anyway," I said, "there's the *real* film in all this. You might even get art-house distribution."

Marvin blinked in confusion, and Deborah knitted her brows as if she had missed the point, and Jay laughed and laughed. All at once, I realized that he had thought that perhaps a real orgy might grow out of all the talk about the fanciful one, and I shut my mouth. But it was too late. Waxworks only come to life in fantasies.

* * *

Outside, the feeling persisted that there was something elusively different about London now, and I finally decided that it was the absence of the acrid smell of soft coal and chemicals that had characterized the city ten years before. Then, the days had been perpetually murky, yellow, leprous, and the dim streets stank like so many pissoirs, dizzy with disinfectant. Now the breeze was full of river-smells, bus-exhaust and frying plaice. The trees in the squares no longer looked vaguely asphyxiated, and the September sky was Della Robbia blue.

Off for the day museuming, Shirley and I walked down the placid Thames, through the Victoria Tower Gardens, to have another look at the Turners in the Tate. In no hurry, we approached them through rooms of English watercolor, in which copse, hamlet, lane, and river were rearranged over and over again until they took on the symbolic quality of the boat, the mountain and the crooked tree in Oriental prints. The Turners (many more of them than had been hung ten years before) occupied several rooms, together with a display of memorabilia—his palettes, his paints and inkstands, his smock.

Perhaps only an island people, a northern people—like the English and the Japanese—can become so absorbed by the relationship between nature and weather. It may be the only thing about which the English, a nation of gardeners, have ever become openly mystical. In any event, their finest painting is profound with a sense of the passage of the seasons over countryside—summer's bee-thrummed noons, the bracing canter over autumn's frosty fields, winter's shroud on thatched roofs, spring choking the throat with the odor of daffodils—the whole *drama* of weather as experienced by a people not so far removed from the nature-worship of Stonehenge, after all. And, in Turner, this national trait finally found its great visionary.

We took a turn through the rooms in opposite directions, because I knew Shirley wanted to be alone. Turner had always had a curiously visceral effect on her. I walked and paused, paused and walked, watching Turner's eye, as it came to know itself over his long career, penetrate beneath appearances, until the eye became the prism of his soul, and its images swam outwards from the picture and somehow *through* the retina of the viewer. His lurid sunsets blazed up, molten as furnaces; his somber dawns seemed to have been daubed in the dew itself; mists as evanescent as reveries unfocused his distances; storms heaped up, black as fate, over the channel-ports; Venice shimmered like a faint promise through the fawn greys and pinks of its lagoon; and everywhere the horizon-line dissolved into little more than a luminous hint of the freed eye's search for limits.

It was painting decades ahead of its time, as prophetic as Blake's poetry, and you saw Turner making *visible* what had lain under our very eyes all along with the raw pigment snaking out of the tube. When we stood on Millbank a little later, waiting for the Westminster bus, his power to transform one's own way of seeing became instantly clear. Everything was in motion. The great Thames moved as vast and formal under the dappled skies as the centuries since Spenser had memorialized a wedding in the image of its seaward flow. Moored boats rocked gently on cloudy reflections. A breeze wafted the leaves into an ineffable, delicate flutter. The air brought a deft glow to the skin. Across the broad sweep of the river, beyond Lambeth and Battersea and a wilderness of bed-sitters, you sensed all of England stretching away south towards forest and moorland and cliff, until it sheared off into the sea. A quiet admiration came over me. The portly, affluent Turner of the last years, eccentric and reclusive, was as dead as a doornail in St. Paul's crypt downriver, and yet he had bequeathed to this day, this year, this London, the rarest gift of all—particular vision, a singular man's unique eye.

Shirley was staring out over the water, her face averted from me, still enclosed in the experience. I realized that she was just inches from tears, and said something glancing. She gave me a look of embarrassment and pique.

"Don't worry," she said, "I won't blubber on the bus ... But he gets to me. He always does. Imagine *seeing* that clearly! It could change your life ..."

After lunch at the Museum Tavern on Great Russell Street, we went across to see the Elgin Marbles. The British Museum was still as sedate, musty and sepulchral as it had been years ago, but now shafts of dark-gold sunlight fell through the high windows on the massed booty of the Empire, and long-haired students bent, transfixed, over an exhibition of Marx's manuscripts a few rooms away from where he had written *Das Kapital,* and the paneling glowed with the rich and luminous patina that comes to gloomy rooms into which the light of day has been allowed at last.

The looted marble friezes, set above eye-level in a vast, empty hall, no longer seemed so much like those spectral, shrouded figures, sitting massively still, legs slightly apart, that Henry Moore had sculpted during the war. Their classic style, blurred by centuries of weather and neglect on the Parthenon, came out clearly, and they reposed in all their huge nobility, shades of a vanished Attica, profound, austere, and mysterious in the echoing silence. As so often with Greek art, I felt at once impressed but not *moved,* as if sensing a consciousness utterly different from my own. These were images of non-human perfection before which History seemed to blow away like ashes. Had we lost something since their day, or had something been gained? I couldn't decide. I only knew that standing there in mod London, so many obliterated empires later, those monumental shards disturbed me with an awareness of the transitory nature of our contemporary vision of human existence. What was it but a fixation on the particularity of each face, spirit, experience? Something else was limned here, something earlier, something unearthly, something that seemed indifferent to our either/or conception of the soul.

Then I became aware of a vast, distant moaning, like a chorale keening a requiem in some subterranean cathedral beneath the building, a sound that somehow became inaudible when I concentrated on it, but returned, like certain bass figures in Bach, the moment I listened to the footfalls and murmurs in the room. I peered up at a tall, impassive Caryatid, her face expressionless and aloof, her body gigantic and somehow roofless, and sensed the sound again—eerie and muffled, as if all these statues were petitioning to go home so they might stare out over Athens, forever blinkless, towards that condition of timelessness about which no one even speculated any longer. I realized that the sound was probably only the air-conditioning, or the Underground vibrating up through tons of stone, or some acoustical anomaly, but it was *there* nonetheless (though no one else seemed to be aware of it)—a massed, barely discernible lamentation that ceased the moment we left that hall. I accepted it, for whatever it was.

Dismal rain in Notting Hill. A morning of raw nerves after a late, unsettling night. Splashing up and down bleak streets looking for the gallery where Yoko Ono's show had opened the night before.

"It's just like her to pick a place that nobody can find," Jay said. But we did.

The smallish white room was as deceptively empty as a Japanese print. The few things in it were as modest and enigmatic as Zen Koans—gentle nudges towards reality-truths. I stood a long time before a glass hammer that was meant to be used to drive a nail into a gleaming metal plate. A sense of white transparency, of the lucidity of a calmed mind, was everywhere. Downstairs, inside a sort of tent, you sat on the floor for two minutes of circling lights. Upstairs, above the gallery, there was a half-room—that is, half-a-bed, half-a-chair, half-a-shoe, half of a perfectly every-day life. The partialness of the contemporary personality, of the splintered self stumbling along on its one leg, came over us all without a word. An ominous quiet possessed everything there, the whiteness became emptiness, and the rain outside the window suddenly sounded as strange as all familiar noises sound when we take notice of them with a new ear.

Then, as we were about to leave, Yoko happened by. She slipped in through the door in an askew rainhat, an old trench coat, and slacks. The small oval of her face, as pale and wet as an orchid floating in a bowl of brackish water, was shy with surprise. She stood dripping on the floor, like a school-girl interrupted in an inner-monolog by visiting relatives, and yet her dark eyes were sharp with cunning, a cunning successfully banked behind the patient, winsome mask. Jay and Fran joked with her, and she laughed a modest laugh with them. Agitated as I was that day, I felt a rush of fellow-feeling for her, and fancied I knew her mood on waking, her engrossed afternoons, her supper pots. Imaginary empathies, of course. But privately I trusted such feelings, and waited for them, so that as we left, I went up to her, aware that everything I was doing was blurred by nerves, and leaned over, kissed her hand, and announced: "You're a princess who got out of the tower." Those quick, watchful eyes noted the tall, flushed, obviously disturbed American, and she smiled half-a-smile, as if she knew that in an hour he would be sitting in the York Minster in Soho, drinking pernod and grenadine, his day a little clearer for her try.

The night before, she had met John Lennon for the first time.

* * *

But America kept intruding on our pleasures and our dreams. Under protest, we were dragged off to a Vietnam Protest Meeting, chaired by Robert Bolt, in a small, modern theater off

Shaftesbury Avenue. It resembled such meetings in New York two years before—natterings about the "rice lobby," "social revolution," and "U.S. Imperialism"; the senseless, self-serving jargon of logic-chopping intellectuals adopting a disaster that is not their own. Endless statistical analyses of who had done what, and to whom. Nary a word about the moral catastrophe that had knocked such wordy bullshit out of most of us back home. I remembered the ravaged look of complicity-in-Suez that I had seen on left-wing English faces ten years before, knew the self-same look was on my face now, and realized that perhaps the only truly educative political experience of these times was to be a little tainted oneself. As Brigid Brophy delivered a flawless lawyer's brief against the Domino Theory, I realized for the first time how far her American counterparts had been driven, by that taint, beyond such theorizing. We were all involved, our ready-made explanations had been rendered obsolete, and the moral squalor of the war had entered us as viscerally as Asian flu. Back home, Susan Sontag ground her teeth on her bed at night, nostalgic for an anger unsullied by anguish.

"We had to turn down Norman's *Vietnam* novel. Regretfully, of course. But it's simply impossible, too obscene for words."

I was lunching in a quiet restaurant in Wardour Street with the lady-editor of my English publishers. She was an attractive, intelligent woman, a fine writer herself, who had thoughtfully seen to it that I had ice in my whiskey, and who occasionally flashed me a challenging, inquisitive smile that I found pleasant.

"Norman may be finished, on the basis of this book. I'm so fond of him, and he's such a vigorous stylist, but he can't *think*. He never could, really. Don't you agree?"

She wasn't being snide, there was genuine regret in her voice, even a hint of saddened expectations, and perhaps a not-unwelcome sense of her own integrity in having rejected a book by so best-selling an author.

What could I say to that? Rationality, wit, and emotional propriety were still highly prized in England, and engaged, intuitive thinking was considered the province of precocious adolescents. They'd been burned by Colin Wilson, hadn't they? Mailer's wild and courageous swings into all the contemporary darks made the Engish uneasy. The mysteries of Being—indeed, the whole existential viewpoint without which it was impossible for an American writer over forty to confront the automated kaleidoscope of his times—were still a locked-closet in the psyche of this island, and I realized that moral labyrinths had never occupied the English overmuch. A tradition-directed people become outer-directed when those traditions fail, and fashion— what the traffic is baring but not a centimeter more—had become, here, the operative guideline, whereas in the America of the late 60s, all intellectual movement was tending remorselessly inward. So all I said was this:

"I'm afraid I think Mailer has the most exciting intelligence in the English-speaking world right now," giving her my most candid smile, because her expression appreciated the disagreement, instead of viewing it as a blunder in the delicate maneuvers of the author-publisher relationship.

"Perhaps I ought to read the book again," she said, with no intention of doing so. "But I found nothing but scatology in it."

"Perhaps I should read it for the *first* time," I replied, "thinking, as I do, that there's a powerful amount of *shit* in the world just now."

I liked her for laughing as she forked up the last of her steak-and-kidneys.

"What *I* often wonder," the Austrian-born historian asked

with an air of lofty hauteur that was even more English than the English, "is why *they* just don't go back where they came from?" He was talking about London's current inundation of Jamaicans, and the rising crime-rate, and we were sitting in the small, neat, white living room of his house in a Kensington mews.

"The impossible racial situation in the States is probably responsible for it," his wife said, an old friend of mine whom I hadn't seen in a decade. "Don't you think so, Johnnie? Rap Brown, and that lot."

They were threatened with the promise of a prestigious job in an American university, which they would accept if it came through—even though the prospect was odious to them.

"It's odd," I said, as evenly as I could manage. "You blame Rap Brown on race prejudice in America, but then you blame your difficulties with the blacks here on *him*—as if he was an American export, like some moral equivalent of Coca-Cola."

The historian gave me a sour look of non-comprehension. After all, you couldn't expect *bon mots* from Americans. The question of America had been settled long ago, hadn't it?

The moment you walked into the Playboy Club on Park Lane you were in America again. The American smell of air-conditioning, and sizzling steaks, and foam-cleaned carpeting; the American look of emphatic primary colors, Leroy Neimans on the walls, and glossy Bunnies in their invisible cellophane—breasts, thighs and buttocks held together around the middle by a swatch of blue satin; the tall American drinks with lots of big American ice-cubes, the tasty American piano-jazz coming out of the chandeliers, and the elusive American mood that seemed made up of equal parts of money and nerves and booze and hope and indifference-to-discomfort.

Vic Lowndes was giving a cocktail party for Cy Coleman,

whose musical *Sweet Charity* had opened in the West End that week. Jay sported a four-inch-wide psychedelic tie; Fran looked ever-more like Zelda in a fur-trimmed, 1920s coat of her mother's; Shirley's paisley-print shift did justice to her classy knees; and I was invisible in my only suit.

In the dark-blue grotto of the V.I.P. Room, you had to keep reminding yourself that Hyde Park was just across the street. You were astonished when your Bunny spoke in the accents of Manchester rather than Winnetka. The nip in the syrup of the Jack Daniels brought the taste of Tennessee back up into your mouth, and you couldn't help recalling a drive across the Cumberlands in a blizzard the year before, nursing a bad generator, having to be in Memphis by nightfall—all that excitement and exhaustion of vagabondage in vast America. You reminded yourself that there was gambling downstairs, that you could be in Paris in time for midnight-supper, that all this lavish waste of canapes and cocktails was only part of the dream America was dreaming at the moment, from which, presumably, it must awaken soon. You maneuvered your drink, your wedge of salmon on toast, and your bit of piping *quiche,* among the likes of Farley Granger, Dorothy Fields, Juliet Prowse, Terry Stamp, Brian Jones the Rolling Stone, and the Guinness heiress.

You laughed, you gossiped, but, for some reason, you had no taste for it. You noted the couple that Vic pointed out through the crowd, who "run orgies in Temple Bar": the husband in his impeccable dinner jacket and ruffled shirt, his handsome, sun-lamped face, his cigarette holder, his entire *manner* pomade-smooth; the wife in pink, ankle-length silk, standing *inside* herself, petite, bejeweled, gesturing languidly with a token Bristol Cream—as, separately, they propositioned the Black, the Ingenue, the Rock Star, the Two Beards, the Drunken Poet, the Girl from Biba's, and the Secret Foot Fetishist—casting that night's revels. Petronian ruminations stirred, unwanted, in your head.

At that moment, it seemed that you had spent years in this room. You had joked its bitter jokes, you had hoped its lecherous hopes. You had tasted the salt of boredom in its hors-d'oeuvres that only a dollop of licentiousness could sate. You had awakened in some of the beds to which it served as an antechamber. You had cured its various hangovers with Fernet Branca and resolutions. You knew its scabrous litanies down to the ultimate wicked anecdote. But here, in London, at last, its fatal magic died. Your Balzacian ambition to know it all, taste it all, survive to write about it, disintegrated into a simple acknowledgment that even Balzacs must pay a tab. You became aware that you hadn't said a word in ten minutes, and that your wife was looking at you as people look at people who are no longer much fun. You looked back at her, speechless, out of your utterly commonplace discovery, and could think of nothing to do but have another drink.

Jay, at your elbow, was saying with a cocked eye: "Come on, I want you to meet the guy who cuts my hair. He's got the line on this whole thing . . . Split ends, teasing, replacing lost body . . . The hippest man in the room."

* * *

During that balmy autumn of 1967, when the days were mild and blue and the nights were green with grass, you ate the tender artichokes in the San Frediana on King's Road, with yellow tablecloths starched as stiff as boards and a bottle of Frascati with the cellar-dust barely wiped away, while outside the crowds of flower-children and mod-freaks and tourists perambulated up and down in an unending flow, and people drank on the sidewalk in front of the Queen's Elm, and Ben Carruthers, who had once acted in an experimental play of yours, appeared out of nowhere in wild skins, ju-jus, and an immense "natural," to spook the citizenry. You lunched in La Gaffe in Hempstead, upstairs above the kitchen, where the *coq au vin* was watery but the *vin de maison* was not, and the prams were on the brake going down the cobbled hill outside, and you talked the best of talk—the talk of tipsy poets. You ate beef and brussels down in the depths of Grumbles in Pimlico where the waitresses, in baby-minis, exposed sky-blue panties with white frou as they leaned over to take away the plates. Or you simply went up to the Chapel Street Market with a string bag to buy prawns, cockles, Stilton, endive, and a dozen of ale, and bring them home, and put Sergio Mendez on the phonograph, and, later, nap the deep naps of surfeited afternoon.

That autumn, you had pints in the Kismet, a private drinking club somewhere near Charing Cross Road, negotiating the narrow staircase down to the bar where there were always out-of-work actors, and counterfeit Brendan Behans just getting started on their day, and a cheery bar-mistress who always drew full ones. You checked out the Indica Bookshop to get that week's copy of *International Times* or *Private Eye,* and gossiped about theater in Berlin, and then you whizzed off on the Suzuki behind Jay's Wild West buckskins and leather World War I pilot's helmet with the goggles down, to Jim Haynes' *Arts Lab,* still under construction then (and gone now), which was planned as a version of the old, idealistic, MGM bromide,"Let's all get together and put on a show!"—in this case, "Let's have us a theater, a film-house, an art gallery, a disco, and a restaurant—all under one roof," an idea predicated on the assumption that something might become clear if everyone pooled their separate muddles. In the drizzly nights, you went to the Roundhouse to see "The Crazy World of Arthur Brown," which was embodied in the chalk-white, half-demented face of a rock ghoul that materialized out of the murk of that enormous, cold shed of worn brick and long-carless track. You took a turn up Carnaby Street where all the boutiques played the same records, and the clerks arrived in proper suits and methodically changed into that week's gear, and tourists stood on the sidewalks taking home-movies of the famous store-fronts, and you felt the end of it coming even then, the smell of money as rank as chlorine in the nose.

That autumn, too, you found yourself in the house of a girl-painter near Kentish Town, whose bed was surrounded by black mirrors, whose kitchen was wallpapered with images of sex, war, irony, and death, staring through the bottom of an upturned whiskey glass at a large apothecary jar on the sideboard in which a brindled snake floated in a weightless coil in the formaldehyde. Those early October afternoons, you often ranged far afield in Islington, looking for cigarettes among the discount stores. But the tobacconists mostly kept pub-hours, and the dismal blocks passed in monotony, and you were marooned in the Sargossa Sea of endless London, and trapped (as you often felt that year when you were alone) in unbidden thoughts of what was happening back home, unable to enjoy the experiences you'd come for, as boring to yourself as fanatics had always been to you, realizing that, still, damnably, you valued character over personality, significance over fun, and were not, at the moment, spectacularly tolerant about the differences. That autumn, too, the team horse went astray, as the *I Ching* had predicted.

You walked by yourself in the never-ending variety of London worlds: the cavernous "marbled-halls" of the Central Market with its medley of damp smells; Soho Square, still sedate and proper, with the sex-films grinding on, upstairs, two blocks away; Bloomsbury that was nice and seedy, and somehow suggestive of doe-eyed Indian students writing economic histories of jute-cultivation in Bengal; the Italian food-merchant on

86

Compton Street where you bought salamis and Gorgonzola and a gift-case of wine; Madame Tussaud's where the girl-painter remarked that President Kennedy's face, in the wax, looked as smooth and pink as a baby's ass. And in the center of all this, a feeling of the privileged coziness of London artistic life. The same faces appeared at all the dinner parties, you saw everybody every three days, rock stars and journalists and actresses and poets milled together around the Beefeater's. But despite this, London had no feeling of the murderous concentration of reputation-building and pecking-order that characterized America's compacted New Yorks. London was the city-as-universe, rather than island. You floated in it. There was little sense of important peaks and valleys in your day. Everything seemed possible, available, so why hurry? As you thought back on it, New York took on the fevered aspect of a boil about to burst, and you learned something about its addictive effect the day you realized that London—so supportive, so pleasant, so inexhaustible—had begun to bore you. You felt like a soldier after an armistice, for whom peace was harder on the nerves than war. And didn't like the analogy.

Jay and Fran were off to visit friends in East Anglia for the weekend, and we stayed on in rainy, late October Islington, packing up for Paris on Monday, so exhausted by the last week's socializing that we slept for ten hours Saturday night, grateful for the silence of the empty house.

Then, as Shirley fixed a small supper on Sunday, images of home came onto the Telly's evening screen: a vast crowd moving across a bridge; the faceless, blunt façade of a prison-like building; Dr. Spock's Romanesque head over the files of marchers; troops in staggered rows moving purposefully into the disorganized throng; the arrested being led away, Mailer in his shysterlawyer's suit among them; a few American Nazis chanting "Sieg Heil!" over the uproar—the mad, gleeful rage of the voices turning the soundtrack into a ghastly replay of thirty years before, and sickening the heart with the suspicion that perhaps nothing much had changed, after all. Thousands had tried to invade the Pentagon, there had been sympathy demonstrations in Berlin, Paris, and Amsterdam, several people had been arrested outside the American Embassy in Grosvenor Square, and I was there in London, out of it.

It all came back over me again in those two minutes of TV film: America! An Egyptian land! Despair and bayonets! No way to reach the seats of power and appeal to their "better angels"! The demons of history bargaining for the American soul!

I sat there in London as *My Man Godfrey* followed the TV news with its madcap, good-hearted version of the 1930s, and drank a little Scotch against the feelings. I wanted to be out in the streets, but only, I realized, in the company of other Americans, and there were none. I honestly wished, for the first time, to be *there* again, back in the Crazy House, because that night it seemed as if our national Passion had come at last, the issue—the war itself—clearly drawn, our finest selves driven into the streets as a last resort, fearful that our government had been taken from us, no uneasy truce with it possible anymore—make it listen, take it back, clear its name! But the obscenity only seemed to have intensified, and there was something fateful in the air, as if gigantic, blind forces were contending in the confusion of events, and the country had had a bitter destiny all along. Had our so-called "innocence," for which others chided and patronized us, lain in our refusal to admit that we were flawed like everyone else? Such dire and foolish thoughts seemed unavoidable as I sat there in frustration, watching William Powell and Carole Lombard conduct an amusing love-affair across the social abysses of the Great Depression.

Shirley and I didn't talk very much about it. We ate our supper to the soft splatter of rain through trees in the Duncan Ter-
race Gardens outside, and finished the packing afterwards. I
stood for a while before going to bed, having a last cigarette at
the long front windows, beyond which London was all wet
brick, black leaves, Laird Cregar-squares, smoky pubs, the foggy
wharfsides of Dickens, the enormous heart of an empire—a
destiny—that had had its noon and twilight too, but had survived the night that followed them. I was content enough, at
that moment, to accept that God was on nobody's side, and that
the mad vanities of the powerful were as ephemeral as the de-
cencies of the righteous. The Elgin Marbles, Turner's water-
scapes—the politics of eons had come and gone, but *which* had
remained? It seemed a thought that, at the very least, promised
the possibility of sleep, and I was ready for Paris now—for a
new language, different people, the next leg, during which one
might store up reserves. I went to bed, remembering Robinson
Jeffers' line, "Thin snow falls on historical rocks," never having
expected to be *warmed* by it.

Paris by the next night! Most of us had lived on less.

FIVE

A Wake in the Streets of Paris

I was walking
in Montmartre, and the steep tangle of its carnival streets, where
few but seekers after the rawest pleasure ever came, seemed to
promise an anonymity from which even the most painful memories might eventually ebb away. One could just take a room in
one of those narrow, lobbyless, ten-francs-a-night hotels, wedged
between a café and a *tabac,* and disappear. One could simply
drop out of sight, and be living an entirely different life in an
hour. The temptation of what Henry Miller had once called

"quiet days in Clichy" tugged at me, because the mail that morning had been full of death back home.

It was Paris, it was a crisp, sunny nine o'clock, and the American friends with whom we were staying off Boulevard Malesherbes had just separated, and were talking about divorce. Francesca thought she still loved George, but he didn't know whether he still loved her, and couldn't expect her to put up with that, so he had moved out of their large, white studio the week before we arrived. Both of them insisted that we stay there anyway, and we were sleeping in their room, while Francesca bunked on the guest bed. We lunched with George, and dined with Francesca, and tried to maintain the concerned neutrality of go-betweens whose "good offices" are not really wanted by either party. The evenings tended to get maudlin with scotch and reminiscences of times we'd all had together in New York and London and St. Tropez ten years before. Francesca was being brave, and some kinds of pain last longer if you're brave. She made frothy, light soufflés, and served the rough country paté I liked, and we made spectacular inroads on their wine cellar, and she never cried. But after a week of it, I was depressed. I liked them both, and had hoped for warm reunions and a taste of their Paris, and I was losing it in all the acrimony. And now, this morning, those two letters lay on the floor below the mail-slot, announcing that by a grisly coincidence two close friends from different periods of my life had died within a day of each other.

First, there was Nick, an ex-student of mine whom George and Francesca didn't know, gone to cancer at twenty-eight; and then there was Stu, just my age and as old a friend of theirs as he was of ours, dead in New York of a massive coronary. Cancer and heart—assassins of the age of stress and cigarettes! What could I write to Stu's wife and Nick's parents? And how could I begin another of Francesca's difficult days with this further loss? Stu was a dear friend with whom she and George had once talked of sharing a house in Chelsea. Besides, after five years away, could she really understand the awful inner-costs of living in America now?

My problem was simple: I had a hangover, and I needed time with my own wounds before coping with anyone else's, and so, leaving Shirley still asleep, I went out and walked, looking at the cheap little hotels, and imagining absolutely eventless days of morning-coffee, croissant, and the Trib, wandering remote arrondissements through pastis-tinted afternoons, chanson-bars where gypsy-fingers spidered along the frets of huge guitars, and early nights of neon-flicker on the ceiling, and none of those long thoughts about death and change that gave so many Americans in those days a vaguely haunted look. There are backstreets in Paris that offer the careless oblivion some of us long for when life has turned a cold corner, for Paris still receives the miserable stranger like the good-hearted prostitute of all the myths: you can always sleep on her floor.

I turned down Rue de Maistre, going nowhere. Breads as long as your arm were stacked in wicker baskets on the rain-fresh pavements. Pinball machines stuttered and ting-ed in the dark bars where Algerian hustlers drank and smoked after a night of working the lushes on Metro platforms out in Saint Cloud. The cheap movies advertised *The Girls of Soho*—most conclusive evidence of the puritanical Paris of Madame de Gaulle that looked to London for its sense of sin. Ten years ago they would have played *The Girls of Montmartre*. The whores behind the shuttered windows turned over in their dreams of the small café, the prim black dress with the lace collar, the reassuring grumble of the cash register, the bourgeois Sundays of bickering in the Bois.

The night-towns of most cities are best seen in the morning. Only then does the flesh show through the mascara, and the finest time to be in any tenderloin is when the strippers, and the bus-boys, and the musicians are having their last drink, and you can eavesdrop on the quiet murmur of the most candid talk there is—the talk of night-people once another night has been negotiated. I drifted along with my burden of personal woe, looking for a likely place to repair last night's damage, and let the soiled streets do their work.

It was good to realize that no one that we knew in Paris (the ad-man, screenwriter, fashion-coordinator expatriates of ten-years'-residence there who, among the anti-American French, had grown defensive, chauvinistic and hawkish) would come around the next corner and interrupt my dismal mood by pronouncing my name. I looked into faces too busy or too weary to notice mine.

Death and change—I was sick of them. But here they had found me in Paris where good Americans were supposed to come to die, but where, in fact, they lived on (like our friends), out of touch, sentimentally homesick but afraid to go home, suspecting that something strange and terrible was happening there. Nick and Stu: there was no one in Paris to whom I could explain what had killed them, and yet later I would have to try, and later still write those letters that do no good but in which my friends would become irrevocably dead to me, and so I walked deeper into streets whose very unawareness of their lives was something of a consolation.

I ducked under a sooty, striped awning, and went into a café that was cheery with sunlight, that day's wine-casks coming up on a pulley through a trap door in the tiles, the cashier-girl behind the racks of Gauloises Bleu buffing her nails, the waiter bringing me a fresh bottle of Perrier water with the Ricard. I had two quick ones for my head, and nobody there paid any attention to me, and I sat back in a shaft of warm sun, understanding at last why Hemingway's ideal had always been "a clean, well-lighted place." In Paris, such a place can be comforting, supportive, pleasant, whereas in New York one always searches for a *dark* bar, a safe burrow in which to hide from the American glare. I watched the motes of dust from the cellar circling upwards in the light as the bartender swung a cask of *rouge* away from the trap. The ankle-length apron on my waiter gleamed waxily with starch, crackling as he walked. The oysters in a just-delivered bushel near my table were studded with pearl-like drops of water, in each of which I fancied I could glimpse a concave miniature of that sunny room, that morning world. I felt better enough to think.

Death had never been a personal matter to me when I was younger. People died out of one's life, and left an empty space, but a few nights of barroom elegizing with friends soon filled it. It wasn't callousness, it was simply the stubborn fact of youth, in which Time is always a burgeoning, never a winnowing. But after forty, you register the loss of friends in your own secret fears, in the days that are relentlessly diminishing ahead of you, in the sense of vulnerability that makes you pay attention to a cold, and shift to filter cigarettes, and go to bed when you are tired. There is nothing that can be done about a death, except to pass it down into yourself, and work it through the mazes of your nature, so that you can move on with your eyes open. But that sort of confrontation is a private, even a *modest,* act, and after certain losses you learn to know your degree of tolerance, and go off, and do the job out of sight.

Stu. I'd seen him the last afternoon before we got the plane. Labor Day weekend, Third Avenue, Daley's. We wondered why we didn't get together more often, and traded news since the last time.

"I'm moving the office. Need more space. It's the goddamn war . . . I'm a Vietnam-profiteer, you know," he said with a sick, bitter smile.

"Well, we plan to stay away for as long as the money lasts. I honestly think the country's having a nervous breakdown."

95

"I know," he said, "Christ, do I know."

We had been friends for seventeen years. His field was aero-dynamics, and (along with George and Francesca) he was part of the hard-drinking, wise-cracking crowd among whom I had managed to get through the company-picnic banalities of the Fifties. Both of us had a life outside that frivolous world—his, designing aircraft systems; mine, writing novels—and this gave us a feeling of complicity in the larger issues of the day that were mostly taboo in our group. Sometimes, like conspirators, we would discuss those issues through an afternoon, and Stu's point of view was at once less radical and more ambivalent than mine. "You have no idea," he would say darkly after a session at the Pentagon, "what moronic hands this country is in. But maybe it's always been that way."

What struck you first about Stu was his intelligence and his control. He had the capacity to absorb vast amounts of techno-logical data, together with a special kind of awareness of the concentric circles of implication radiating outwards from tech-nology into, for instance, history, which he read for relaxation. And there was something else too—a fatalism, an unflappa-bility, that made some of his friends say: "Stu? Oh, Stu's Victor Maturity. I'd like to have his cool if I ever grow up ... Did I ever tell you about the time I saw him change three flat tires in a hundred miles and never say so much as 'Damn!'?" But Stu was torn, and his level-headedness in a morally unstable world was paid for by steady attrition to the already-taut nerves of a secret idealist.

Increasingly, as the sixties passed, his contracts were military, and his spare time (increasingly devoted to the American Civil War) began to evaporate. And sometimes the ominous strains of this life showed. His jaw would clench white under the perma-nent shadow of a twice-a-day shaver, his eyes would bulge and widen, and a cold, rebuking harshness would enter his voice:

"Don't you think I'd like to quit sometimes? But I'm trained for this. And I love *design*. Why should I have to cope with all the goddamn politics?" the word an obscenity in his mouth.

He and his wife, Mary, moved to Great Neck, and had two children; they ascended the economic ladder, and he worked too hard. But all the time I think that Stu, who had been taught to think of integrity mostly as it concerned the performance of metals under stress, was haunted by the older, the squarer implications of the term. He didn't feel that he had sold out. He took a grown man's pride in his work, and was sensible enough to know that it was good, but often he had the abstracted, fretful air of a man trying to find a mistake in what he knows to be a perfect equation, and he kept away from some of us, as if avoiding arguments he knew that *he* would initiate. He lived in a society that had only one use for his gifts, and the product of those gifts held up under the stress of combat-conditions. But Stu broke down.

I lit the last of my London, free-port Kents, and breathed a little of its blight down into my lungs. It had the taste of plastic fibers spun in a cyclatron under the dead light of fluorescents. I thought of Stu, who had moved out of Manhattan, policed his drinking, quit smoking, settled down, had children, stayed cool, and then dropped dead anyway, as casualty of an America that bought a man's personal tranquility along with his public skills. I remembered Stu saying that last afternoon, with a raw edge of conviction that somehow hinted at uncertainty: "Sure, Sherman burned Atlanta, Sherman tore up the railroads, Sherman was a monster. But it was Sherman who said that war was hell! And it was Sherman who ended it!" Only the bulging eyes, faintly yellow in their whites, indicated a man whose moral options were remorselessly chewing him up. The damned war had killed him as surely as it was killing other Americans in the DMZ, and how could George and Francesca comprehend that?

They had been gone for years, and unhappily defended American policy in Vietnam against the pot-shots of their complacent French friends, and had never seen that look of being backed into a cage that had become grafted onto Stu's face. And Nick? Would Nick, whom compromise had never tempted, have understood it either?

The powerful need to move came over me. All at once my body craved exertion, as if that "clean, well-lighted place" was immobilizing me into unwanted thoughts. Besides, I had to make American Express before lunch to change money.

Place de Clichy was a bedlam of traffic. The gendarmes, in their ominous capes and white forearm-gauntlets, stood in the midst of snarled Citroens like impatient matadors in a corrida full of cows, screaming at jaywalkers, summoning on hesitant taxies, furious at the chaos that seemed to demean them in their power. I didn't like their hard, contemptuous jaws, the angry, chopping gestures of their arms, their air of self-righteousness goaded by incompetence towards violence. After London's mild and courteous Bobbies, they were a shock, a shock reminding me that I was in a republic once again where the citizenry is assumed to be restive with egalitarianism, and the police are armed against them, and the streets are the ultimate arena for civic disagreement.

Cabs were in short supply, and I joined a queue of modern-day Madame de Farges with their net shopping bags and that air of personal chic (the simple dress, the stylish shoes, the lone piece of tasteful jewelry) with which all Parisian women seem to be born, along with their Francoise Sagan-expressions of independence and hauteur. When someone tried to horn in near the head of the line, these ladies would cry in chorus: "Mais non! Arrêtez! Déshonneur!," forming ranks against the intruder, shaming him with their reproaches, some sense of feminine justice so outraged that they became in an instant a remorseless sisterhood. Seven months later when Paris rioted, and the authoritarian *flics,* strutting around the intersections, collided with the smoldering democratic wrath of the cab-stands, it was the children of these women who tore up the cobblestones, and almost tore down the government.

In the taxi, I considered the fact that I had never had a good time in Paris. Ten years ago, it had been winter, and there is a clammy touch of the morgue to Parisian streets in winter. I had gotten trivially sick, and slumped around the bitter quays, telling myself that I didn't feel rotten, and feeling rotten anyway; and after only four days, we had given it up and headed south. And then, this time, I had fallen into the morass of my friends' unhappy situation, and seemed always to be cabbing from one to the other, doing no real good, but somehow stuck in the role of go-between nevertheless. And now, today, the staggering pointlessness of those two deaths back home. And yet, turning into the Place de l'Opéra, I decided, on cool assessment, that Paris was still the most beautiful city that I knew. That beauty lay in the republican width of its boulevards and sidewalks; the subtle change of character, arrondissement to arrondissement, that kept one's attentions poised; the presence on most blocks of a *tabac,* a café, a wine-shop, and a range of markets, evidencing the Frenchman's concept of life's priorities; the sense that every street would eventually converge on some broad Place of iron balconies, into which all the energy and style of that particular district would spill, so that every place in Paris had a feeling of centrality; and above all, the dazzling, open-vista-ed *heart* of the city, lavishly spread along the Seine, where everything exuded that air of intellectual breadth and sensual possibility that is the unique Parisian mood.

But I seemed fated never to quite capture that elusive mood (which may be the reason why Paris still *feels* more cosmopolitan than cities with stronger claims to worldliness), because, once through the revolving doors of American Express, I was in America again, Nick's America. The lobby was thronged with kids. They might have been Nick's students, as Nick had once been mine. Young, exhilarated faces came streaming up the wide stairway from the mailroom, faces at once vigorous and faintly quenched, faces whose open, trusting expressions revealed, around the eyes, that hint of secret hurt, of baffled hope, of stubborn resolve, that first appeared on U.S. campuses after the Kennedy assassination, the faces of our uncertain future.

Young Americans were everywhere in Europe that year: civil-rights activists trying to forget their rejection by the Blacks; hippies on their migratory wanderings towards the Ultimate Cool; peaceniks in whose war-haunted dreams the fantasy of American concentration camps had taken on a paranoid reality; dropouts from the huge, lock-step education-factories, who had enrolled in Europe as if it were a university. They flowed up the stairs to the Money Exchange with their guitars, and skiis, and bedrolls. They waited patiently on the teller's line as if they had been queued-up all their lives, each holding the green-and-gold passport and the book of traveller's checks with which America arms even her most defiant children, thinking thereby to get some purchase on their idealism.

Adult Americans always look vaguely homeless in Europe, a little confused, eternally between psychic trains, but these kids seemed to have been *born* in a waiting room, and they were involved in something vastly more complicated than simple placelessness. Four years ago, Nick had said to me: "Never forget. Money's not our thing. We've always had it. And travel-for-itself isn't our thing either. Everyone I know has been everywhere. Our thing is changing our heads around. And that's going to change the world," giving me his widest, goofiest, canniest grin, as if he didn't expect me to understand, and didn't mind. I laughed, remembering Nick's grin. And then remembered that it had been wiped away for good by a few cannibal cells that had run amok. I changed my money, and felt querulous, and cheated, and old.

I walked. I had an hour before I was due back for a lunch with Shirley and Francesca that was bound to be grim with my bad news, and in Paris, on a good day, the place to do housework in your soul is along the river. Narrower than the Thames but wider than the Tiber, feminine compared to the Mississippi but not slatternly like the Liffey, less somber than the Hudson but more dignified than the Chicago, the Seine is the most satisfying of all city-rivers, and that day high, gusty skies, across which turrets of epic cumulus moved, had turned it into a cloudy mirror where fat-beamed barges rode upon their own reflections. Everything I saw—the chestnut trees scattering their leaves along the walks, the wide bridges clustered with bookstalls at either end, the medieval town of the Île de Cité over which Nôtre Dame raised its ponderous, Gothic stones—evoked that strange pang which even first-time visitors to Paris recognize, with some astonishment, as *nostalgia*. A buried memory seems to stab at your consciousness in Paris, and you follow in the steps of an elusive phantom of *déjà vu*, but never quite catch up. So deeply embedded in the world's dream of freedom, youth, art, and pleasure has this city become, that the feeling that the stranger in Paris is a feeling of *return*. Perhaps one misses friends so keenly there because all of one's senses are pitched to such a keen note of receptivity, and one vibrates with an awareness that one longs to share. In any case, I thought of Nick.

I don't think he had ever been to Paris. That had been put on the back-burner along with his novel. Four years before, he had been my student (and sometime-assistant) at the Writer's Workshop of the University of Iowa. He wrote wacky, perceptive, Black Comedy stories with titles such as *I Make My Manic Statement,* and he lived with two other guys in a noisy, ramshackle house on a bad street where there always seemed to be a party going into its seventh hour.

Nick was as short and compact as a lightweight fighter who will have a little boy's paunch at thirty-two. You knew he was from New York the moment he opened his mouth because that mouth, large though it was, could never seem to handle the thick flow of words that always taxed it. His verbal style was humor, and he had his generation's jugular-instinct for the shams and absurdities of America in the sixties. He knew there was something comic about himself—he talked too fast, his features were outsized, the grin was distinctly horsey—but like Fernandel, he exaggerated all this with such charm and winsomeness that you always thought of him as attractive, even handsome. He couldn't drink, and yet he insisted on drinking, and got immediately tipsy, and then hilarious, and finally affectionate, and all at once turned green and threw up on the table. "Well," he would say by way of explanation, "I must have been having a good time anyway." He knew just who he was, and what he was after, and so if you had something to teach him he was willing to make a fool of himself to learn it. I came to rely on him in my seminar, grew to admire his talents, and gradually, rather carefully, we discovered that we had become good friends.

He loved literature, but, like so many young people then, he was courting politics. When I chided him about this, he grinned slyly and said: "First things first. I can always write that book when I get old and cynical," his eyes adding from behind the glasses, "like you." The political passion of those years was, of course, civil-rights, and Nick had marched, and sat-in, and sung, and written for the Movement as a simple human duty. He was never rhetorical, or self-righteous, or boring about it. It was an obligation which his age and his intelligence had placed upon him, and he discharged it, skipping the ego-massage of moral superiority. He felt none of the sentimental, folk-song identification with blacks that was typical of many white activists then. He simply recognized a mess, and did his part to clean it up.

One day he came to me and said: "Hey, would you write me a big, phony recommendation for a job? But I need a real rave, John, so if you can't bring yourself to lie a little, don't sweat it." It was for a teaching position at Morehouse College in Georgia, a black school with few whites on the faculty, and I didn't have to lie, and he got the job.

Thereafter, he would often phone me on his way to Boston or someplace during the summers, and stop over for the night, sometimes with a black girl-friend. He was still very funny, even about the scrapes such relationships got him into with blacks as well as Southern whites, but somehow the humor wasn't as lighthearted as before. In his face, I saw the bleak deferral of that splendid dream of reconciliation, in which his generation was losing its innocence, occurring line by line, and heard him stubbornly insist: "All right, so I'm getting mine. It's fair, we earned it, but it'll pass, and then, man, I'll *write*." I admired his tenacity in going back to Morehouse year after year, his willingness to live out his commitment no matter who was offended, and his courage in risking the violence which the despair of a divided America was bringing out on both sides like a tragic native flaw. And when we were together, I tried to curb my pessimistic suspicion that an awful disillusionment lay in his future like that inevitable paunch, and I did this because I couldn't stand to think about it. And now that future, bitter or sweet, had passed.

The death of the young is peculiarly appalling. There is something so obscene about it that even atheists tend to stare up resentfully at the empty heavens, only to realize how deeply they, too, have believed in some pattern of completion, some proper dying-fall to the stanza of a life. Nick wasn't one of those friends whose abrupt absence from my time would taint it for years.

There are only two or three such people in a man's life. But I hated his death with a fury nevertheless. Old Bitch America was still devouring her young, and here I had counted on Nick, and on his kind, to save the country from itself! I stopped in my tracks. The callousness, the pompousness, of the thought disgusted me. Good God, was it only some representative of a generation I would miss? Had America's current turmoil so befuddled me that I didn't even realize what had been lost? It was the *grin* that I would miss, Nick's canny grin. That grin was the specific, personal loss. I would never be able to enjoy watching his face again, I would never again be able to look forward to him. Only *back*. That was the simple, brutal fact of it. That, and the letter to his parents, whom I had never met, that had still to be written.

All Paris was spread out around me, unaware of this. The hour of luncheon was approaching, and the exquisite sauces of the city were nearing their moment of truth. I watched a couple strolling hand in hand down there on the embankment. The young man drew the girl along after him, and she languished back from his hand, as if her whole being was taking its life from that single point of contact. They half-danced along the walk, like two encurled leaves in an eddy of wind, and plainly it wasn't the idea of food that moved them. They were completely absorbed in that subtle, urgent, sensual hunger that Paris rouses, and there was no touch of death in the light, tranced swayings of their young bodies. I watched them until they vanished under a bridge.

My two friends were dead now half a world away, and I wasn't going to see them again. I wasn't going to drive to New Hampshire with Stu and Mary, and line the wine bottles up before the picture window of a mountain cabin, and build a big fire, and sit down for a two-day binge of talk. I wasn't going to pick up the phone and hear Nick saying: "Got a bed for a New

Left, outside-agitator, nigger-loving weirdo?" But I had done these things, and remembering them, I succumbed for a moment to that outrageous nostalgia for my own hopeful youth that turns so many Americans into drunken, maudlin boys in Paris.

Nostalgia! In these years in America, it threatens anyone who has paid attention long enough to be worried. Nostalgia for the past, for the good years that are gone; for simpler times and simpler choices; for cameraderie, and horseplay, and loyalty, and sentiment; for the innocence of America itself before its days of empire faced us with moral dilemmas that could so break the heart, and immoral conditions that could so abrade the nerves, that Stu's coronary and Nick's cancer could become only another occasion for holding a wake over the corpse of the Republic; that stubborn reflex of nostalgia that is, finally, our immaturity.

In America, we had built a civilization that didn't allow someone like Stu to enlist his talents in the service of life. But it was also a civilization that compelled someone like Nick to give his talents to that very cause. Still, they were dead because of an absurd, quirkish bodily flaw, and *not* because the country was foundering. Stu's troubled eyes, Nick's canny grin: at the last, nostalgia was so simplifying the human richness of a man's life that even his death could be turned into a cheap symbol of some fleeting national crisis. It was a habit I resolved to break, because, like most bad habits, it was self-serving.

I turned away from the river. A hint of *vinaigrette* seemed to waft on the breeze that stirred among the chestnut trees. The Louvre was as immensely long and formal and austere as the Pentagon, and I seemed doomed never to get inside either building. For the last three days I had been trying without success to arrange our schedules so as to get to the Louvre before closing-time, and now taxies were pulling up before the west entrance, and I thought of calling up Shirley, begging off lunch with Francesca, and spending the afternoon there. I could find a Rembrandt, and settle down in front of it, and let the mending come. But I had indulged myself in enough evasions of what had to be done, and the Louvre would be there later, so I got into a cab instead.

The studio was in the middle of a quiet, leafy block of six-story, mansard-roofed buildings. It was on the far side of an inner courtyard of white gravel and flower beds that you reached through a cobbled passageway. It was a new structure, connected to the other buildings in the courtyard only through the wine cellars. Its entire roof was a vast skylight of wire-meshed glass, and it always reminded me of those chic, Americanized flats (complete with Milt Jackson and Johnnie Walker), in which Roger Vadim sets his slickly shallow films.

Both Francesca and Shirley were sleeping late these days, so I used my key, only to find George mixing a second martini at the tiny, black-marble bar, as Francesca sat, one nyloned leg scissored tensely over the other, in the fishbowl light of that cavernous room. The aimless electricity which is generated when people are being too tactful to speak of their emotions, and so talk about money instead, flickered in the air. Shirley came out of the bedroom, dressed for lunch, and I saw my gloomy expression transform her face.

"Well," George said, adding two ounces of gin to the shaker without even asking, "I—I just dropped by to pick up the bills." He was flushed, and embarrassed, and irritated.

Francesca produced one of her stunning, set smiles, openly theatrical, which stated that the show would go on, and she was a soldier, and she wasn't going to cry, so don't worry.

"So what did you do this morning, darling," she said distractedly. "George was just saying—"

"Yes, it occurred to me, John, that we've—well, *I've* been so damn busy that we haven't had a decent night on the town."

"What's happened?" Shirley said as I took the two letters out of my pocket.

I had a good dollop of martini, and told them about Stu, leaving out the embellishments.

"Stu! No! When did it happen!"

I saw the hole open in their memories. I saw the indigestible fact lodge in their throats. I saw their difficulty in accepting it produce a reflex of aversion. George, who had grown florid, and weary, and pressured after years of conducting business in a language not his own, did what I remembered World War II sailors doing when they heard of buddies, sunk on the North Atlantic runs: he lit a cigarette, and made a glancing remark about something else, and swallowed the hateful foretaste of all the deaths-to-come (perhaps culminating in his own) with the martini that kept his mouth occupied.

"Also," I went on, "Nick—he's this ex-student of mine, maybe I've mentioned him—Shirl, Nick got it with cancer . . . Yes, *Nick*."

"No!" she said. "Not Nick, *too*."

Francesca began to cry all at once. Her strong, intelligent, womanly face didn't collapse; it didn't become contorted around the mouth the way a face does when the will-to-endure caves in. Her eyes simply gave up their tears, as if she'd had enough, as if, in Nick, she'd found an impersonal object on which she could safely expend her grief in the open.

"Christ!" George said about nothing in particular, and made a move towards her, and then checked himself as if he had given up the right to commiseration too. "What the hell's going on back home anyway!" he snapped out, and lapsed off into a frown.

Shirley brought me another drink, and I realized she wasn't going to give in to her own feelings until later.

Francesca was embarrassed by her tears now, mostly because she had allowed herself to cry at last, and was crying as much for herself, and George, as for anything else, and didn't know where that might lead.

"Look," I said. "Let me buy us all a lunch. Can't we just go around the corner?" There was a small, awninged café there, under a flutter of Parisian trees, and they would bring you a dozen oysters on a bed of cracked ice, and oven-warmed bread, and sweet butter from Normandy, and as much chilled white wine as would make you sanguine about your day once more. "Come on," I repeated, knowing that memories of happy meals we had all shared in the past made George and Francesca feel sentimental and affectionate. "We'll start with a small bowl of onion soup just to warm the cockles, and then we'll go on from there."

"Yes," Shirley said immediately. "Oysters, too. And then a pastry."

"That sounds marvelous," Francesca said. "Unless—" looking evenly at George. "Well, you probably have another appointment."

"Nothing half so pleasant," he replied, with a little of the old guardsman-smile with which he used to acknowledge his admiration of her. "Just let me make a phone call."

They set about getting ready to leave, and the air flickered with a subtler kind of electricity, as if they had carefully negotiated an invisible obstacle, and could breathe.

"Stu," Shirley murmured to me, as we waited. "And then Nick . . ." She shook her head: "We always have a rotten time in Paris."

After lunch, I thought, I'd come back, and write the letters that would do no good.

SIX

Encounter with Myself in Munich

"We can't *bear*
America," my hostess was saying with the uneasy casualness of
a Smith graduate dismissing her coming-out party. "My mother
says in every other letter, 'You've been gone eight years. You're
going to be one of those Americans who never comes home.'"
Her gesture with the glass of champagne-punch was in shorthand. "But if you can't *stand* living in America, why feel you
have to do it? Why *apologize*?"

What could I reply? It was her apartment, and her party, and her evening. Or rather it was her husband's. He was a professor of drama at the branch of an American University outside Munich, and we, the twenty-odd guests, had just attended the first performance of his psychedelic production of Pirandello's *Henry IV,* and then had blundered about through the Bavarian night (full of that piney, astringent odor, those fierce unblinking stars, and that hint of hoar frost in the November air that so powerfully suggests the presence of mountains nearby) trying to locate this particular apartment in a rank of identical project-like buildings, no different from their counterparts in Denver or Seattle.

My hostess was the tall, horsey type, glib and genial and assertive in her black lace mini-dress and silver-mesh stockings, adroitly maintaining, at that moment, the balance between expatriate snobbery and native enthusiasm that seems to overcome the wives of American intellectuals abroad. A nice young woman blurred by chic.

The professor, in his solemn tuxedo, was indulging himself in criticisms of his own production that were so unreasonable as to instantly elicit heated objections from his friends. His theatrical ideas were mostly derived from Artaud via Peter Weiss, and he dropped them into his conversation with the casual italics of a radio announcer in Topeka mentioning "Liz and Dick."

"Of course, I couldn't have done it *this* way in any university at home," he was saying with the tone of an orphan rejecting what has rejected him. "Can you imagine mounting this production in—in Iowa City?" looking to me as the most recent escapee from America's bleak shores.

I gave him back a dim smile, and kept my own counsel, because, though I had liked the play and the young actors, both had been so fatally encumbered by an overlay of psychedelic gimmickry that my mood at the final curtain was irritable. What in God's name had Pirandello *failed* to say about guilt, and psychic identification with the past, and the mysteries of human responsibility, that all these masks, and strobe lights, and slide projections could better illuminate? My host's conception of the play involved such a misunderstanding of its content that it constituted the most urgent reason for his hieing himself back to the artistic upheaval in the States on the next possible plane. But one does not carelessly mar anyone's moment of triumph, and I barely knew the man, and was drinking his liquor. So I escaped to the punch bowl, refilled my glass, and found a spot out of the conversational line of fire, to savor a not-unpleasant sense of dislocation.

Forty-eight hours before, we had been gaining altitude over the sparkling pattern of Paris boulevards below, laid out (like some incredibly intricate lavalier on a piece of black velvet) in strings of tiny, pearl-hard lights radiating outwards from the bright pendant of the Arc de Triomphe. Just that afternoon, I had had an encounter on chilly Ludwigstrasse, the meanings of which were still to be sorted out. And this very evening, while tooling along the autobahn out of Munich, on the way to see a modern Italian play performed in English by a group of "army brats" on an American Armed Services complex that had once been a Nazi military installation, I had found myself listening (on the car radio) to an Israeli folksong sung in German by a Frenchman. So I was full of the time-and-culture shock for which I had come to Europe, and I was in Germany—the one leg of our trip which I had undertaken as a duty, rather than a relief, to the state of my nerves.

Germany! To a man of my age (World War II vet) and persuasion (radical without an ideology), Germany had the unhealthy fascination of Sade's *Les 120 Journées de Sodome*. It was a dark part of all our nightmares, and there hung over it that aura of the Nadir, that faint stench of the mystery in the Pit, to which only the morally unimaginative can feign indifference. I knew intelligent and talented men, who (these twenty years after the war) still refused to go to Germany, and said so with the complacent disinterest of people stating that they loathe escargots on the basis of having tried them once at sixteen. I knew others, like myself, for whom Germany (with its myriad associations—Nietzsche, Himmler, Schweitzer) was an embodiment of a contemporary human problem of such huge and indistinct proportions as to be inexpressible in any terms less stark than Malraux's, "Is Man dead?" The source of my attraction to Germany was precisely the testing of old aversions and new knowledges that it demanded, and I wanted to walk German streets in this autumn of Vietnam, and see if any shred of America's fatuous sense of moral superiority remained in me.

Germany! Aside from the above, my relationship to it was especially ambivalent. My grandfather had studied medicine in Berlin in the nineties, my grandmother had been raised there, and German was often spoken in their home. Two relatives-by-marriage from Alsace, brothers, had fought through the brutal wallow of the First War, one for the French, one for the Germans. The bitter, romantic, carnival-nihilism of Berlin in the twenties had always exerted a stronger pull on me than the Bohemianism of Paris during the same decade, and on troublous summer evenings in 1937, a second-cousin, just home, had described Nazi Youth Rallies in the mesmerized voice of Trilby trying to shake off an evil spell. Hitler's guttural, hypnotic rant, seeping through the static of the transatlantic radio, was as much a part of my adolescence on the Eastern Seaboard as the Lone Ranger; and I found that I had read Erich Maria Remarque too early, and listened to Marlene Dietrich too closely, and studied George Grosz too long, to view the Second War, when it came, with the simple, two-dimensional ethics of a Western. If most of my nineteen-year-old idealism did not survive the unspeakable revelations of the concentration camps, a few of my emotions matured forever while listening to scratchy Kurt Weill records smuggled out of Amsterdam.

I suppose, at the last, Germany was modern history to me, a capsule history of my own era, encompassing both the human lampshades of Ilse Koch, and the human eye of Bertolt Brecht—an eye that, to this day, stares at me off my wall, keeping me honest; a deeply thwarted land that found its true voice in the totalitarian sentimentality of music like the *Horst Wessel Song* and Paul Dessau's score for *Mother Courage,* by both of which it is impossible not to be stirred, despite your politics; a terrible laboratory of extremes in which Wedekind's Lulu and Jack the Ripper had murdered and copulated ceaselessly throughout my lifetime.

In Paris, James Jones had told me: "Go to Munich. Go to Dachau. It's an experience you owe yourself—particularly this year," and here I was, in an apartment full of expatriates, in a Germany that had been occupied by Americans for twenty-two years, in the Munich where Thomas Mann had written *The Magic Mountain* and Hitler had established National Socialism, where Jews had died by Nazi gas, and Germans by American bombs, and where, ironically, no one but me seemed to feel disturbed. I looked around the room with the cold, abraded heart of Lenin turning off the *Moonlight Sonata.* I swallowed the urge to spoil everyone's evening by swallowing champagne instead. If the truth be known, I felt silly, perplexed, cheated, morbid, square, and the reason was that afternoon's encounter on Ludwigstrasse, about which I hadn't told a soul—not even Shirley.

The best way to absorb a city in a short time is to map it with your feet, and my habit was to drift without specific aim towards the center of a town, turning down every street that looked intriguing. We were staying in a small hotel next to the Armed

Forces Network on Kaulbachstrasse. Our room was up under the roof—large, alcoved, dark, with casemented windows looking out over those broad, blunt Munich rooftops that are so indefinably Gothic after Enlightenment Paris. A fountain riffled all night in the paved, leaf-strewn back court below (where Peter Lorre crouched in the shadows with his pathetic fantasies), and the bed was smothering and womblike with goose-down. Nevertheless, I was up early, and impatient to be out. But Shirley lingered under the quilts. I smoked a cigarette, and studied maps. She kept dropping off.

"Come on," I said. "We've only *got* today and tomorrow. We'll change Traveler's Checks, and book a flight to Venice on Saturday, and then find a restaurant around Marienplatz somewhere."

She stirred, and blinked, and turned over again.

"Listen," I repeated, "let's get going. It's already after nine. What's wrong anyway?"

I looked down into her face and realized that she was wide awake, and had been for half an hour. And I knew the shifty, distracted expression in her eyes. She was frightened. For the first time in her life, she was in a city where she could not understand a single word that was spoken. She hadn't much wanted to come to Germany anyway. There was something ponderous and gloomy about it that was antithetical to her Mediterranean soul. Its air of logic baffled her intuitions. Its streets were without nuance, its people strangely shrouded, its language lugubrious with abstraction.

The afternoon before, as we walked through the dense, still woods and open meadows of the Englischer Garten under a dreary, somehow stricken sky, she had seemed depressed, and bewildered by her depression. It was cold there, the paths wound on and on, the sad rustle of leaves only accentuating the melancholy silence of Bavarian autumn. The hunting-lodge restaurant in the center of the Garten was shuttered-up for the winter, the huge mastiff chained by the service entrance (strings of slaver hanging from his savagely-barking jaws) explaining the *Achtung!*-signs that were posted on the trees. There was a forlorn hint of early snow, and twilight fatalism, and muffled Beethoven in the air. She was shivering, and wanted coffee, and it was all deeply alien to her. That night, when I attempted to thank the hotel's Frau Muller for calling us a cab, only to be told with humorless rectitude, "But no. Do not thank me. It is my *duty,*" Shirley had visibly winced, something in her recoiling, as if from a glimpse into the heaviness, the narrowness at the nation's heart. And now, vulnerable with sleep, she simply couldn't bring herself to get out of the bed.

"I can't. I just *can't*. Not this morning. I feel like that woman in Bergman's *Silence.* If anyone looked at me, and said something, just anything, I'd break into tears." She was furious with herself, but she was even more unnerved. "But you go on. Don't wait on me. I just can't make it."

If I was a little miffed at this, I suppose it was because, since I spoke no language other than English, I had gotten used to functioning with my hands and eyes, and didn't clearly remember any longer the stifling sense of absolute estrangement that can overcome you when you cannot even ask the way to the john, much less understand the directions if they are offered. So I went off by myself.

I walked. The teller at the Deutsche Bank in Schwabing spoke English, and so did the girl at Alitalia. They conducted my business with dispatch, without small talk, correctly. But they weren't cold, they were *shy.* Their reliance on form was the result of an inhibition, rather than an absence of emotion. They eyed me distantly, but there was hunger in their eyes—the hunger of the socially-unpoised, the over-sensitive adolescent who is excruciatingly polite. It is why so many Germans love music. They are as full of chaotic, unclear feelings as seventeen-year-olds, and music expresses the inexpressible.

I walked. Munich was in the midst of completing the subway that had been begun by the Nazis, and making one's way along Leopoldstrasse was like navigating in a modern city after a devastating air raid. Huge craters yawned in the middle of the sidewalk, you had to detour at least once in every block; at one point I could see all the way *under* the street to the other side. Drills stuttered, dust rose in a weird unfocusing haze, men crawled about below the pavements in hardhats, traffic snarled around temporary excavation-fences plastered with posters, rubble was heaped in neatly numbered piles.

In the vicinity of the University, throngs of easy-hipped, long-haired students milled about among the wan-faced Hippies, who, with their knapsacks and scarred boots, looking as blank-eyed and passive as DPs, crouched against posters asking *Marx-Mao-Marcuse?* in that attitude of eternal waiting for Godot that was characteristic of certain streets all over the world then. Munich was an important way-station on the caravan-route across Europe along which Dutch Provos, American Diggers, English Mods, and French Drop-Outs moved towards some remote Mecca in the desert of their psyches. A kind of walking-madness seemed to have afflicted youth everywhere, a lemming-like migration of the young with their pot and guitars and copies of Hermann Hesse, as if some crucial tap-root had been pulled in everyone under twenty-five. They were the first flotsam of an as-yet-undeclared war, refugees from an inhuman future and an impossible past, LSD-Trippers on the chemical thumb, gypsies who had kidnapped *themselves* out of the straight world. And they looked at the strafed arches, the dreary institutionalized buildings and the disembowelled streets, and did not see them. But then they had never seen anything else.

I walked. There was the idealistic green Volks with the sticker, *Make Love Not War,* and, a block away, there was the Citroen that countered Gallicly, *Make Love Not Babies.* There were the amputated stumps of Bismarkian linden trees, and the brightly lit windows of aluminumized stores where everything was dirt cheap, and the steamy, jammed gastettes where *all* speculations could be numbed by wurst, and dumplings, and strudel, and lager. There was the street corner in the canyony Wall Street bustle of Marienplatz where I paused to watch the eleven o'clock *Glockenspiel* up in the Rathaus tower, the two opposing files of life-sized knights and peasants moving with the precise, automated jerks of figures in a silent movie; the crisp, thin air of mountain-girt Munich on that cold morning pierced by the clear pealing of silvery bells, and the strong sense beneath everything of some Black Forest in the German soul, stranded at last in reality, but unreconciled.

All was hurry, commotion, chill. Early Beckmann faces were everywhere—thick, secretly sensual, metallic. Platzl struck me with a sharp pang of *déjà vu,* which, upon investigation, proved to be grounded in Fritz Lang. An old infatuation with Expressionism hallucinated me with the feeling that I understood everything I saw—the heavy overcoats muffling the body but not the will, the gluttonous menus stupifying both, the mood of public propriety and private quirk, of unexamined urges and a damning sense of social distance. All this framed itself into an unhappy question as I walked. Why did I seem to know, instinctively, how to function in a German city? It was everything about myself from which I wanted to escape.

I started back up Ludwigstrasse, pondering again the awful mystery that had obsessed my generation twenty years before, and (in another context) had set the Hippies wandering: the eruption of barbarism at the very core of Christian civilization, the mass slaughter of concrete human beings so that a few abstract ideas might live. Dachau. Hué. Concentration Camp Commandant Hoess with his love of dogs and Brahms. The American Captain who said of the Vietnamese village he had just burned, "We had to destroy it in order to save it." If these people passing me in the street were "good Germans," who hadn't known what was going on just ten miles away, what did that make of me, who knew too well the horrors that were being committed half way around the world in my name? Would anyone see the conscience under *my* overcoat?

I looked into the faces around me with an unpleasant understanding (new to Americans, educative) of how terribly difficult it is to hate one's own country, to force it to live up to its dream or judge the dream inadequate, to isolate in all the welter of policy, ego, blunder, and avarice that make up a nation's acts, the germ of future evil, and to stand against it, no matter what. Some of us had been standing against America's current "evil" since 1964, and I thought, with a pinch of guilt, of friends back home, still *there,* refusing to relinquish stewardship of the dream to its debauchers, and felt again the old dull pulse of that resentment of America's leaders that had driven me away. But no matter how uncompromisingly one opposed the sickness in one's own land, one could not avoid a feeling of guilty complicity in it. It was as if one had discovered a murderer in one's immediate family, but remembered the carefree, winning youth he had once been. Dachau? Hué? Though different, both posed an identical moral problem, and one's anguish was not lessened for knowing the answer. The awful mystery was within.

"Is colder than New York?" a voice said.

A small, dishevelled man had fallen into step beside me. He had the eager, worried, paunchy face of a bank clerk proving his trustworthiness with every over-friendly "Good morning, Sir." At that moment, the face had a high flush from the cold, and it hadn't been shaved in a day. His watery, agitated eyes begged my patience with his skeletal English, and his wan smile revealed a mouthful of neglected teeth. He wore a thin black raincoat in need of re-proofing, a baggy-trousered summer suit with that junkie-rumple at the crotch, a frayed white summer-weave shirt buttoned to the throat, no tie, and a shapeless felt hat that had been handled by greasy fingers. He talked steadily, stubbornly, falling over his words, picking himself up, falling again, laughing at his mistakes, encouraging me to laugh too. Though there was a certain charm about his comic self-deprecations, I had been accosted in half a dozen foreign cities by then, and I was on guard. Nevertheless, he seemed to be only interested in talk, and as the talk was in English, I went along with him.

He was, he said, a Polish refugee, a teacher, who had been in Dachau during the war, and worked as a laborer in Munich just afterwards, and now, after years back in Poland, he had managed to get out, and was waiting in a relocation camp to go to America.

"Student?" he said, and at my "no," "Teacher then, too?" concluding this, I suppose, from my glasses, and Loden coat, and rugged walking shoes.

He had thought so, yes; and, of course, he realized that *he* could not expect to teach in America, but just last week the refugee-committee had gotten him a job in a library on Long Island. Perhaps not as a librarian in the beginning, perhaps only as a janitor, but he didn't mind.

"I don't know even where *is* Long Island," he said with an expressive shrug. "But it pays two tousand. Can live in America, with family, for two tousand?" to which, at my faint "perhaps," he added hastily, "Well, I want roof, and to be in blesséd America, it is enough . . . But can live on two tousand there?"

Somehow I got the impression that he knew you couldn't, and

that there was a question within the question that his rudimentary English could not quite frame, but then he said: "You like Munchen? Have seen the sights? . . . No? Must show you something then. You have a few minutes? One more time before I leave Munchen, *I* must see too. I show you, and then show you bus to Schwabing. Just over here."

We turned off Ludwigstrasse, and he talked on and on, asking the same questions over again, opening the raincoat to show me his suit. "They give me suit, committee. Worn before," fingering a fraying lapel, "but what do I care? Only to get to America. Sail in fifteen days now. I tell my wife soon we be all right . . . But tell me, you think I need scarf—you say it, *scarf*?—in America? Is cold there too?"

He laughed, but he *was* cold, his teeth actually chattering as he blew on his raw, chapped hands, the tears standing in the corners of his weary little eyes, his ears as red and numb as a rooster's comb.

He hurried me along through the empty, formal Hofgarten, with its austere pavilion, and withered flower beds, and pebbled walks. The sky was aching with snow, and the city seemed bleak and unfriendly. Winter there would be bitter if you were poor: slush, cold doorways, leaky shoes; all that heavy, spiced food behind the steamy windows, all those accordions and violins. Then, over a high privet hedge, clipped with a precision that seemed fanatical, I caught sight of a large, official building at the back of the garden, once a palace of the Bavarian kings, and now a modern ruin: that is, bombed-out twenty-odd years ago, and left as a monument to—what? the disasters of Nazism? the barbarity of the Americans? Grass grew out of the wide, smashed steps, the ornate stonework was fire-blackened, a dead sky showed through gaping windows where direct hits had been made on the walls beyond. There was that echo of rats scuttling over littered parquet that haunts ruined buildings of some magnificence. A rusty, chain-link wire fence had been erected around it, and just in front, at the bottom of what appeared to be an empty reflecting-pool, there was a mausoleum made of blunt, modernistic slabs of concrete, and it was to *this* that my friend, who had identified himself as Adam, and who was now calling me John several times in every sentence, was leading me.

We walked down into it, and there, in a damp, chilly, oppressive crypt, a massive bronze figure lay, almost buried beneath wreaths of dead flowers. The walls were carved with casualty-figures—18,000, 30,000—but I could not read the epitaphs accompanying them and learn who these people were, or in what manner they had died, or why they were memorialized here. Germans or Jews? Victims of the bombers or the ovens? An old habit of mind made it seem to matter.

My friend's English could get no closer than "innocent dead," somehow leaving the suggestion that they were workers from Dachau (why else would he want to have a last look?), but not excluding the possibility that they might have been Münchners killed in the raids. I stood there, sobered by the grim arithmetic.

But all at once he had seized my hand, his eyes had watered and averted themselves from mine, and he was saying in a stumbling little speech: "America must aid the Polish people, John. They would do the same. I bless you forever. Americans—such good people, so generous. See, they send me this suit. Help the Polish people, John—"

And I was moved, and a little shamed by my recent thoughts, because, yes, I believed we *were* generous; I still believed that at bottom we were good; and the old tarnished dream of haven in America lived on in him, despite what we had made of it. I felt a secret reflex of pride in my country, in its instinctive decency (now so bafflingly obscured), its honesty (now so appallingly

WALKING AWAY FROM THE WAR

compromised), its idealism (now buried in a file somewhere in the antiseptic warrens of the Pentagon), but there, still *there* in the hopes of Europe's displaced and uprooted. I was moved enough (in that place of the "innocent dead"—so solemn, so unimaginative, so German) to grasp his shoulder, and say, just as solemnly, that I would tell people in America, that they would help, that I wished him a good life there, a happy life, only to hear him say with redoubled urgency: "But I kiss your hand, John. I never forget you. There are still fifteen days. We have to live. Do not forget the Polish refugee . . . a few marks—"

It had been a con, a pitch, all along.

I suppose I was afraid that he might actually kiss my hand. I suppose I was embarrassed by the tears (were they real?) that started out of his beseeching eyes, and my own chagrin at having failed to realize that he was asking me for money, and had brought me there for no other reason—there to that evil spot, from which no memorial could immunize me against the knowledge that thousands had died nearby, senselessly, in terror and despair, a-flame (whether at *their* hands, or ours—no matter), our century forever indicted by such butchery, none of us ever to be quite whole again because it had happened. I registered the suffocating pall it had laid over my own life, and the fierce hunger for human solidarity that human viciousness always arouses.

In the midst of these lofty thoughts, I saw him realize that I had misunderstood him, and abruptly change his tack.

"One more thing you should see," he said insistently, "and then I put you on bus to Schwabing," hurrying me up the steps, out of the crypt, and along a path, almost babbling now, towards nothing more than some gloomy bushes along a wall bordering the gardens.

Suddenly I stopped in my tracks. All musing ceased. I re-entered the moment. The suspicious vigilance of an old Central Park walker came back to me. He wasn't a refugee at all. He might not even be Polish. He was a con man, a thief. He was desperate, he might be half-cracked. What did I know of the Munich underworld? And he intended to rob me in those bushes, by force if necessary. (Or was it only some further reminder of the obscene past that waited there—some plaque, some grave, some bullet-riddled statue—with which he hoped to finally shame my pockets open? I still don't know.) But I stopped dead, and he knew I wouldn't go any farther. He could feel me bridling, and so he talked on, stubborn pridelessness replacing the charm, wet eyes searching the pebbles at our feet.

"No food . . . I tell my wife about the kind American professor . . . Could you think to yourself about the Polish teacher, who only wanted to get his family to America? . . . And my little girl—what does she know of the bitterness of life?" A sad and desperate ramble. Was it true? Did it matter?

"Look," I said, interrupting him as you interrupt someone who is embarrassing you by humiliating himself. "Would it insult you if I gave you money? I don't want to insult you, but if it would help—"

And if he was a con man, working the oldest dodge in postwar Germany (evoking guilt or horror in feckless American tourists), this must have amused him mightily when he recounted it later to his cronies ("Ah, the Americans—always so naïve, so child-like, so trusting. To wonder whether it would *insult* me! How can you respect such conquerors?"). But dare you treat a man as if he is not a man, as if he *cannot* be insulted? Dared I assume that conning was not demeaning, even to a con man? Somehow I couldn't call him on the truth, whatever the truth might have been, and so I kept up the fiction, if it was a fiction.

I thumbed out fifty marks ($12), which he pocketed without even looking at the bills, thanking me effusively but with embarrassment now, and, that being over, his agitation eased a little, and he walked me back through the Hofgarten to Ludwigstrasse. A certain formality, a certain chatty reserve, entered our conversation. One could not keep the image of the post-transaction whore and client out of one's mind, for we had trafficked with one another, we had reduced whatever emotions we shared to a crude exchange of money, and it was necessary for both of us to act as if it hadn't happened. Each of us felt that sudden recoil from the other that results from some kinds of intimacy.

We reached the bus-stop, eager to part, and, though it seemed painful for him to have to mention the money again, he said: "I never forget you. And do not worry. This go for food, only for food ... Who needs a scarf—you say *scarf* in American?" gesturing at his throat in such a way that I realized it was probably a necktie about which he was so concerned. "But now," he said with a curious, sly, almost comradely hint of humor in his voice. "Now *you* broke." That was the very word he used.

I assured him that I wasn't, and we said a quick goodbye. He turned on his heel, and went off into the crowd streaming in and out of a haberdashery, and the last glimpse I had of him was when he paused to inspect a window-display. Something had caught his eye. Perhaps, after all, a necktie.

I turned off Ludwigstrasse, and walked towards the river, searching emptier streets. I felt foolish, like the All-American-Sucker, the good-hearted boob so ignorant of the modern world that any reminder of the years of suffering and death there in Europe would automatically evoke the corniest sort of pity, *and* the money with which to buy it off. I had fallen for one of the oldest European cons, no less callow than a Jamesian hero from Duxbury, and allowed myself to be bilked out of the cost of a full day of our trip, a day I had worked, schemed, and, yes, *conned for* myself during most of the preceding year. Money, money, it always came down to money—and didn't *I* understand that? Did every European think every American was rich? As an American writer, a little honored but without profit in his own land, I seethed with resentment, only to realize that I was mostly furious with myself for proving such an easy mark.

The nightmare of modern history had always been my secret albatross. But did it show on my face? Had these last years of anguish and dissent put lines there that anyone could see? Was it so clear that I had come to Germany, as to some heart of contemporary darkness, hoping to ease one guilt in the presence of a greater? Was it even *true*? I didn't hate the Germans, I never had. It was likenesses I looked for, not differences. I was not at odds with my conscience, I was at odds with my century.

But how could Adam have known the burden of human complicity that some of us feel, even in crimes for which we bear no responsibility? How could he have known that, at the last, I would rather *stay* human than act hip? I hadn't known it myself. I hadn't known it until the moment when it no longer mattered to me whether he was telling the truth or not. For he was a man too, and even the shabbiest of sob-stories is an appeal to a common condition, a common consciousness. It assumes that we are all indissolubly involved with one another.

I walked along the Isar escarpment where delicate, pale-yellow leaves fluttered down into the fast, cold, murmuring rush of light-blue water over rocks. The few old men on benches seemed distracted by smoky, half-obliterated memories of pre-Sarajevo days. A black-coated woman, with that look of a stern governess that is typical of some German women over forty, waited patiently by a tree for her dachshund to finish. Across the river from me, rising stolid as a headstone out of the feathery trees, there was an official-looking building, cold and somehow spirit-withering as official buildings in Germany often are. A vague air of sadness without cause, of exhaustion in the hopes, of some perpetual autumn in human affairs, hung over everything. It was, I must confess, not unpleasant to me. It was one reason why I had come to Germany: to experience as keenly as possible my own relation to the strengths and weaknesses of my species in my time.

I thought of Adam, and decided to believe in him, realizing with delight that I had the choice. I had conned to get away from America in order to save a part of my American-ness that seemed in jeopardy, and Adam was conning to get there before something of himself was finally lost. Our spur was the same: to survive, to avoid hating life, to remain human. I settled it that way in my mind, and relinquished the fifty marks with some relief. They had bought something, after all.

Standing with my glass of champagne amid the brittle, literate talk of fortunate American expatriates, living the privileged lives of Romans in Gaul, it seemed a trivial incident. Undoubtedly something similar had happened to everyone in that room. But what had *they* felt?

The professor was talking to me about Tuscany, where he and his wife had a small country house, and scribbling down the names of friends for us to look up once we got to Florence.

"Italy—," he said, a warm, surprisingly boyish smile coming over his face. "What can one say? You'll know the minute you get there. You'll *rest* . . . Germany is a strain for Americans now. It's too much like home." He eyed me, wondering what I would make of this. "Of course that's why some of us like it."

"*I* rather like it," I said. "I think it's been valuable to me."

"Yes, that's the word," he replied immediately. "It's valuable. Americans should have the experience of Germany. If they can receive it . . . And if they can go to Italy afterwards. By the way," he added, "did you get out to Dachau?"

"No," I said. "Well, not *exactly*."

A look of recognition flickered across his eyes, which he understood I understood, and, liking each other immensely at that moment, we turned to the punch bowl.

SEVEN

"Venice About Which Everything Has Been Written—"

On our second morning in Venice (our first in that jewel of a hotel on its quiet campiello in back of the Teatro La Fenice), I sat trying to write in front of a window, the heavy wooden shutters of which had been creaked back to reveal a mottled pink wall across the way, and a small iron-fenced garden below it where a large black dog was confined, ears expectantly alerted, who glanced up at me now and then out of his mid-morning boredom. Beyond, through rusty palings, there was a glimpse of a bit of narrow back-canal the color of cloudy jade, flower pots trailing begonia over a carven sill, and a leafless vine that had worked up a drainpipe out of a chink in the exposed brick. It was Venice in the blear of a chilly November morning, seen from the window of a large room at the back of the red-and-gold, paneled-and-glassed Hotel La Fenice; a room up to the windows of which the exaggerated human sounds of Venice backstreet-life rose with the acoustical clarity of a stage whisper: a carpenter hammering, his mate calling out ribald comments, a barge-man whistling, somewhere in the cavern of the theater next door a trumpet attempting a glissando, high heels pattering along the flagstones, the lapping of the canal against a bridge-pier—all reverberating up between steep walls to distract me from my words. I didn't feel like writing. I hadn't come to Venice to second-guess reality. The very act of putting pencil to paper seemed absurd. Still, the habit persisted.

We were just back from morning *cappuccino* and croissant, and the purchase of a large bottle of Campari Bitter which, at the moment, I was sampling against the dead taste of the cigarettes, while idly trying to find images for the impressions of the past two days. Images for the first sight of Venice from the air as we swerved in a steep bank over it—a risen Atlantis in the blue and gold lucidity of late afternoon, floating as weightless as a fading, brocaded glove on its wide lagoon. Images for the ugly Eighth Street-feeling of the Lista di Spagna (where we spent the first night), and my certainty once I threw open the single window of the tiny room we rented there on blank walls, soiled light, and the dead breath of an airshaft, that we could not stay in it if Shirley was to wipe out the memory of a bad Venetian summer, years before, and if I was to encounter the Venice (and the Italy) my mood hungered for, and so got us together and onto the vaporetto to come all the way along the twilit Grand

Canal to check out hotels and pensiones nearer to the center of things.

Above all, images for nighttime Venice itself—for the wash of shimmering lights on black water in the autumn dark, for the silhouettes of crenellated cornice, intricate grating through which lampshine flickered, and gondola-prow fretted like a glass-cutter; for the Rialto Bridge suspended like an Oriental saddle over the back of the canal; for the whitish pile of Santa Maria della Salute as huge and empty as Grant's Tomb in the damp night-wind off the lagoon; and for Piazza San Marco that instantly reminded me of that immense, sinister ballroom in *The Masque of the Red Death*, figures moving through it with the slow-motion perambulations of tranced waltzers, to be suddenly arrested by the sight of the famous church, indistinct and vaguely elephantine in the luminous dark, at the farther end of that civic square that resembles no other in the world, because it cries out for a Goldoni to stage its inaugurals.

Venice that was like frozen Mozart, symmetries and a-symmetries fusing and separating in restless visual counterpoint until the eye, unfocused by such a feast, riveted on one single *facet* of a building (an arch, or balcony, or a bit of Loew's-72nd-Street colonnade)—unusable, frivolous, needlessly ornate, the decorative sense having simply overflowed utility, ornamentation laid over ornamentation, as if nothing in that town had ever been torn down, only added-onto. Venice that was exactly the sort of city that bored and introverted boys once built in their imaginations on rainy afternoons, its streets only eight feet wide, and none of them straight for more than fifty yards, its canals narrow and pestiferous and meandering, a city fulfilling perfectly the boy's idea of illicit freedom in that it offered a thousand places to hide with a girl, a thousand routes of escape over its broken plateau of rooftops. Venice that was a rabbit-warren of alleys, and bridges, and vest-pocket squares with the plash of fountains playing spectrally in the dark as you crossed them, startled by the sound of your own footfalls.

For it was not a noisy city at that time of year; it was simply that the only sounds were *human,* and they were somehow amplified by the inward-lean of the buildings and the almost total absence of the whirr or putt-putt of machinery (motorboats on the larger canals being the single exception), so that it was the only city where I had ever been where you were always aware of people. You could hear them *walking* three streets away. Even in an empty alley, you heard ghost-like voices, or an echo of vinegary laughter, or the *vino bianco* of some fugitive song; and at night, hurrying through a shadowy campo with something of the delicious stealth of a bravo, the insistent rustle of specters moving off an empty stage under a single worklight of low wattage, that weird rustle always approaching or receding.

It was the intimacy. You wondered what delicate adjustments to the nerves would be necessary for a man habituated to the thousand small anxieties of normal city-life, to live for very long in such astonishing intimacy, realizing how much the grid-like character of most modern cities walls people away from one another into the isolation and anonymity of spaces fragmented by cold pavements, roaring traffics, and automated cross-walks, for here you *brushed* the person who passed you, you drifted as if in a crowded bazaar, and only in a few of the larger squares was it possible to see your fellow stroller from a distance of, say, thirty feet, so that this was a city of faces rather than bodies, of closeups rather than longshots, of gestures large with drama because they were seen in such sharp focus.

Venice, at the last, resembled nothing so much as a gigantic movie-set—as tawdry and grandiloquent, as concentrated and somehow miniaturized, as much the *essence* of a particular reality (rather than that reality itself) as a movie-set always is—and it looked exactly like one's most farfetched, book-nurtured idea of it. One was constantly trying to shake off the feeling of theatricality, façade, fantasy, spectacle, and penetrate to the actual, day-to-day life of the city, only to realize that Venice *was* a theater, as impractical as its location (a mirage afloat on a lagoon), as quixotic as its modes of transportation (could anyone board a vaporetto with the same feeling of vague depression and instant claustrophobia with which one always boards the Madison Avenue bus?), and as histrionic as its history, for this once-powerful and unscrupulous city-state had been the stage upon which operatic dramas of greed and lust and pride and connivery had been played out, and coming from bleaker, more rational streets, one's bruised hedonism stirred into life again at the sight of a city that seemed fully commensurate with the most excessive human appetites. There was no escaping it: The Venetians had produced an environment equal to their own vivid emotional colors, whereas our imperial American passions seemed to have become as mechanistic as the cities we had unwittingly built to express the meanness to which our original vision had come down.

"Venice," I wrote in my notebook that morning, wearied in advance by all the words that lay ahead. "Venice about which everything has been written already—." I broke off. It was not a city that was on my mind, but a man. Not an Italian, but an American. And properly, in that least prosaic of all the towns of Christendom, a poet.

Immediately, I had known the Lista di Spagna area wasn't possible. Even off-season it had the garish, cash-register look of a cheap street in Atlantic City. Tourists, bandoleered in their cameras, wandered bewilderedly among its trinket-shops. Visored hustlers for the hotels seized one's bags and hurried off with them. The smell of sweaty lire hung like burnt coffee over the arcades. And besides, it was too close to the mainland, and some of Mestre's housing-project, supermarket, mass-man bleakness had spread across the causeway and washed up there. We wanted distance from all that. After mod London, and puritanical Paris, and shrouded Munich, we hungered for some final severing from all reminders of the modern world; for an absolutely isolated week alone; for islands, water, strangeness, and above all for the comfort of a past that wasn't ours, and thus was usable. We didn't know a soul in Venice, and were glad of it.

After finding nothing in the San Marco district, I remembered someone mentioning the Hotel La Fenice, and we made for the modest Campo San Fantin, over which the Teatro loomed like a tiara-ed dowager in a mews, and then went on a little farther down the dark side-street and saw a small marquee dimly lighting up the end of a tiny square, quiet and shadowed under a vine-covered lattice.

One look at the room decided me, and we booked it for the following day, which turned out to be a mild Sunday. A wan sun bathed the tottering palazzos in a milky light as we came down the Grand Canal among chattering, church-bound families who no longer noticed them, and wistful Indian tourists who seemed speechless and overwhelmed at the sight. We struggled our bags off at the Fenice stop, and worked our way through back alleys and into empty squares where prides of Venetian cats sunned themselves with placid unconcern, and espresso machines hissed on the zinc bars, and bells tolled sonorously over red-tiled roofs all across the city.

There was that feeling that you get in Catholic countries at a certain hour on Sunday: that vast hush, that quivering suspension, of Mass being said everywhere; a hush which, at any moment, will be broken, once the spiritual meal is over, and people flock the streets and squares again, strolling, promenading, to crowd into the gelaterias and the bars. *Caffès* will be drawn from the steaming machines; tall, heavy-bottomed shot-glasses of Stock 84 or Campari will be poured; children's mouths will be a smear of sugary pastry-filling; the air will be pungent with cooking chickens, with squid frying in deep fat, with the strong breath of cheese and oil and wine. And ahead, the huge, leisurely, stupifying human meal, the talk, the laughter, the watchful women and the boastful men, the kids; and finally those two shuttered hours of blissful drowse that break the Italian day. And mend it. In short, that taking of sustenance into body and soul, that immemorial communal rite that has made Sunday such an ordeal for those of us who live fretfully on the margins of smashed faiths, consoling ourselves with the bitter rusk of our "evolvement."

The pang of Italy is that the old, natural order of things has endured there and still nourishes, and at that moment I rejoiced in it, for I was in flight from too many Sundays of bad hangovers and grim headlines, and the scotch sours that made both seem bearable.

The room was just as fetching as the night before, and out of the window the bas reliefs on the balconied building beyond the small canal shimmered with watery reflections, and we went out (while the hotel's "Maria" made the twin beds into a single wide "matrimonial") to see Piazza San Marco in the day.

Every turning revealed a vista of quiet, statuaried courtyard or graceful bridge beneath which idle gondolas rocked, that seemed too perfect, too staged, too damnably *Venetian* to be believed. A strong imagination, fueled by a lifetime's reading, produced a discovery at every step. Byron, Browning, Howells, James, Baron Corvo, Pound, Hemingway rushed into my head, and out of my mouth. I was the only person I knew who had, at nineteen, struggled through all three volumes of Ruskin's

Stones of Venice, a work as recondite and eccentric as Venice itself, and I was intoxicated with fancied recognitions. Shirley, who had suffered not a little through my dour mood of recent weeks, relaxed. Besides, she was discovering it too. "Last time," she said, "it was August, it was Holy Year, and—Well, wait till you see San Marco. I loved *that* even then."

The Piazza seethed with motion like the floor of a stock exchange. Crowds flowed through the colonnades, eddying in and out of Florian's, swirling around the base of the Campanile. People took pictures of other people, vendors hawked "views"; the hubbub was tremendous. Over it all, in the middle air, the canny, curious, proprietary pigeons of San Marco circled and swooped, lighting on the arms, the shoulders, even the *heads* of astonished tourists with the same arrogant familiarity with which the guides and souvenir-sellers accosted them. If Venice (even off-season) was a carnival, this was the outdoor Hall of Mirrors in which you saw yourself on every hand, distorted, caricatured, but all too recognizable as a gawker.

In the bland, thin sunlight, the church itself was terribly ornate, all white, gold, pink and blue, all painted and domed, like a nineteenth-century canvas pavilion at a garden party. It looked squat and almost garish at the end of the severely black and grey Piazza, and its rotund, Byzantine splendor was as alien to me (after the Gothic severities of France and Germany) as if it had been a mosque. I was a little disappointed, and we turned into the sea-wind that wafted over the thronging Piazzetta from the lagoon.

Suddenly we seemed to have walked directly into the Venice of the Doges. Bearded youths in multi-colored doublets lounged before the Ducal Palace, staring at nothing. Girls with long flaxen hair and paintless lips strolled by in sweeping capes. Slouch hats with peacock feathers were pulled low over the pale, impassive faces of draft-age bravos. Flared jackets of vaguely military cut, emblazoned with gold buttons, milled among velvet bodices, thigh-high leather boots, and the dangle and chink of enormous earrings. Stringed instruments thrummed under a babble of tongues from across a dozen frontiers. We had stepped through the fun-house mirror into the world of Marco Polo.

Nowhere does an outright hallucination seem more commonplace than in Venice, which constantly tugs at the moorings of the imagination, and for a moment I failed to recognize this gaudy crowd as Venice's complement of the wandering Hippies we had been encountering all across Europe. But here was a city so bizarre that no one in a proper suit ever looked quite natural traversing its bridges, and so the Hippies, for once, seemed the perfect citizens of the place.

In the States that year, theater (in the hands of the Hippies) was taking to streets much less dramatic than these. Costumes and incantations and symbolic gestures were erupting in the most blighted urban parks. But Venice, which was as psychedelic as the Hippies themselves, as hallucinatory as the destination of their Trips, nevertheless seemed to bore them. Here everything from which they had uprooted themselves—the earthquake of change that was shuddering up through modern life, leveling our cities, our traditions, and our very sense of ourselves—had done no damage more serious than a few Coca-Cola signs, and a general aura of forthright Con. Here life itself was viewed as theater rather than as struggle, and any change was no more permanent than the tides that rose and fell in the canals with their cargoes of empty Chianti bottles, orange rinds, and dead cats. Yet the Hippies seemed mostly indifferent to the rich tangle of human history all around them, as if here they had no modern drabness against which to appear more vivid, no hypocrisy from which to secede in the name of a higher truth, and realized that in this city even *their* philosophy was provisional. They looked around expressionlessly, or laughed their half-derisive, half-bewildered laughter, or merely slumped against their knapsacks. They might have been slouching through Disneyland to be bored. The Venetians (who had seen everything, after all) streamed out of the churches, paying them no mind, and went off to the pasta, and the fish, and the wine.

Among these sights, I suddenly saw a face I knew I knew. It was a face as crisscrossed with lines as an Elizabethan mariner's map by its meridians, and it seemed made of a parchment as weathered, and salt-yellowed, and perishable. It was an austere face, an eloquent face, gaunt, somehow burnt-away, with a wispy grey-white beard neatly shaped to its lean chin, the clear remote eyes of a wordly man who no longer saw what he did not want to see, and a mouth set in a pursed, acerbic line I seemed to recognize. It was the face of an immensely old cavalier, unhorsed but still upright. It was the face of a saddened, stubborn Quixote, who had long ago survived his windmills. Wearing a double-breasted camel's hair coat, a maroon silk scarf, and a Russian fur hat, carrying a cane he did not lean on so much as port, he was moving through the crowds at a measured pace, taking his constitutional. A small, trim, pretty-faced woman, also in a fur hat and holding his arm, walked beside him the way women used to walk with strong-minded men—deferential, protected, quietly proud. "My God!" I exclaimed to Shirley. "I think that's Ezra Pound!"

I worked through the crowds until I was ahead of him, and turned, not wanting to gape, and gaped. Incredibly, it *was* Ezra Pound—the late Pound of the Avedon photographs, the Pound who still resembled the famous Gaudier-Brzeska sketch, the Pound whose very first book of poems had been published here in Venice in 1908—strolling with a friend in the Piazzetta on a Sunday noon these sixty years later!

I was as astonished as if I had come upon Henry James among the teeny-boppers in Washington Square. The mood of the day was instantly altered by a sense of *presence*. I didn't stare at him, overcome by a sudden reflex of ridiculous discretion, but I was electrically aware of him there, not ten feet from me, in that strange Venetian intimacy.

"I can't believe it," I said under my breath. "It's like seeing a family ghost. I knew he was alive, I knew he was back in Italy, but—well, somewhere *else,* out of reach . . . Lord, I wrote poems based on lines of his of fifty years ago!"

Pound and his friend had reached a cluster of small, iron tables in front of a bar facing the lagoon, and they stopped to chat with an acquaintance. That is, the friend sat down for a moment and exchanged pleasantries. Pound stood there, something about him as eminent and anonymous as if he were an exiled Russian novelist in nineteenth-century Wiesbaden, an expression of quiet, intense, perplexed concentration fixing on his face the look of a man in whom memory and reality conduct a continual, musing dialogue on which he is always eavesdropping. The sun came out a little, the noisy throngs moved by him, and I studied him avidly.

He had meant so much to me. Art and politics were the opposed-religions of my time, and he had worshipped simultaneously in both their churches—a poet who deserved the Nobel Prize, a propagandist who had earned himself St. Elizabeth's. But in this third year of Vietnam, political virtue no longer seemed the measure of a man (we had all been wrong too many times to rest easy in our convictions), and it was his stubborn eccentricity of mind, his merciless standards when it came to art, his undeviating fixation on the *life* of words, his piratic beard and his crankish eruditions, the very longevity that had seen him outlive all the movements and most of the men who had created "modernism," that fastened my gaze on him that day.

At the time of his trial twenty years ago, I had found myself (despite the stern demands of my own anti-fascism) simply *unable* to dismiss his poetry along with his politics—an "inconsistency" that I eventually came to accept as a sign of maturity in this ambivalent age. Besides, there was something so—well, so *native* about him. His passion for the arcane, the obscure, the antiquated; his love of lingo, statistics, theorizing; his infatuation with the past and his scorn of the present; *even* his crack-brained political follies—all this had somehow struck the quintessential American note, and to my generation he had always been Uncle Ez, the maddening, unorthodox *Literateur Terrible,* from whom we had learned more about the vocation of language than most of us could accurately assess. And to me, the man who had written of the First World War, "There died a myriad, / and of the best, among them . . . For two gross of broken statues, / For a few thousand battered books," was a man who had educated me in the monstrous disproportions of a civilization that later would produce, in the same twelve months, the Pisan Cantos and the holocaust of Hiroshima.

His years of incarceration in army stockade and mental hospital (a blot on the national conscience), and the flow of work which he had allowed neither experience to interrupt (a subtler rebuke than any made in his behalf), had more than a touch of quirkish heroism to them, and for almost fifteen years I had suspected that there was something that Ezra Pound could teach us all about surviving in what he had once called "a botched civilization." His continuing presence in a world so utterly changed from the world of his youth was, in itself, something of a consolation to those of us who had grown up amid the sounds of all the traditional sets being struck, and now, amazingly, here he was, waiting out the amenities of a chance encounter in a public place. He had outlived everything, including *himself,* and my own cantankerous awareness of being forty-one, and tired, and at odds with the world, fell away before the fact of his incredible old age.

I would just go up to him (I thought suddenly), and pay him the respect of an American writer, of whom he could not possibly have heard, but whose work and life had been vitally affected by him for twenty years; not wanting to intrude or insinuate myself into his day, but relying on the truth of the gesture (the intuitive truth of my urge to make it) to smooth over the interruption of his Sunday stroll, uncomfortably aware of how often I failed to do things that I *knew* were deeply appropriate because of a fool reflex of propriety which, at that very moment, was already framing the question, "But why should Ezra Pound care one way or the other about *my* respects, no matter how tactfully tendered?"

So I hesitated, losing my nerve by the second, and then noticed that Pound was being photographed as he stood there, his stance as indefinably aristocratic as if he were Louis Calhern playing a Czarist Grand Duke down on his luck in Paris. Two men, with hand-held movie cameras, stood at different distances recording the moment. A third, the harried director, crouched and sweated among the shoes of the strollers, framing Pound between his thumbs and forefingers, only to get up after a moment and approach Pound's lady-friend. A quick conversation ensued, a finger suggested a move down the Riva Degli Schiavoni, and this was transmitted to the impenetrable Pound. It was evidently a crew from Italian TV, filming the concluding sequence of a cultural documentary: Ezra Pound strolling in the Venice he had known intimately for sixty years, the Venice where he had published *A Lume Spento* at his own expense so long ago, and here, now, the taper not yet extinguished! One could feel the director's secret pleasure in this juxtaposition. Impervious, Pound obviously intended to endure it all.

I moved Shirley along after him. The breeze was crisp and lightly salted. Far off, the Lido shimmered like a mirage over the limpid surface of the lagoon. A chestnut-seller poked at the blackened, pungent nuts on his brazier with bandaged fingers. The Hippies muttered to one another with that glum cool, that somehow pathetic air of aimless disdain, that always made me wonder why they traveled at all, finding (as they always seemed to) nothing but the same drag everywhere. Pound stood near the edge of the quay, silhouetted against the glassy brightness of the water, and, drawing closer, I saw that same curious expression of perplexed concentration on his face. *Which* Venice (of all the Venices he had known) did he see? The comic opera Venice of D'Annunzio? The somnolent, plague-ridden Venice of Thomas Mann? Peggy Guggenheim's jet-set Venice? Mary McCarthy's? Or some older Venice that existed solely in his own fancy?

It was impossible to tell, but there was a certain courtliness in the way he declined his head to listen to his friend's remarks, a certain quiet fatalism (suggesting that fame and ignominy involved precisely the same degree of discomfort) about the way he turned back towards the cameramen, and a certain elusive dignity about the way he strolled more or less *through* them, as they gesticulated with that frenzied dread of the "lost moment" that is the nightmare of all photographers. Did he really see them? Was he only playing out some role? His eyes were as clear as moonstones, and as unfathomable.

"Speak to him," Shirley said. "You ought to go up and speak to him."

I knew she was right, but somehow I hesitated, all of a sudden remembering the lines, "Down, Derry-down / Oh let an old man rest," which he had scribbled in a cage in Pisa amid the ruins of 1945. The photographers were maneuvering him this way and that, moving in for closeups, shooting over the shoulders of passers-by, and, as he turned into the Piazza-proper, flocks of dirty pigeons, like *scugnizze*-angels in a Tiepolo canvas, flapped brazenly about his head. He walked among them, upright and unblinking, a man too isolated in himself to be dissuaded any longer by anything short of death.

The Hippies, to whom he might have been something of a culture-hero after all, hardly noticed him, or, if they did, saw only an eccentric, rather out-of-style old gentleman (perhaps an obscure Balkan diplomat) being badgered by a couple of newsreel photographers. To most of them, Ezra Pound was probably nothing but a fabulous name out of the murky past who could not be imagined walking the unpoetic streets of their world. I felt a sudden flush of resentment and protectiveness. "There is no organized or coordinated civilization left, only individual scattered survivors," he had written forty-five years ago. "Darkness and confusion as in Middle Ages; no chance of general order or justice; we can only release an individual here or there ... Only those of us who know what civilization is, only those of us who want better literature ... better art ... can be expected to pay for it."

He had paid (as much for this conviction as for his "treason"), as he was paying now at the hands of the cameramen, who jumped around like pygmies baiting a wounded lion, while he made his way, unrecognized, among the broken children who had "released" themselves, but no longer spoke of art or literature. His short, careful, deliberate steps, his curious air of having been so buffeted as to be reduced at last to the essential strengths, but above all his scuffed, brown, vaguely 1940-ish shoes, so moved me that I was momentarily *enclosed* within the feeling. No, I wouldn't go up to him. I, at least, would let the old man rest, paying my respects to his lifelong expenditure of sensibility by leaving him alone.

As it happened, this failure to go up and speak to him would come to haunt me when, some months later, I learned that just then Pound, far from being secure in his great fame and even greater age, was enduring agonies of doubt about the value of his accomplishment. This man of eighty-two, who for over six decades had thrust his finger into every cultural pie with the confident certainty that his taste was infallible, had been deserted by the sense of his own gifts, and words, by which he had lived as a monk lives by prayer, had become a notation as incomprehensible to him as notes of music are to people who play by ear. Some buttress of pride had crumbled within him, and this most maddeningly loquacious of modern poets had relapsed into almost total silence. He would listen, he could hear, but he rarely spoke, and when he did, the bewilderment, the confusion, the pathetic refusal to ask for reassurance, was terrible to those who cared for him.

I learned all this too late, and remembering his clear, perplexed eyes studying the lagoon, I realized that probably he was seeing a Venice that he had never seen before, the Venice of an old man who had survived beyond images, beyond the artifices of language, beyond that sense of Ego that views the world as perfectible in the theater of art; an immensely old man, cruelly deserted by his illusions, who found himself beached in what Yeats (an old friend) had called "the desolation of reality." What difference would it have made if I had spoken to him? Could anything I might have said at least have flattered him back into his famous irrascibility? Perhaps, after all, the fundamental pointlessness of this, *all* this (the crowds, the photographers, the fame, the infamy, Venice itself), was a more penetrating truth than any he had ever enunciated. Who can know?

But the debt one human being owes another who has enlarged him *should* be paid, and the filial respect a younger writer feels for an older *ought* to be acknowledged, because such insignificant acts may be all that remains of the old communions in this era of endless, empty Sundays. Who can know whether the gesture I failed to make would have awakened a momentary flicker of egoism in him? What I *do* know is that I consider my trepidation to be a pettiness of spirit. "I am homesick after mine own kind," he had written once, a feeling every American artist learns to live with year after year. But in Venice that day there was no kinship. There were only individual, scattered survivors.

"Venice about which everything has been written already—." Re-reading the line, I no longer liked it. The admission of surfeit and impotence that it contained had lain like a shadow across Pound's eyes, a shadow that had lengthened until it had all but obliterated the faces of the Hippies. Nothing more to be written, nothing more to be imagined, nothing more to be done.

Sitting at the window having a second drink, and staring down at the large, black, bored dog penned in the garden below, I discovered that I was still *this* side of such "wisdom," if wisdom it was. As a troubled American writer, whose country was at war with its own soul, I had come to Europe, as Americans always have, looking for native strengths, for the old American breadth of vision, for ancestors. Did it all come down to a baffled old man, a gang of bombed-out youths, and no more words?

I couldn't accept it. Pound had once believed that artists were the frail bridges across which the past escaped into the future through the upheavals of the present (a belief in the continuity of human experience that was the source of his *own* survival), and perhaps the act of putting pencil to paper, in an attempt to salvage a few words before their meanings were lost, *was* the ultimate civilizing act, as he had said. In any case, I was too old to dismiss it as frivolous, and not yet old enough to decide it was futile.

No, there *had* to be more to be written—even about this unlikely city out of whose lagoon had sailed as many books as merchantmen. I thought back on the day before, remembering that after we had watched Pound stroll off into the crowds, we had gone into the huge, dim cave of San Marco where Mass was being chanted in a harsh singsong that rose insistently over the echoing footsteps of hundreds of sightseers. Staring up into the cavernous darkness of the domes that were peopled with flaking blue and gold mosaic-figures, as awesome and primitive as the cave-paintings in Lascaux, I had tried to be impressed. But Pound's questioning eyes and weary shoes were still too much with me, and I could feel no hint of reverence, only the suffocating dead air of centuries of exhausted hopes, only the multitudinous prayers (like so many poems) that had vanished upwards within those unavailing walls, only the abject knees that had made of that wavery, inlaid floor a mute tablet of unanswered supplications. At that moment, the place seemed as irrelevant as Madame Tussaud's.

But then I noticed that a pigeon had wandered in with the rest of us. Plump, dirty as an urchin, with a metallic, purple sheen on his wings, he was waddling about among the myriad feet, pecking at specks of dust, tweaking shoelaces, and sidling out of the way with a ruffle of feathers and a soft, exasperated little coo. His black eyes gleamed like beads in the candlelight, and he strutted about with alert, inquisitive undulations of his neck. He was as self-satisfied, and engrossed, and warming to behold as one of those fat, jovial little priests you see in the third-class carriages of Italian trains, who darefully thumb up every crumb in the corners of their lunch boxes, and drain their wickered bottles of *rosso* down to the last drop, and only then, with a little sigh, reopen their breviaries. Like them, he knew exactly where he was, and why he was there. He was in his world, he was within himself, and the play was continuing.

Friar Tuck (I thought), a pompous, winning little Friar Tuck-of-a-pigeon, and had to laugh under my breath, for the sheer stubborn wonder of existence—*all* of it—had come back.

Shirley looked up from her book: "What are you doing?"

"Writing."

"About what?"

"That pigeon in San Marco," I said. "And Pound, and the Hippies . . . Just a few notes for later," and finishing my Campari, I settled down to the notebook.

"Venice," I rewrote the line, "about which there is always something more to be said—"

EIGHT

Flesh and the Machine:
Thanksgiving in Florence

It was Thanksgiving
Day, and in a few hours Americans all over Europe—even the
most resolutely expatriated of them—would be getting together
over makeshift banquets to experience, many for the first time,
the meaning of that first Thanksgiving: strangers celebrating
their survival in a strange land. But we knew no one in Florence,
and so we had arranged to have our little feast that evening in a
quiet restaurant a block from Dante's house.

"Yes, this is still the best view," Shirley said, puffing a little from the climb. "Now you can get an idea of what it was like when I was here before."

We were standing at the parapet up on the Piazzele Michelangelo, a little surprised by the distance we had come, for we could just make out what we took to be the roof of our pensione beyond the far-off Duomo. Down there, across the milky-green Arno at low-water, Florence lay spread out in a shallow bowl of hills—its pale-yellow piazzas, and walls of earthy pink, and tiled-roofs in terraces of faded ochre as graphic as a high-definition photograph in the startling clarity of the Tuscan morning.

"From up here, in this light, you'd never guess that it's become a madhouse," I had to admit.

The light was the pure, emphatic light you saw through the windows of Quattrocento paintings, and of course the landscape was the same. The cloudless blue sky was as keen and scoured as tempered steel, the cedars were that black-green that seems the very essence of greenness, and the rooftops looked as if they had been kilned out of the red earth itself. It brought back a forgotten memory of California foothills in the smogless, early thirties when the air was still as clear and cool and rational as a glass of mountain water.

"Yes, *this* is how I remember it," Shirley said with a trace of the returnee's pensive recognition of how much had been taken for granted before. "In 1950, it was poor and cold, and there was still bomb damage then, but I had my best times of all here."

From that wide, sunny height, Florence looked as splendid as one's bookish hopes for it: the queen-city of the Renaissance—as marvelously anachronistic in a world of urban blight as an exiled Empress punctiliously holding court in a slum. Out of the maze of narrow, zigzag streets, the Duome, the Palazzo Vecchio, and Santa Croce rose above the rooftops like a lopsided triangle of plinths in a moiling sea, and from up there the busts in the Uffizi

courtyard, commemorating the artists, philosophers and states-
men who had transformed this provincial town in Tuscany into
a world-city, took on flesh and walked its streets once more in
the imagination. You could visualize them down there off the
busy piazzas, pausing for coffee on that crisp morning amid the
smells of ink and marble dust and wet plaster, and for a moment
the genius of old cities, cities that had grown up naturally out of
a communion of energies and ideals until they achieved their
own unique character the same way that a man achieves his,
came home with an empathetic flash. The communitarian vision
that had once represented man's deepest urge towards civilization, but which in our age had degenerated into a nightmare of
cement jungles, stirred up the powerful nostalgia one sometimes
feels for an experience one has never had firsthand. Community!
A community of men!

But the feeling evaporated with the idiot beeping of a tourist
bus pulling onto the Piazzele. For we had just walked through
the streets down there. Or rather we had negotiated them as you
negotiate the mad swirl of a Dodgem rink, and knew too well
that Florence had become a community of machines rather than
men, a museum surrounded by a traffic jam. At last Dante had
something to scowl about from his pedestal in Piazza Santa
Croce, for he had become the sole attendant of a parking lot full
of Fiats. The eighteen-foot reproduction of Michelangelo's *David*
in the Piazza Della Signoria rose above the motor-scooters and
delivery vans, as vulnerable in his genitals as a sleeper dreaming
that he is naked on Fifth Avenue. The traffic that roared in a
ceaseless drag-race around the Duomo made it one of the most
treacherous places in the world for the culture-prone pedestrian,
and contemporary Florence would have totalled Ruskin in the
first five minutes of one of his famous morning walks.

It had taken us two days to register the reason for our pee-
vishness. If the nerves were as taut as guitar strings, it must be

the result of anticipation, excitement, or our ten quiet days in Venice. If the attention wouldn't concentrate on a building or a picture, it must be because by then we'd seen too many buildings and too many pictures. But not at all. Our state of more or less permanent jangle resulted from the sheer impossibility of walking ten steps with our eyes lifted. There wasn't room in the streets for the Lambrettas, much less the Maseratis. The sidewalks were twenty-four inches wide.

The forbidding, windowless walls of palazzos lowered over you like escarpments. You had to walk blocks to find a crossover, and once you ventured out into it the motor-bikes pursued you like berserk lemmings, and if you got across with your legs unbroken you were little better off than a mountain-climber on a ledgefull of Sherpas. Even if you were an old New Yorker, you discovered nerves you hadn't known about, and after a while your gorge rose in the half-crazed, splenetic fury that sometimes overcomes the urban man at that one indignity-too-many. You snapped at your wife, and cursed the drivers with a pumping forearm, and ran like an hysterical turkey the week before Thanksgiving, and your initial discomfort rapidly deepened towards outright paranoia.

A year before, the passive Arno had risen all in a few hours to flood the city. Along the riverside, the high-water mark was seven feet above the streets, a height attested to (in this city that memorialized everything) by classy bronze plaques. In the Duomo (all white and pink and green marble—the largest chunk of Gorgonzola in the world), the central floor had become a fenced-in excavation, in which you dismally expected to see that tangle of loamy ganglia for which Con Ed is always tirelessly probing in New York. The damaged lower parts of the huge paintings in Santa Croce were covered with those ugly plastic shrouds that obscure everything around building sites, and every cellar *trattoria* on the side streets exhibited a Polaroid-shot of loaves of bread or heads of lettuce floating just under its rafters. Still, the more permanent inundation was bound to be the automobile. The city cried out for a traffic-planner, but you couldn't escape the suspicion that he would qualify for a strait-jacket within ten days. The twentieth-century machine had ravaged the fifteenth-century city as remorselessly as a horde of army-ants, turning what had been a citizenry into a fragmented crowd, and Florence had become less a place of human habitation than a kind of claustrophobic, automated Antonioni-land in which the people, souls somehow muffled behind their eyes, seemed as ephemeral as their counterparts in London or New York.

Nevertheless, looking out over the city in the blue and gold November light, unmenaced by animated metal for the moment, I realized that it was a sense of flesh that was qualifying my disappointment in Florence. The massive, violent nudity of sculpture was everywhere. The Loggia across from the Palazzo Vecchio was a bacchantic tableau of thrusting breasts, and strain-ing thighs, and phalluses blatant with power. In the Bargello, the huge nude figures around the inner court were stone so transmogrified into flesh that your own flesh roused towards them involuntarily. The harsh and virile genius of this city dur-ing the Renaissance seemed to have driven its artists so beyond the austerities of their culture (much less the pieties of pope or Medici) that they had ended up, like so many closet-pagans, monumentalizing the ecstatic mystery of the body's life in the very squares of commerce.

A day before, I had stared at the statue of *David* (the civic emblem, miniatures of it available in every *gelateria,* a reproduc-tion standing behind us now), and found myself stirred by a kind of sensual awe, for the beauty of this muscular youth was rendered with an erotic intensity usually reserved for female beauty, and his noble, shameless nakedness—the expressive weight of the hands, the subtle downward curve of the belly, the very cock itself—made me glimpse for a moment the natural perfection of a man's body in all its arrogant power, and understand, as well, something of the secret langour of a woman's response to it—even as I choked on the fumes of the exhaust.

But despite its past, Florence was no longer a sexy city—the way modern London is, or Rome. You didn't sniff that faintly acrid trace of salt in the air that suggests seraglio-excesses behind the closed shutters of Venetian afternoons. There was little sense of a secret, voluptuous life going on nearby, and the contemporary Florentines seemed to be a mannered, snobbish, mercantile and urbane lot—without a hint of hedonism in their high, cerebral foreheads and coldly beautiful eyes. You were always aware of the burden of past distinction that had somehow ennervated the present, of tradition stifling innovation; and the young artist, his imagination just coming into itself, must have felt suffocated by the profusion of Michelangelos, Donatellos, and Cellinis that he encountered on even the most casual saunter after cigarettes, and probably he ran off to Rome to get away from it all. Some cities, in burning their unique vision into the consciousness of the world, seem to burn themselves out in the process—as Athens had, or Boston—and the traffic had done for the rest.

"I suppose we ought to try to do the Medici Chapel this afternoon," Shirley said, "if we're going to do it at all." She wanted to shop for a hat, and we would have to lunch before one o'clock when everything closed up.

"Might as well. After you've seen two thousand Annunciations you've seen them all, but we've only done ten or fifteen chapels."

The Medici was her favorite place in Florence. Years before, as a girl, the Michelangelos there had shaken her awake the way works of art sometimes do, permanently enlarging the moral imagination as they speak to the senses, but she hadn't talked much about it since we'd been in Florence. I knew she was saving it for the right moment, a moment that hadn't come. But now we were leaving for Rome the next day, and it couldn't be put off any longer. "Let's find us a *trat* on this side of the river, and arm the nerves with a liter of wine," I said. "That is, if you can stand a little more broken-field running."

She could, and we started down a terraced walkway through an olive grove that was fenced with simple, oaken crosses with No One on them yet. The old, earth-dun wall of the city toiled over the next rise towards the Pitti Palace, and we passed under a portal where the ancient masonry gave back the warm glow of the sun, and went along a narrow, inner street that was cool and shadowed and blissfully autoless. Dark doorways, fragrant with Romano and olive oil and fresh oranges, stirred up an appetite in me that so far Florence had failed to touch, an appetite for neighborhoods, for local life, for districts where people cooked and washed and slept together. Up to then the city had seemed as unctuously custodial as the guards in the museums. Shirley bought an orange for tomorrow's pre-breakfast hunger in a tiny shop where dusty salamis hung like reeking stalactites and a dog lay among baskets of artichokes, losing to his fleas. My spirits rose a little, and we wandered on into the "better" part of town on that side of the Arno, past the Brownings' house (Elizabeth Barrett got all the billing on the ubiquitous plaque; Robert wasn't even mentioned), but couldn't seem to find the sort of restaurant for which I hankered. Not wanting to lose my temper to the servile hustle of a waiter, I got picky, and Shirley began to weary.

The steel shutters of the shops would be banging down in twenty minutes, and the streets were suddenly crowded with noisy school children, wielding strapfuls of books like so many young Davids brandishing their slingshots at the Goliaths of the traffic. Piazza San Spirito was a chaos of parked cars, and a reef of tall, white cloud moved over the hills across the sun, bringing a sudden chill to the air, like a premonition of the cheerless, urban twilight that was still hours away.

"How about that place?" Shirley said. "Maybe we'd better settle for it."

It was a tiny *trattoria* on the corner of the Piazza. Its dingy windows displayed no menu, no *prezzo fisso* in three languages for the tourist, but only some dusty bottles of *Stock* and a lethargic tom cat. Inside, there was a small zinc bar, and the strong odor of a garlicky soup, and a kitchen doorway full of steam and the clatter of pots. The tables were crowded with workmen finishing their coffees, who took Shirley's measure as a matter of course—the eyes going down and then going up again with that candid and impertinent appreciativeness that is a street-gallantry in Italy. We found a table in the narrow, dim little alcove that led to the toilets. The checkered cloth was a mosaic of wine-stains, cigarette-ash and yesterday's hardened cheese sauce. "Look," I said, "this won't do. Not for our last day. Let's go on a few blocks," wanting the lunch to be as special as Shirley's hopes for the afternoon.

But the Signora had appeared, a large, pretty blonde woman with an amused eye, a supple waist that pasta and child-bearing had thickened, and the slap-slap-slap of bedroom slippers. She eyed us with bold interest as she recited the *listo,* flicking the ashes off the table with her towel, and settling the matter of the wine right off. She liked us (you felt she probably liked everyone at first), but nevertheless her kitchen was closing. Artichokes and eggs? The artichokes and eggs were "molto bene." And perhaps a bit of her own ravioli to start. A nice *ensalata rosso,* and then Gorgonzola and fruit—yes?

Yes.

We drank the white wine that was so dry and tart that you gulped it down like water, and ate her spicy ravioli that was "molto bene" too, and went on to the artichokes and the lightly beaten eggs, and found, once we had gotten to the pears and the cheese, that we had had a fine time after all. Nothing would suit the mood but that we have a Strega with our coffee, which the Signora set down before us with the wise, tactful smile of a concierge renting a room to lovers. The place was emptying, everyone was going home mulled with wine to drowse or to make love, and the Signore behind his bar eyed the Signora as he rinsed the glasses, and the Signora felt the Signore's eyes upon her, and hurried.

It was suddenly *good*. I felt lifted. An absurd uprush of well-being came over me, and for a moment the hater-of-cities went back to his grumpy lair, and I said "yes" to Florence—traffic and all—for the first time. What did I care that the glut and pollution and nerves of the modern metropolis had reached here too? There was still wine, skylarking children, the afternoon siesta, and the wise smile of a woman who knew the important things. There were still a few years left to this city, at least on this side of the river, before it became uninhabitable to everyone, except those who had allowed some part of the machine into their psyches. Beyond the chiselled flesh of the statuary, which seemed to have withered the sensuality of the Florentines precisely because of its extravagant voluptuousness, might there not still be the faint pulse of the old Adam? Wasn't there some meager hope as long as everything came to a stop for an hour or two in the afternoons?

Outside, the emptied streets made it seem a safe bet. The Volkswagens along the curb, and the rank of motorscooters parked on the pavement at crazy angles, had the slightly foolish look of kids' playthings abandoned in a front yard, and, once we turned towards the river, the silence of the afternoon-hiatus restored an air of human intimacy, or architectural coherence to the narrow, Renaissance blocks down which we walked. Up-river, three frigate-swans cruised under the silversmiths' shops on the Ponte Vecchio where, at mid-bridge, the bust of Cellini mused—the patron-saint of all artisans and hustlers. We walked, in a warm envelope of wine, under the dramatic Tuscan sky—the sun coming out and going in as masses of broken cloud scudded over the city, the chic shopwindows along Via Tournaboni alternately gilded or in shadow—and, on a certain corner where the sun suddenly flooded down an old stucco wall in a poignant rush of champagne-light, I knew that I would remember forever every last crescent of tile on that overhang, every bit of window ornament, every single shutter-slat—so absolutely open to it, so unimpeded by the gloomy reflections of the discursive intelligence, was I at that moment.

This feeling of utter lucidity, this idiotic joy I felt in the simple unfoldment of reality itself, lasted through the Central Market where some of the stalls and barrows had remained stubbornly open to catch the custom of lire-burdened tourists from colder climates to whom an afternoon nap was frivolous, if not downright decadent. It lasted through the piles of handbags, wallets and gloves, the ranks of dashboard *Davids* in plaster or lead, the gimcracks and gewgaws, and the whole souvenir-detritus of mass-produced bad taste that may bury Europe one day as it has already buried America. It even lasted through the ritual ping-pong of offer and counter-offer, concerning a Russian-style fur hat, which Shirley conducted with an admiring barrow-man, and it lasted because if the value of an object can still be haggled over, one has remained its master instead of vice versa. But shortly I became aware that Shirley was stalling on the Medici Chapel, which was only a few streets away, as reluctant to risk disappointment (in it, or in herself, or in me) as a divorcée the second time around.

The afternoon had gloomed-over while we shopped, and when the steel shutters rolled up again the lights were on in the *gelaterias* where the espresso machines hissed like toy steam-boil-ers, and the pastry trays glistened with Alp on Alp of glazed icing. The trickle of cars was building towards a stream once more, and you felt the city taking a deep breath, and getting its second wind. I wasn't sure I wanted the Medici Chapel. I didn't feel reverent, even about Michelangelo, and I was enjoying Flor-entine street life for the first time. Shirley wasn't sure she wanted it either, but we were each too poised in tactful awareness of the other to say anything, and found ourselves pocketing those lovely, tissue-thin, pastel-colored tickets of admission that you purchase in museums all over Italy, and following the signs through a crypt, up a dark stone stairway, through the ornate chapel-proper, and into a severe, domed ante-room.

Does this smallish marble chamber, higher than it is wide, and bathed that day in the half-light of late afternoon coming through modest windows far up in its walls, constitute the pin-nacle of Michelangelo's art? I don't know. Though I had known his work for years through reproductions, he was the crashingly obvious revelation of my weeks in Italy—his *David* seeming the perfect emblem of Florence in its boom days: larger than life, self-indulgent, virile and yet somehow narcissistic in its sensu-ality; the wooden torso of the *River God* in the *Casa* on Via Buonarotti, limbless and decapitated though it was, stating with unexampled power that a titanic, Archimedean energy— sufficient to turn us all into gods did we but accede to it—lay somewhere just below the navel; and later (in Rome) the Sistine ceiling striking me as nothing less than the audacious attempt of one supremely gifted man to be done with all the possibilities of painting in a single, gigantic creation that was almost as encom-passing as the vision of Creation that it celebrated, and yet . . . Well, all that was *Art*—great art that evoked pleasure, admira-tion, even awe—but only art, after all. The way *Madame Bovary* is art, or Haydn's *Farewell Symphony.* Whereas *Anna Karenina* is somehow *more* than art, as is Mozart's *Jupiter.* And those statues in the Medici Chapel.

There was a straight-backed chair or two in that austere chamber, to which the ponderous weight of the surrounding marble seemed to impart a special, tomblike chill, and Shirley took one and sat in a corner, while I moved around, studying the four recumbent nudes (representing Day, Night, Morning, and Evening) on the two sarcophagi. Footfalls and lowered voices echoed hollowly in the outer chapel. The traffic outside was a distant, muffled roar, sounding as obsessive as the gabble of game-playing children in the street as overheard from a quiet room. A small East Indian gentleman came in, seemed embarrassed by our presence, did a quick turn of the room with the self-effacement of a dormouse, and scurried away. I could hear my own breath.

But more, I could feel my own body. Those four life-size blocks of marble, which had been forced almost five centuries before to *become* flesh at the behest of a human hand, seemed more mysteriously alive than most of the bodies I had allowed myself to experience in a bed, and waves of sensual understanding swept up through me. A tendon glimmering through the flesh of an upraised thigh, a straining shoulder that limned the banded pattern of the musculature within, the soft swell of a belly firming downwards to the Venus mound, the lax droop of a penis falling to one side: to *know* the body as Michelangelo had—the way it occupies and defines space, the way it tenses and lapses as it discovers its own solidity—and to be able to compel lifeless stone to so awaken the living spectator that the enigma of human sentience that redeems the simple meat came out clear, was to have penetrated to the sacramental core of all sexuality, to have come beyond a fixation on the erotic into the

realm of a deeper longing, the longing of the soul to be a cele-
brant in the temple of the body.

I felt an overpowering urge to touch. I wanted to use my
hands instead of my eyes. My own body trembled with crea-
turely sympathy, and in a flash I remembered watching a ten-
year-old girl in London's Tate Gallery years before, standing in
front of a Dégas sculpture, unconsciously assuming the position
of the dancer out of that same sympathy of flesh for flesh. Suddenly the stubborn, unmoving presence of those four bodies
weighed on my consciousness with all the baffling power of a
primal memory. I no longer denied that I knew what I knew.
We were not broken, *we were whole.* All the ephemeral people
hurrying through the streets were complete and perfect, and
their machines were only rueful evidence of their distrust of that
completeness, that perfection. We humans had recoiled from our
physical selves, as from a mystery our arrogance could not abide,
and the fantastically complicated watchworks we had made of
modern life was nothing less than an exteriorization of that pathetic self-hatred. Standing there, I found myself mourning all
the bodies I had ever trafficked with—their shames, their mod-
esties, their lecheries—all of it: the whole sad illiteracy of our
sensual vocabulary, the dance that was helplessly imprisoned in
every one of us, the intellectual pride that never went before the
Fall, the barren dramas of the ego to which we had forced our
guileless flesh to become the corrupted accomplice. I missed a
dozen girls to whom I had never been the proper lover but only
played the sexual acrobat going through his paces; and half a
dozen men with whom a mutual affection had remained ner-
vously gestureless. We were whole, after all. We had only to
admit it. Witless as a boy approaching a woman for the first
time, I reached up and touched the smooth curve of a female
thigh, and was shocked to discover that it was *cold.* It was noth-

ing but marble, a piece of statuary, the dead image of a living thing, another exteriorization. And yet a compensating warmth spread through me, and I turned to Shirley.

She sat in her chair, back in the shadows, unaware of me (the hardness of the chair, the softness of her buttocks—all of a sudden I *knew* the tactile nature of things that way), and she seemed utterly within herself at that moment, as if some gap had closed in her (a gap in *my* awareness, I realized with delight). Her face was as musingly lucid as the face of a deer turned towards a sunset across which wild geese etch the long, wavering arrows that will get them home (nothing to plumb, no need to translate the expression into the mood), and she sat quietly absorbed in the statues, so completely herself, and so absolutely separate from me, that it was like seeing her for the first time. All the disappointment in Florence had drained out of her face, and her eyes were faintly moist with relief to discover that seventeen years of winnowing certitude had proved insufficient to blunt the truths of twenty-one. She had that look of mingled pride, skepticism, pleasure and irony that the triumphs of the species always evoke in those who are sensible enough to expect defeat, but nevertheless refuse to relinquish hope.

The redemptive power of art in broken times came over me like a revelation. If we could still be roused by the integrity of body and spirit in these sculptures, an integrity that ultimately had nothing whatever to do with aesthetics, it must be because we were still integral ourselves somewhere beneath the cracked veneer. If the powerful mystery of sentient flesh embodied in the marble could still awaken an answering mystery in me, what real power could the automobiles and the anxieties exert? For the first time, it occurred to me that even religion might be only art in another form, instead of vice versa, and I felt a sudden lightness, almost a giddiness, of soul.

The light in the room had waned with the waning afternoon,

the shadows had densened, and I had a strong sense that we were the last people in that echoing building. Shirley got up.

"Ready?" I said.

"Whenever you are."

I took her arm, and we left, and didn't look back. Outside, the chilly streets had the sere, musky smell of damp leaves that always suggests New England autumn twilights to me. We negotiated the traffic hand in hand, and almost overturned a baker's boy, who was carrying an armful of fresh loaves in front of himself like a stack of logs. He shot us an angry, dark-eyed look, which turned quizzical at our smiling apologies, and then dissolved into a comic shrug of the shoulders as he went on, leaving the yeasty fragrance of the oven-warm bread behind him.

"Ummmm," Shirley murmured. "You know, it's ridiculous but I'm *starved*. Let's go home, and get ready for Thanksgiving."

The cars flowed around the Baptistry opposite the Duomo, scooters zipping in and out among them like pilot-fish, and we breasted our way upstream against throngs of secretaries hurrying homewards too. The night before, we had tried to explain to the Signora of the restaurant a block from Dante's house about Thanksgiving. Finally, she had understood that it was a curious American feast, in honor of a good harvest, and she had promised us a delectable *Bistecca a la Fiorentina* and a special Chianti.

Strangers celebrating their survival in a strange land . . . It was true of these Florentines too. It was true of all of us in this brutalizing century, through which everyone was struggling in his own way to bring some vestige of passionate mortality intact.

"We've just got time for a nap," I said, "to give thanks to Michelangelo for making it a good day, after all."

Shirley clenched my hand: "What in the world would I have done if you hadn't dug it."

NINE

Awake in Rome

The yellow light
of the Roman afternoon seemed to have rinsed the walks and
meadows of the Borghese gardens in a pale wash of Strega. The
weather-worn faces of the marble busts along the Viali Magnolie
were streaked with sooty tears, and fallen sycamore leaves
drifted around the pedestals like withered ten-thousand lire
notes. It was a quarter after two, all Rome drowsed in siesta
behind its heavy shutters, and I was already half-drunk.

The luncheon wine shifted in my gut, contending, no doubt,

with the three mid-morning Scotches that had preceded it. I felt muzzy, and stuffed with *cannelloni,* and irritated. The day had turned out like all our Roman days. Rain in the morning when everything was open; fair in the afternoon when everything was closed. But I was damned if I would sleep.

"All right," Shirley had said fatalistically half an hour before, "do as you please. But I'm going home for a nap," and she simply walked away from the restaurant towards our dismal, third-floor *pensione* off the Piazza del Popolo.

We'd be home in a week, and half our days in Rome had been spent dodging showers and changing shoes. Why wouldn't she stick with me? What was wrong with her? I let out a loud belch to illustrate my pique, but aside from the busts under the flutter of the big trees there was no one to hear.

I knew what was wrong with her. She felt at *home.* She'd lived in Rome for a year in 1950. She'd run a house and a "Maria." She'd marketed, and partied, and worked here. She felt none of the urge to "have" the city in a single gulp that made me curse the rain at eight in the morning, and gnash my teeth when it failed to abate by nine, and succumb to the temptation of a drink after ten. She had slipped back into the Roman rhythm as effortlessly as she always slipped back into her accent the second day in Louisiana. So here I was, alone, indulging a morose vision of myself as the only consciousness still awake in the warm somnolence of late autumn in—the Eternal City! I hurrumphed. It was time that was obsessing me, time that was inexorably putting the trip behind me, out of reach.

At the moment, there wasn't *enough* time, and I found myself hating Rome—because I loved it, and I had to leave. Up ahead, there was too *much* time—months of teaching in a backwater college-town in Ohio during which to ponder what in God's name the trip had profited me, after all. Not enough time for Naples ("What's the use?" I'd snapped pettishly that very morn-

166

ing. "If we can't go on down the Amalfi coast, why bother?"),
and too much time, right now, before twilight brought the
promise of—well, more wine.

The concessioneer's stand up ahead, where you could purchase all manner of coffees and pastries, was closed up, and the
metal sign in its window, advertising an Italian version of Alka
Seltzer, bore the slogan *Doppo il Troppo* (After too much), which
gave me no laugh, despite my condition, because I was possessed
by a sense of myself I had rarely experienced before: I was feeling *old*.

I stumbled through the Pincio gardens, and there, beyond the
parapet, all of Rome lay under a vague haze of grey and rose.
Across the river, the dome of St. Peter's loomed like a gigantic,
motionless dirigible in the middle distance, and the elusive melancholy of these last mild afternoons of the waning year suddenly seemed the proper emotional lens through which to view
the frustrating days just past.

From the very first, the girls, silhouetted against the glittering
parallelograms of the smart shops along the evening Corso,
hadn't helped my mood, for there were more beautiful women
in Rome than I'd seen anywhere in Europe—elegant, fine-
boned creatures, quietly eschewing the haughty chic of Paris and
the kicky mod of London, face after face reflecting that refine-
ment of expression, that delicate suavity, which centuries of civilization breed into the eyes of shop girls and contessas
alike—whereas for all I knew I was going back to the lumpy
knees and vacant stares of a gaggle of corn-fed coeds. Below the
Tiber's walls, at dawn, the shuttered dance-barges rode in low
water like bleak images from old Jean Vigo films of the thirties,
films that I had seen over two decades ago. The Via Margutta,
in the artists' district, sported a sign on its corner saying "Carnaby Street," and the *portier* at Max Frisch's house told me that,
no, the Swiss writer hadn't lived there for three years. The dark

rooms in the house where Keats had died were paneled and narrow and hushed at nine o'clock in the morning, and I was appalled by the smallness of the beds in which famous poets so often cough their last. I looked out the rain-bleared windows at the hippies huddled on the Spanish steps like refugees too numbed by frontier-crossings to notice the weather any longer, and the flower-sellers smoking stoically under their awnings down on the Piazza di Spagna, and I became exasperated by the sepulchral voice of the custodian, droning on and on over the display cases of rare manuscripts, and so splashed across the square to the Café Greco for an aperitif (as I fancied Byron might have done) to get away from that tardy deification that does no honor to a neglected artist's life.

After the third day, it became clear to me that the Romans lived among their ruins with a casualness that was positively domestic—but which I, a stranger, could never seem to approximate. Fisted-up packs of *Nazionales* floated in the Bernini fountains in the Piazza Navona where, that month, the two-by-four stalls of a Christmas fair were being hammered-together, and moustachioed workmen, eating bread and cheese, spat wine-dregs in the gutter. The excavation in the Largo Argentina, around which a mad carnival of traffic continually swirled, had been abandoned to legions of Roman cats—fat, streetwise toms sunning themselves Neronically on the shards of columns, lean-flanked females prowling among the cabbage heads with the impenetrable black eyes of Africa—and just a few blocks away the ornate monument that Mussolini had erected in the Piazza Venezia resembled nothing so much as a vulgar wedding cake designed by MGM for the nuptials of a Mafia overlord. The red twilights of December turned the Tiber as lurid as blood, and I regularly gave in to that old American insatiableness (Rome was mostly dead by midnight), and dragged Shirley from one awful Via Veneto café to the next. You heard five languages over the brandy snifters on the Via Sallustiana, and the accordions in the hofbrau on Via della Croce played sour imitations of Kurt Weill. The ghosts of all the conquering armies of the past had re-materialized as tourists—yet Rome's plebian grasses grew stubbornly over the imperial stones in the Forum, and its mysterious, umbrella-shaped pines almost obscured the villas on the Palatine Hill, and I discovered that this was the first city in Europe where I didn't *want* to feel like a stranger. It was a small city, neither stately nor quaint, but it had a certain seedy magnificence to it, and even its cosmopolitanism was cozy. I realized—with a feeling that the realization might have come too late—that I could probably live here. A low-ceilinged flat up under the eaves in Trastevere, a neighborhood trattoria with a *prezzo fisso,* evening walks along the river in the Roman spring. For days, Shirley had been eyeing me, baffled by the turmoil in my spirit. How could I tell her that I couldn't *risk* being happy now, when I still refused to acknowledge it to myself?

Nevertheless, leaning on the balustrade, looking out over the domes and towers and tiled rooftops, that was precisely how I felt. A weary, sweat-flecked horse dragged a creaky *fiacre* of chattering Americans up the steep, winding street from the Piazza del Popolo. A vagrant current of air, wafting up from the broad square below, smelled elusively of the winy breaths of lovers after love, and suddenly I felt spent, parched, *emptied,* as if, for weeks, I had been combating one of those low-key fevers that you only recognize once it starts to wane. I tried to make an assessment.

All right, I was feeling my years. Why? Part of the reason was that I was tired of traveling, but wouldn't admit it. Our *pensione* was impossible—with its stygian lounge, shabby furniture, gloomy corridors, and 25-watt bulbs. The buses on the Via del Corso just below gnashed their gears like maniacal bulldozers till all hours; an out-of-tune bell three blocks away

bonged witlessly in the downpour at five every morning; and a
herd of crazy peasant pipers, in sheepskin hats and leg-thongs,
appeared on schedule during the rush-hours to tootle their dis-
sonant *Buon Natales* at the crowds of hurrying umbrellas. Yet I
was too impatient to look for another place, and spent hours at
the window waiting out the rain, and did nothing. But the major part of the reason for my malaise was the day at Ostia with
Jon and Trish, and the evening with Ginny that had followed it.

Jon and Trish were young acquaintances of ours from Connecticut, just married after several years of living together, and
traveling through Europe in a white Volvo station wagon with a
letter-of-credit that Jon's father had given them as a wedding
present. We didn't know them well, but they left a note for us at
American Express, and the four of us got together for a meal
and an evening of wine, only to discover, as travelers sometimes
do, that nothing makes acquaintances seem more like friends
than meeting them in a foreign place.

They were in their mid-twenties, and could have been my
students of a few years before. They had quit their jobs, and
might stay over a year. Next week they were moving into a
borrowed apartment with lots of room. Why didn't we move in
too? Later they would go to Florence, and there was talk of
Christmas in London. Couldn't we travel with them? In short,
they were full of the planless plans of the footloose, affluent
young. I envied them outrageously: it was just the sort of trip to
Europe that I had not been able to make at their age. Impulsively, I ordered another carafe of wine, and started to calculate
time as against Traveler's Checks. Why not just throw over the
damn job, and wander for a few more months?

They suggested a drive to Ostia for lunch the next day, and
picked us up on the Ponte San Angelo at 11:30. They were al-

ready into a wickered liter of *Frascati,* and were feeling the excitement of being in Italy with new friends. Trish's long blonde hair spilled over the seat-back as she passed the bottle, and Jon got us out of town expertly. As we drove out the Appian Way through all that evanescent, flattened countryside of ancient trees and sequestered villas, whose elusive *triste* (suggesting some enigmatic shift in mood that will occur once you reach the sea) only Fellini's camera has ever captured so subtly, a wan sun came out, limning everything with the soft-focus blur of mist drifting in the wet air. We all grew talkative, and very hungry.

The Lido in Ostia reminded me of Montauk in December, and we sat in a chilly, customerless *trattoria* on the long, empty esplanade of pastel hotels and striped cabanas, and ordered enormous plates of garlicky pasta and a bottle of *bianco.* We sat for a long time, drinking and joking, but after a while the wine brought a decided edge of bitterness to their gaiety. Obviously the trip so far hadn't been the lark they had anticipated. They began to bicker, making light of it, but bickering anyway. I tried to strike the note of what-the-hell, we-might-as-well that seemed proper to Americans in Europe that year, but wasn't very successful.

Then all at once they began to speak heatedly about conditions in the States. They had been involved in the peace movement, social work, civil rights. All of it had come to nothing. The war was tearing apart the fabric of life in America, and it was pointless to *try* to help any longer. They spoke of all this with that combination of public aversion about what was happening *there* and private guilt about being *here* that I knew so well by now, and it occurred to me that perhaps they had finally gotten married because that letter-of-credit was their ticket out of it all. They brightened with their bitterness exactly the way expatriates in a Fitzgerald novel invariably brighten as the impossibilities accumulate with the cocktails. They were through

with city-life in America, they said; they were through with turmoil. When they went home, they would live in the Berkshires
or on Monhegan Island. Jon would work for a local newspaper
or teach in a country school; Trish would make ceramics or
weave. It might be a *possible* life for the next bad years. But the
echo of wounded idealism sulking in its tent, of youthful scorn
for history and its compromises, of naïve hopes having been
cruelly *cheated* by the realities of a violent era, so clearly underlay
their plans that my mood dimmed. The war, always the damn
war. It waited at the end of every good time like a hangover.

Outside the open double-doors, the sea was grey and cold, the
thin light of the afternoon sun fell in a finger-smear of dull gold
across it, and that feeling of quiet desolation that muffles seaside
resorts at the onset of winter edged in over all of us. I suggested
that we drive farther down the coast, and find a way out onto
the beach, and finish the wine there. We were all a little drunk
by then, and made attempts to resurrect the good spirits, and
finally turned into a sandy road between palmetto-thatched cottages. In the eerie light of the failing afternoon, I watched Trish
scuffle a tipsy little dance across the cold sand, cradling the cum-
bersome bottle in her arms like a new mother with her baby,
her long hair streaming out behind her, as she crooned a Joan
Baez ballad. Jon seemed quenched, thoughtful, and irritated by
her antics. We sprawled in the lee of a dune, and passed the
wine around. The sea-breeze had stiffened, Trish's hectic eyes
were red-rimmed now, Shirley's face darkened as the sun sank
towards a range of cloud on the horizon, and I talked on
hopelessly.

There we were—four pensive, wine-fumy Americans, huddled on a chilly beach like the last survivors of an autumn picnic,
intent on having fun and glad to be together, but all of us contending with our own very different thoughts once the conversation lagged. I wanted to get away from there, and acknowl-

edged to myself that some kinds of fun were over for me, for now. I wasn't twenty-three any longer, when banding together with friends around a bottle could constitute a temporary armistice in the war between dreams and responsibilities. I was going home, and I didn't want to talk about America. They were free of it, and wanted to indulge their feelings of disillusionment. I wondered whether two decades of work and crisis had established solid enough reserves of patience and cunning in me to outlast that *cheated* look that I had seen everywhere in the kids that year, a look which, in my cups, exasperated me, because it seemed evidence of how easily their commitment had capitulated to the first defeats.

The sun had just been snuffed out by the horizon (it was inexorably sinking over that immense, troubled continent four thousand miles away, as well), and we lingered on, out of step with one another now, but refusing to acknowledge it. I took a final swig out of the bottle. I was weary beyond belief with my own thoughts. In ten days, I'd be back in all *that* again. Why couldn't we just be reckless, and forgetful, and gay?

"Has Rome changed that much since *you* were young?" Trish asked Shirley as we drove, in twilight, by the Farnese Palace a little later.

Jon actually winced: "God, Trish, you talk as if they were *old!*"

"No, I meant when she was here after the war," Trish hastened to add, "the other war."

Shirley laughed: "Rome survives the wars, *child,*" she joked. "It's automobiles that may do it in."

We said goodbye in clouds of steam billowing out of the doorway of a laundry on narrow Via Laurina, Trish's eyes suddenly become the muddled eyes of a girl whose party is over, Jon asking us again why we didn't just stay on, knowing that we couldn't. As we walked back to the *pensione* along the pockmarked walls of a Roman sidestreet, Shirley said: "I like them. They pull their weight."

"Listen, it's easy enough to pull your weight when you have a white Volvo station wagon, and all the time in the world. But I'm a little bored by this survivor-of-the-Lincoln-Brigade act."

"Oh, come on," she said, eyeing me carefully again. "They're just kids . . . Christ, they're almost young enough to be *our* kids."

An hour later, fortified by a large Scotch, we met Ginny in the Piazza Colonna, Ginny who actually *could* have been my child. She was the second daughter of my oldest friend, and I had seen her, hungry and squalling for life, an hour or two after she was born. Now, just twenty, she had been living in Rome for a year. She shared a flat with an English girl on the Via Monserrato, worked as a typist for an importer, and was in love with her Sergio—just like so many of the Daisy Millers of those years.

She was an optimistic, good-hearted girl, full of outgoing family affections, and when she had decided not to come home after a summer-trip to Europe I had been surprised. Her older sister seemed more the type to strike out on her own. Ginny was one of those pretty, awkward girls that Lynn Redgrave plays so well, who are naturally loving but sometimes awed out of their good sense when they receive love in return, and recently her letters had been mentioning marriage, and I was more or less on commission from her parents to scout out the situation. But after our dispiriting day, I couldn't have felt less like a wise and steadying uncle when she emerged from the evening crowds, all smiles and kisses and eagerness.

We were to meet her Sergio at an *hostaria* in Trastevere— their special place—and I flagged down a taxi. Ginny was proud to be so at ease in Rome, and joked with the cabby to show off her Italian, and told us all about Sergio, and wanted family news, and squeezed my hand in the half-dark in lieu of words.

174

The restaurant was just off a little piazza full of motor bikes, and it was one of those small, clean, modest places, delectable with smells, that you instantly know will be good. We were early, and I ordered two liters of wine, and detected just a hint of nervousness about the evening in Ginny's rosy and expectant face, flushed as it was in the candlelight. She so wanted everything to go well, and kept glancing over my shoulder towards the door.

Punctually, Sergio arrived—a tall, proper, nice-looking fellow, a good five years older than Ginny, sober-sided and solemn, who lived with his mother out in the Flaminia district, and was about to take his examinations as an engineer. He sipped his wine meagerly, prolonged a decision over the menu, and quietly, but firmly, corrected Ginny's Italian.

The evening was arduous with language difficulties. Sergio spoke almost no English, and my Italian was mostly limited to the purchase of food and lodging. I drank, and pretended to understand more than I did. I nodded, and laughed, and drank some more. Shirley bantered in Italian with Sergio, who plainly wasn't used to bantering women, and he became punctilious with the waiter. It was clear to me that any wedding was a year or so off, and that nothing would come of it in the end.

But Ginny's china-blue eyes were wide with his presence; she touched his hand secretively under the table. Her emotions flowed with simple, innocent ardor out of her, flustering him somewhat, and I so strongly fancied that I could see the indifference, tears, arguments and wrench-of-feelings that lay ahead for her that I resigned my commission as Lambert Strether. She would weep and feel bereft, but in a few months she would meet someone else, and in a year would wonder what she had ever seen in Sergio.

I knew this as surely as I knew that I would have a hangover the next morning, but when I looked at her—at her mouth that was no longer a child's mouth tasting the sugary confections of the day, but a mouth that was moistly parted with that sensual hunger that assumes a future—I didn't want her generation's cheated look to twist it. I wanted her to be deluded and happy and young for as long as she could. Deeper in my liquor than I realized, I experienced the fierce, unreasonable protectiveness of fatherhood. And then, of course, its immediate reverse. For I had no child.

Sergio drove us home in his Fiat. The black Tiber snaked sluggishly under empty bridges. They would go back to Ginny's, and, one supposed, make the good love that was probably still between them. It was midnight. Our corner of the Via del Corso was as deserted as Lexington Avenue at dawn.

Tipsy, emotional, I took Ginny by the shoulders there on the pavement, and said something foolish, and seasonal. Suddenly, she came apart a little. Those eyes teared up. She caught at a little girl's sob—she was alone in Rome, she missed her family, she had strong and sentimental memories of Christmases in the past. She put up her mouth, blindly, to be kissed. I held her for a second with an urgency that would have done anything to keep ugliness out of her young life, if it could, remembering the pettiness of my reaction to Jon and Trish. She sniffled, and wiped at her cheeks, and mended in an instant, and they drove off.

"I guess you can't save anyone from anything," Shirley remarked as we crossed the street. "Besides, what a joy for her—an affair in Rome! Suppose she hadn't had one."

The carriage-horse, with his cargo of Americans, had reached the top of the hill now. His lips, bruised pink on the bit, dripped strings of slaver, and his flanks were glazed with sweat. But his dumb eyes beseeched no one, as if that hill was his daily fate, to be negotiated endlessly until he dropped. Just below me a fountain plashed, and I could smell the sour reek of palm-fronds baking in the sun. It was very warm now. The indistinct line of hills beyond St. Peter's shimmered in a heat-haze. The wine grumbled in my stomach, and a dull throb of headache quietly set up behind my temples.

I'd come to Rome too late, I concluded. Like so much of the trip, our days here had been wasted, consumed by my stubborn insomnia, obscured by avaricious thought. I was forty-one, and blurred with wine, and I couldn't sleep. Already the imminence of America had tainted the last days as an operation taints the hours before you go into the hospital. Damn it, I thought, not to care was best. What did it matter? I'd go over to St. Peter's again, and climb up through the skin of the dome itself, and get a final look at the city from the very top.

But then the sick ambivalence of vertigo (fly, or cry, or die) that had overcome me there five days ago, swept its wash of premonitory fear through my stomach, making the very idea impossible, unsteady as I was. Vertigo! I, who had teetered on ledges in the White Mountains in the past, feeling nothing but a keen exhilaration! I, who had scampered up and down seven-story fire escapes on a dare years before! I was getting old, and intractable, and—no way around it—somehow I'd reached middle life without really noticing. I felt alone in a new way, marooned by a knowledge beyond communication, with nowhere to invest the primitive, familial longings whose sudden discovery in myself, at that moment, made me gulp at an obstruction in my throat. I hungered for some simple richness—of continuity, and Christmas, and children—that I had never prized before. A wave of unspecified regret broke over me, and I turned in the direction of Trinità dei Monti, shuddering with bewilderment.

Fat pigeons waddled in front of the façade of the Villa Medici, and a blond young man was leaning against the parapet, staring at me with an expression on his face that was indisputably an expression of shocked *recognition*. To my surprise, I recognized him too—the handsome, spoiled face, the slender surfer's body, the look of baffled innocence. It was Tab Hunter, the golden-boy movie actor of the Fifties, now grown out of the appealing callowness that had accounted for his brief career. We had never met.

He wore rust-colored corduroy slacks, a rumpled jacket, and no tie. He was unshaven, red-eyed, and feeling awful. Probably he was in Rome making "spaghetti westerns," capitalizing on the time-lag that keeps a reputation luminous in Brussels long after it has dimmed in Brooklyn, and had wandered over here from his hotel on the Via Sistina after a drunken night.

Caught staring at me, he turned away with embarrassment, and looked down at Rome, studying it as he might have studied a plate of tripe or octopus. He was willing to eat it, but he wasn't going to *understand* it, and I fancied him missing the simpler options—of a hamburger and fries, and later a spin out to Malibu for a dip—that made such queasy afternoons possible in Southern California. He looked debauched, numbed to nuance, beset by new and disturbing moral experiences, and he had that battered-by-Europe expression that a certain type of depthless American face takes on as it travels, giving up its naïveté a lire at a time, and condemned by the utter strangeness of everything around it to the travail of an unaccustomed degree of consciousness. I stared out over the city to share his view.

It drowsed, it basked, it stirred in the blandness of the day. The churches and the ruins and the monuments spread away into the haze with an appalling permanence, as indifferent to human fret as a desert to a footprint. What were celebrity, youth, politics, or even age, in the face of stones that had outlasted the lusts and ambitions of the Caesars and the popes? They were as

ephemeral as smoke. Of course, the questions assailing Hunter
(I was sure) were far less grandiose: Why was he alone like this?
What was he going to do tonight? Had anyone thought to make
arrangements?

I swung my gaze back to him, only to find him staring at me
again with that self-same expression of shock and recognition.
Had we ever met? I searched my memory in a panic, as if I
could no more trust it now than I could trust my balance. No, I
was certain I'd never set eyes on him in the flesh before. Then
all at once I saw my own face reflected in his expression—a
forty-ish, raddled, out-of-place American, insatiably awake in
Rome. What he had recognized in me was nothing less than
himself in ten years! Too much liquor blurring the features, too
much speculation blurring the mind. The losses and the costs of
some native fixation on ephemerality must have been as plain in
my face as the fact that I was half-drunk at three o'clock in the
afternoon. I became cold sober in an instant, an instant during
which we looked at one another—I at the past, he at the future—and then, both recoiling from the insight for our separate
reasons, he meandered off down the way he had come, and I
turned and started down the steps to the piazza around which,
now, the Fiats had begun to circle again, and people were strolling back to their offices.

The sun was as warm, the air as soft, as a boy's Mediterranean
reveries of thirty years before in bleak New England—yet this
was real, this was Rome, and in between those reveries and this
moment the years had interposed half a life which seemed to
have sealed me off from both. Had Jon and Trish, had Ginny,
seen the same haunted look in my face as Hunter? The middle-
age prisoner of worry, doubt, vanity, habit, time? A life-buffeted
Lear at all of forty-one? Suddenly, I seemed as addled to myself
as I must have seemed to them. If I couldn't seize the day, how
could I survive the years?

I was passing the open doors of a bar, inside of which one of Rome's countless Anna Magnanis (the black dress, the sensual lips, the life-old eyes) was doing her nails behind the cash register. I went in and ordered a *cappucino* at the counter. The place had just re-opened after the siesta, and I was the only customer. After serving me, the young barman went on unravelling long streamers of tinseled rope while the sixteen-year-old sandwich girl, frail in her smock, tremulous, plain as pudding, unpacked tiny tinfoil bells from a dusty carton. They were decorating the place for Christmas. I sipped my coffee and watched them for a while.

The barman balanced on a stool, stringing the tinsel, while Anna Magnani, carefully painting the edge of a nail, made brief, sardonic comments on his aesthetic sense. A delivery boy staggered a huge tray of fresh pastries through the door, and joshed the little sandwich girl for her wide-eyed delight in each new bauble retrieved from the bottom of the carton. Everyone ignored me the way happy kids ignore a teacher while decorating their schoolroom for the holidays.

All at once, I felt a fine, reckless uprush of freedom. Everything was funny and interesting. The young barman knew he cut an agile figure on the stool, and that no corner of the place was out of his reach. Anna Magnani knew that everything would get done in time, and in an hour the cash register would be ting-ing with pre-Christmas excitement. And the sandwich girl loved the feel of gaudy, fragile things in her fingers.

She noticed me looking at her shy eyes, she saw the smile of warm encouragement on my face, and she smiled back with the distracted look of a child who has been caught in the thrill of an innocent pleasure. I seemed to know her life down to its last, most special dream. *What's the use of going to Naples?* My own voice echoed as querulously as a voice from another room, and at that moment my peevish four months of wandering through the capitals of Europe seemed like nothing compared to her ten minutes of wonder with those Christmas bells.

The barman had every loop of tinsel just right, according to his lights, and jumped down from the stool, putting it out of his mind. Anna Magnani blew on her nails with a soft little poof of breath, inspected them, approved, and was ready for the evening. The sandwich girl's modest joy was as impervious to time as art. They were all utterly alive in the moment. They would age, and shudder with bewilderment, and have no way to communicate it, but it didn't matter to them now. To them, the bells of Christmas signaled the rebirth of a new chance, a new intensity of life.

Of course we'd go to Naples, I decided. We'd take the *Rapido* in the morning. If it didn't matter, its "not mattering" didn't matter either, and so I ordered a *Cinzano* to go with the end of my coffee—a nightcap—because, finally having come awake, I could admit how sleepy I really was.

TEN

See Naples and Live

"Money," he repeated in the same tone of flat demand as the first time, suggesting even more strongly than before that the word constituted the nucleus of his English.

I continued to ignore him, staring out the glass doors of the new Stazione Termini into the piazza from which the statue of Garibaldi had watched so many armies, military and otherwise, invade the city.

"Money," the word this time accompanied by a hand held out,

palm up, at the level of his face, the voice this time decidedly remonstrative.

"No," I said, shaking my head. "Niente, niente," the nucleus of my Italian when out in the streets.

There we stood: the tall American in the tan raincoat too lightweight for the gloomy chill of late afternoon in winter Naples, guarding the luggage while his wife was in the *gabinetto,* and the sockless ten-year-old boy in the man's jacket he inhabited like an overcoat, with the large, black eyes and piquant mouth of a Murillo urchin, and all the savvy of a street-psychologist.

"Money," he repeated impatiently, as if I was wasting his time, and took the edge of my raincoat between his thumb and forefinger, all the while subjecting me to the gaze of those enormous eyes that were at once so soulful and so insolent. He felt of my coat, appraising the fabric.

But my back was up, and I was furious. I knew it was a game, but I had been playing that game for weeks, and had lost my cool. "Basta!" I exclaimed too fiercely, and wrenched my coat away. "Basta! Niente!"

He took my measure in an instant. There was no resigned quiver of the lips, not even a contemptuous smile. He simply shrugged, and gave me up. He simply turned as if I had never existed, already picking out his next mark, and left me standing there in the puddle of my own foolishness.

Shirley came up, and we went out through the doors, and got the bags into a cab.

"Christ," I said irritably, "no one told me Naples was colder than Rome at this time of year! Why in hell didn't we pack my duffle coat?"

"Hey, what's wrong with *you?*"

What indeed! Certainly it wasn't the kid. It was that Rome had been rainy, and I was surfeited with churches and museums, and our trip was all but over. It was that we were flying home in less than a week, and home meant Vietnam, riots, work, nerves, and an election year too crucial to the future of the country to be ignored.

Also, Naples occupied a special place in the landscape of my imagination. Like many Americans in their forties, to whom the current war was a squalid and dishonorable adventure, I sometimes found myself longing for the older, the juster, the more innocent war in which I had once served. And Naples, perhaps more than any other European city, held memories of that war for an American veteran—even one, like myself, who had never gotten there. And now it was cold, the streets were a drizzly blur, and the Neapolitans seemed intent on taking back, lire by lire, whatever reparations the G.I.'s had incurred twenty-four years before.

First, there was the cab driver. Pulling up before the small marquee of the Hotel Rex half a block from the bay where far-off lights on Capri winked and the feel of deep water nearby came in on the wind, he wanted 800 lire, and was disinclined to turn on his meter-light. Caught between languages, I established (with the help of my Zippo) that the fare was actually 440. Shirley acted as translator. Oh, well, the man mumbled without a flicker of the eyes, all right, 700 then. There were two of us, there were the bags, there were taxes, there was—something else that was lost as his dialect thickened. I knew it was a con, I knew he was simply seeing how much the traffic would bear, I was outraged, and I paid. The bare-faced audacity of it put me in check.

Then, there was the desk clerk. No, the room was not 3,100 lire, as the list from the Italian Tourist Office in my pocket stated. "3,100 lire for *this?*," his flourish of the hand seemed to say. For these bland, pastel reproductions of "romantic" Neapolitan scenes? For these pipe-and-leatherette armchairs? For the now-international smell of plastic and chlorophyll and disinfectant that typifies Motel-land? No, such up-to-date splendors went for 3,500, and were cheap at the price. I whipped out the list, and indicated his hotel and its rates with an irate forefinger. He frowned, and spluttered, and threw up his hands, and argued, and beseeched the ceiling in a long harangue. Then he acceded with a shrug, and huffed out of the room.

"What was that all about?" I said.

"Winter, as far as I could tell. The cruelty of winter for the hotel man."

A cold seawind stiffened as we walked along the Via Partenope a little later. Behind us, the *Leonardo da Vinci* (pale, lavish, garlanded with lights, and between cruises) was tied up amid the ghosts of rusty transports. Ahead, the opulent hotels, fronting on the water, each exhibited the empty lobby and *fumetti*-reading bellboy of the onset of mid-December. Beyond them, the esplanade curved gracefully around a bay so ample that all the world's navies could have dumped their crews and garbage there. Above it, Naples itself was spread out in a fantastic, terraced semicircle of sparkling lights on its shadowy hillsides. "My God!" I exclaimed, as we turned away from the water and climbed into a maze. The spot had so obviously cried out for a city to be built on it.

To the refugee from the cheerless suburban rectitude of middle-class America in search of the picturesque or the quaint, back-street Naples at night must appear like the Lower East Side of New York in the bad old days—festooned with loaded washlines, littered with stale vegetable greens, ill-lit, pestilential, a filthy rabbit-warren of steep alleys raw with onion, and tenements as noisome and noisy with the stench and uproar by which the poor insulate themselves against despair as Hogarth's London. It is all of that, and it excited me. The greatness of a city is best measured by the vividness of the life in its slums, and Naples, by that yardstick, is a very great city indeed. Despite its hustler's eye, and thief's fingers, and con-man's spiel, it remains as life-shrewd, hot-tempered, tough-hearted, and indefatigably gay as a De Sica whore. What other city could have overcome my pensive mood simply by trying to fleece me at every step?

Coming down a narrow, cobbled street, slippery with spittle, headlong as San Francisco, where kids smoked and yelled and gesticulated in restless groups, and spectral grandfathers sat silhouetted in the doorways of mysterious, dim bedrooms opening right onto the pavement, I became aware of a strange ambiance that I remembered from my first days in New York after the war: it was the feeling of *neighborhood,* of a community created out of passions, appetites, and dangers suffered in common, of a mean life that somehow was not demeaning, and I felt a pinch of grudging envy for these people, and for that old, raucous (as against riotous) city-past that was all but obliterated in America now. Then suddenly an engine revved up at the top of the street, and the single idiot eye of a motor scooter's headlight zigzagged wildly down upon us, the rider pelted with mouldy lettuce-heads, a succession of forearms—obscenely chopped by wrists—leveled in his direction, and insults as spicy as pepperoni clamoring up through the fluttering bedsheets. We jumped into a doorway a split second before he flashed by with a cackle of sportive laughter. It wasn't a town that encouraged woolgathering.

We descended out of the murky honeycomb of that quarter by a series of steps. Muffled radios behind shuttered windows tinkled with phantom mandolins. Delivery boys with baskets of vegetables or bread loaves balanced on their heads hurried past us, lurching down the perilous inclines with the same reckless leaps as the scavenger cats that trooped after them, hoping for spillage. At the bottom, the restaurants on the Via Santa Lucia were thronging. Cashier-girls stared out the plate glass at the dark, preening young men—peacocks of the night—who ambled by, their coats thrown like capes over their shoulders, Fellini-style. It was very cold now, it would rain again later, and we were suddenly ravenous.

We went into a place that had a reasonable *prezzo fisso* that included wine. It was overheated, pungent with odors, not crowded, and very brightly lit the way modest Italian *trattorias* mostly are, as if to say, "See, we have nothing to hide." The wine that came with the scallopini was bad, sour as vinegar, with strings of mother stirring in it, but the waiter only looked at it casually, smiled, and gave a particularly cynical version of the Neapolitan shrug. I countered by ordering a *mezzo litro* of Ruffino, which, I concluded, must be the next move in the ritual. For her part, Shirley looked apprehensive, as if expecting a bitter editorial on Italian venality, not a few of which I had delivered in Rome. But I was in unaccountably good spirits. Somehow the cheerful air of swindle had become invigorating.

Besides, there was going to be music. A middle-aged man, with the wiry pompador of a one-time peacock (now gone quite grey), and one of those indescribably urbane faces that you see all over Italy (the sheer weight of experience stamped into it as indelibly as tank-tracks into macadam), was shouldering on an accordian. His young wife swept the long fall of black hair away from her pale cheeks to accommodate a violin, and, after tuning up briefly, they began to play. And the song they played was *Lili Marlene.*

They moved among the tables slowly, the man singing the verses one after the other in a clear, unsentimental tenor thickened by cigarettes, and the young woman following behind, the poignant line of her chin canted into the fragile wood of the instrument. They paused at each table, offering it the challenge of their dispassionate eyes, and the man would half-turn at the end of each chorus to direct the listeners to the delicate, taut wrists of his lovely young wife, inviting them to admire her, and be moved to generosity.

It was at this point that I noticed two similar parties on either side of the room—the same gruff, florid-cheeked father, the same past-forty, well-dressed mother, the same bored teenage kids. The two fathers were undergoing an identical experience for which they obviously were not prepared. A rush of nostalgia seemed to be gripping them both, and when they turned and spoke offhandedly to their wives in an effort to regain composure, it became clear that the man nearest us was German, and the one across the room was an American.

Veterans! Veterans making that strangest, saddest of all sentimental journeys: taking the wife and kids back to the battle-field on which, like absentee-landlords, they had a permanent claim because they had fought for it, and survived. In this case, probably Caserta. One tried not to draw any of the easy conclusions about the quality of a peace in comparison to which war retained all the misty aura of youth's springtime camarade-ries, but nevertheless there they sat, twenty-five years older, paunchier, and more vulnerable, undone at the moment by that old song that had belonged to both armies, and, all unawares, fraternizing at last in the no-man's-land of a common memory. The bittersweet taste of 1943 was in their mouths (I fancied), bringing back war's most unmanning moments—the moments of leave, the moments of being weary and young and homesick and bored and alone in a foreign city. Perhaps, separated by only a few weeks, each had eaten lonely suppers in this very place a quarter of a century ago, for the expression on their faces now was identical: they were haunted by their own dead youths. I fancied, as well, that both of them were thinking that they hadn't had enough to drink. I knew I was. But the musicians had finished up, and were passing among us with a salver, and in a moment they launched into *Roll Out the Barrel* in case there were any English in the room.

"They don't miss a trick," I decided, taking a deep swallow of the wine. "They'll do *Bless 'Em All* next, what do you want to bet." It seemed such a cynical trafficking in emotions, the moral equivalent of the larceny that ruled the streets.

"But it's what all you men want to hear," Shirley reminded me, "so that you can remember—well, all *that*," which was true enough, though I didn't want to know it.

No, I wanted the sad, wine-fumey, bravely maudlin song to go on and on, I wanted to believe the unexamined feelings that it aroused were real, I wanted to be a veteran of a time, and a war, that was safely past, safely over, instead of a civilian-soldier in that newer and nastier kind of war—the war *against* the war that was tearing up America's streets and soul, whose leave was almost over.

"But don't they remember?" I complained unreasonably. "Christ, even that German remembers what it was like!," suddenly hating the fact that one must grow out of the easy simplicities of the completed past into the uneasy complications of a future that has still to be *made*.

"What makes you think they don't remember?"

"Well—well, damn it, then they don't care!"

"Maybe they care about something else."

Something else. Something other than bitter memories, or the sentimentalizing of the dead. Something other than history. But what? I was up at seven o'clock the next morning, pondering it.

It had snowed on Vesuvius during the night, the upper slopes wore a scapular of white, and the volcano resembled the Fujiyama of all those happy postcards from traveling relatives in the thirties. The sullen sky was breaking up over the long arm of the Sorrento peninsula to the south, and dirty, optimistic Naples had been awake for hours, relishing the Big Deals of a new day. I headed for the Galleria Umberto to have a look, John Horne Burns having bequeathed the spot to all literary-minded folk of my age, and crossing Piazza del Plebiscito (now a parking lot) I passed the series of large statues that face it from niches in the façade of the Palazzo Reale. German marauders, Spanish viceroys, Anjou kings, a Bourbon or two: all the foreign tyrants who had ruled and squabbled over Naples for a thousand years. They were blunt, unattractive, brownish statues, subtly mocked by the sculptor's hand, somehow set-at-naught in the very act of their commemoration, and they gazed out impotently over the brash cartops of the city that had survived the worst that they could do. Had a place been saved for General Mark Clark and the Nazi commandant whom he succeeded? Of what were they supposed to be a reminder? It was as curious a way to solemnize one's history as if Atlanta had erected a memorial to Sherman.

Working girls thronged the Via Roma, bold-eyed, dark as Moors, smoldering in their flesh, loud as a treeful of magpies, hurrying along towards morning *cappuccino* and gossip. The Galleria faced the opera house across a narrow street of pell-mell traffic—a huge, splendid black and gold arcade with a steep curve of sooty glass roof that suffused the chilly interior in a pallid, underwater light in which every mole, every trace of feminine moustache, stood out as graphically as a secret vice in the impersonal glare of a lineup. I wandered back and forth among the crowds that milled around, dwarfed, at the bottom of that immense, five-story room pretending to be a street.

I had a coffee in one of the little bars where you buy your ticket first and then present it to the boy at the machine, and watched the cashier-girl ring up double the amount and pocket the difference, and then, a moment later, ring up 130 lire for a 180-lire tab, and pocket that too. It seemed marvelous all of a

191

sudden, admirable, the way some kinds of lawlessness in our time seem to strike a blow for an older law. Everyone cheated everyone else as a matter of course, and yet that peculiar lechery, that lascivious quiver of wet-mouthed greed that contorts faces along 42nd Street, was not in evidence here. No, the confident audacity of Neapolitan pillage seemed a triumph over the glum seriousness of money itself, thereby restoring some human balance; the poverty of Naples, like its bitter history, mocked, set-at-naught. In the States, the poor and the outraged marched and rioted. Here, they boosted from the till, and set up statues to their oppressors. But what in God's name did they *care* about?

I wandered back to the hotel, picked up Shirley, and we went out for breakfast. Toast, butter and jam, at extra charge, arrived with our eggs for the simple reason that we had failed *not* to order them, and by the time we were finished, the day had faired-off. The sky was a milky blue, the air mild and aromatic as Vermouth, the rain-washed pavements smelled fresh with possibilities, and we decided to go up into the Vomero quarter where (we had heard) one got the most lavish view of Naples and its Bay.

The *Funiculare Centrale,* in which we were jammed chest to breast with chattering school girls, was a subway-on-a-slant that clanked ponderously up its sloping mineshaft, the chain that pulled it vibrating up through one's shoes. On the top, out in the sun again, the drama of the city's setting became clear. Naples appeared to float in the air in the same way that Venice appears to float on the water. We looked down on all the tangled warrens we had wandered in the night before; down over diminishing levels of roofs, terraces, stairways, balconies (everything built on top of something else, house on house, street on roof, stairs, stairs everywhere); down through the stupifying complexity of myriad lives which we viewed, as a god might, in a stunning, vertical perspective—the balconied lives of a *Mediterranean* people, a people in thrall to the sun. We looked down, down, and then *out*—out over the wide lucid expanse of that great Bay (pale blue as an April sky) that had the power that all truly breathtaking places possess, the power to so awe, to so humble us, that we become for a moment saner, soberer at the very sight, aware that, after all, the inmost drive of our nature is to yearn for Beauty, and to suffer the knowledge of our own smallness in its presence. Capri was haze-shrouded, distant, beckoning with the witchery of all islands; Vesuvius was the powerful shoulder of a slumbering, brown giant on the left; and the long, generous, shimmering horizon southwards to Amalfi opened the heart like a lens.

Poets used to rhapsodize on places that seemed "blest" by God (an uncomfortable idea in our Godless, unpoetic times), and Naples—dirty, brawling, thieving Naples—is such a place. Something stirs in you when you see it from above, an old languor that is not without an even older reverence. The extravagant humanity of the Neapolitans, the avid appetite for life, sheer sensual life, that drums so insistently in their streets, must result from that beckoning island always before them, and that threatening mountain behind. No cause, no ideology, no fanaticism can survive for long the sight of Naples' Bay, and with all the surprise of an important discovery, I realized that I had forgotten what it was like to be completely happy.

The rest of the day was vivid with this emotion. We walked in the park around the Villa Floridiana where the sunless, meandering paths were cold with that deep and penetrating chill that makes you feel keen in your own flesh, all a-tingle with the damp, verdant *green* of shadowed places on a warmish winter's day. Mothers wheeled babies, old men sat offering wizened faces to the sun, the city was dazzling below us—tile-red, earth-brown, palm-green, its seething life only a faint echo in that upper air.

We walked without direction, searching for a way down, no-ticing everything with delight, following our noses. It seemed enough. We came down out of that quarter on a long, steep succession of stairs that weren't on our street-map, calves aching towards the bottom from the effort to keep upright on the inclines, famished now, wanting fish, cheese, bread, wine, our hunger somehow so *perfected* that we could relish it as if it were food.

As we came out at last onto the level of the Riviera di Chiaia and began looking for a likely *trat,* a woman coming towards us, modestly but neatly dressed, carefully made-up, not more than forty and rather pretty, with a Giaconda-like smile in one corner of her mouth, suddenly extended her left hand as we converged. Nothing more: no plea, no expression of pitiable des-titution, no huge-eyed baby thrust forward as a prop. She simply held out her hand for alms, all the while smiling mysteriously and with just a touch of distant irony, as if to say: "Why not? This is my city. And if you're not a sentimental American, per-haps at least you can be embarrassed." I was too astonished to respond in any way, and she passed on with an indifferent, pri-vate little shrug. Had she hated, loved, trafficked with my coun-trymen as a girl? Had we killed her brother, laughed at her moustachioed father, bought her sister with a chocolate bar? The guilt of history stirred up for a moment, and then died. I turned and saw her chatting with a man who was furiously try-ing to back his vegetable truck into an alley too narrow to ac-commodate it. An attractive, self-possessed woman in the mid-dle of her day! I had the strong urge to run back and give her all my money. I wanted to acknowledge some new Neapolitan insight that had come to me. I craved a gesture as Zen-like as hers had seemed, and then realized that gestures were simply that—self-serving, and in Naples you pushed reality a little, seeing if it would give, but no city could be less metaphysical. So instead, I laughed to myself, and admired her.

We ate deliciously and at length—*zuppa di pesce* thick with mussels and shrimp for Shirley, *fritto misto mare* for me (so that I might savor one last time the virginal squid in their delicate peignoirs of batter), and two ice-cold *mezzos* of *vino de paso* that digested our food for us as we walked down the long esplanade towards our hotel, the sun westering now over Ischia, the sky ribbed with strange ladders of Turneresque cloud. That good day was darkening, the wind was harsher off the water, the Capri-boat came cresting in on the rising sea, and a fisherman, standing in his big, double-ended dory, rowed, double-armed, against the weather, wearying a little. I felt complete.

"Tomorrow," I said, "we'd better go to Pompeii."

The *Ferrovia Circumvesuviana* was four or five jolting Toonerville trolleys hitched together, and my stomach was already unsettled by a pat of rancid butter I'd wolfed down with my breakfast roll. It was a warm blue-and-gold morning, with just a hint of snap when you were out of the sun, and the cars were crowded with laughing young people off for the day to Castellamare. But again death was on my mind as we rattled out through plaster-and-pastel housing developments in the suburbs, and I kept looking beyond the orange groves, and the patches of feathery, lacelike *finocchi,* to Vesuvius—so close, right over there across the fields, partially crested with snow, its treeless slopes as bald as a burial mound. My guts were rumbling uncomfortably. I'd never been in a dead city before, and I was arming myself against analogies to my own era that seemed bound to come.

Then we were beyond the suburbs and the mountain, and the

heavily-cultivated, tropical land ran right down to the Bay on one side, and a plain opened out on the other, ringed by a far-off range of lavender hills with a sparkle of towns on their sun-drenched lower reaches, and we were there.

There was nothing but a small depot of peeling and exhausted stucco, a few dusty palms, and, across a road jammed with horse-carriages, the grey heaps of ruin that were all that was left of Pompeii's outer wall. Guides, souvenir-sellers, and carriage-drivers swarmed around us, each trying to out-perform, out-promise, out-hector the other. But a man with indigestion cannot be conned, and we made for the tiny coffee-bar in the station, and a Campari to settle my stomach. There, as the oily, bitter liquid did its job, we listened to a man with a superior pitch. He pointed up the road to the official entrance, told us the prices in the *ristorante* in the ruins, laid a simplified street-plan down on the bar, and then fell silent. Three-hundred lire, and no sales-talk.

Off we went. What struck me immediately (as it had in Na-ples) was the perfection of the site. *I'd* have built a city there too, and damn the broken-pated mountain less than a mile away with its jagged crest ominously suggesting a crater! Here was a level, sunny plain, well-watered, on a strategic road from the south, the Bay not too far off, with pleasing views on all sides, and a salubrious climate. Life in Pompeii, before the holocaust, must have been good—that was my feeling.

We wandered. It was a smallish city for smallish people. We saw some of the people in the museum on the site (the famous plaster "positives" that have been made from the "negatives" left by the ash), and none of them was much over five-foot-three. These bodies did not strike me as particularly anguished, our century having accustomed us to that vaguely fetal crouch that people assume when they are about to meet death raining out of the sky, and it was a dog, sprawled on his back, lips retracted into a snarl, legs higgledy-piggledy in a convulsion of agony, that unnerved me most—the old Protestant assumption that animals are somehow more innocent than humans, and their deaths thereby less warranted, coming back despite decades of disbelief.

We saw the city too—the one-chariot-wide streets, their paving stones deeply grooved by iron-rimmed wheels two thousand years ago, the houses with their cool, fountained atria within, a modest temple or two, the granaries, the Lupanare with a padlock that read in English, "Made in Italy," the public baths that could still function so little demolished were they, and the small *Foro Triangulare* with its frail, candle-flame cedars that had proved so much less frail than the city itself. And almost everything was roofless, shorn off, leveled at a single height as if by an enormous scythe (the level of the suffocating ash), and at the end of every westward-running street, the glowering, mute hump of the volcano.

I waited for the solemnity, the "long thoughts," that seem proper in the presence of a human catastrophe, but they didn't come. Names, street-numbers, and even graffiti were still scrawled on the walls of wine-shops. Frescoes depicting delicate, Dali-like figures (all black, sienna, green and orange), and rendered in a style, like Dali's, that suggested canny borrowings from older, better cultures, had survived inside some of the grander houses. But it was the sounds of *life*, by their very absence from these streets, that impressed me most—the clatter of rush-hour chariots, the street-seller's hoarse cries, the hubbub of the markets, the careless twist of a song. I had a strong feeling of Pompeii as a provincial city, not very important, not unusually corrupt or sophisticated, a little vulgar, certainly humid in the summer, predominantly mercantile, impatient with "speculations," sensual but not particularly decadent, as *pushy* as Dallas used to be, until one day—

We went into the *ristorante* ("*Government* restaurant!" the hawker in the pin-stripe suit and porter's cap bawled out, as if to reassure travelers suffering from Neapolitan battle-fatigue), and had a good lunch, our waiter wheeling up the most expensive meats on a cart, the bartender saying, "I know what *you* want, Signore—Cutty Sark!" But what we wanted was wine, and so we had a bottle of Lacrima Cristi, very cold, very subtle, and—tears of Christ!—very ironical on that spot. I thought of the old novel by Bulwer-Lytton, in which the twilight of paganism had hung over this city like a judgment of the gods, and realized that he had missed the point of Pompeii and its last days, which wasn't superstition but absurdity. It hadn't been destroyed, it had been entombed, and in point of fact the ash had *preserved* it from the demolitions of time that had worked such damage elsewhere. Wine-presses, oil-vats, cooking utensils, even blackened, petrified loaves of bread—all buried, an entire city and its unique lifestyle buried in an afternoon, and thus fixed forever. There was no way *not* to think of the smashed cities of my own time, the Dresdens, Coventrys, Hiroshimas—all obliterated beyond recognition. There was no way *not* to realize that the difference was simply this: nature was capricious, but man was vindictive, and after this most murderous of centuries, we could glimpse what had eluded Bulwer-Lytton. At the last, *his* morality and *our* politics had less substance than the cedars of Pompeii.

"They certainly know how to carry things," Shirley said, indicating the cocky bar-boy, with a case of *Aqua Minerale* balanced on his head, who passed our table at that moment, as graceful as a stag beneath his antlers.

"Disasters," I said. "That's what they carry so well." I could have said, "Defeats," but what I really meant was the burden of history—that burden of violence and anguish in the past that bows the backs of so many of us over forty now, that burden of intolerable memory that increases in direct proportion to our

198

awareness of how futile all the losses, all the ideologies, and all the horrors have been. Looking out the long windows that had been adroitly placed to provide the diners with a view of Vesuvius, I had an inkling of what it was the Neapolitans cared about, and realized how fitting it was that our trip was ending among them. Their calamitous coast—so beautiful, so "blest"—remained, despite everything, a reminder of a harmony older than history and all its discontents.

The sky was bruising-up as we went back to Naples in the twilight, past empty depot platforms with their fly-specked lamps, through dark groves where one sensed that the earth was still warm, alive, mysteriously fecund. The sun was going down under rain clouds beyond Capri, a single vast beam of light pierced through (pure, white, lucid as the eye of God) to fall between the island and the mainland, and Naples was an exquisite necklace of lights strung out in the dusk around the throat of the Bay. We didn't talk much, the moment had its own privacies. It was one of those rare times when life seems to shift its direction, and we were aware of it.

That night, while Shirley dressed for dinner, I chanced upon this bit of wisdom in a Victorian travel-book by Augustus Hare from the hotel lobby: "The treatment of the dead shows the character of this idolatrous and self-seeking people in its saddest aspect. When the funeral of a friend passes, a Neapolitan will exclaim with characteristic selfishness, 'Salute *a noi*,'—health to ourselves—without a thought of the departed."

I had to laugh. If one's attitude towards death illustrated one's attitude towards life, and vice versa, whose view had proved the least idolatrous? How could the pious Mr. Hare have known that a scant seventy years after he wrote, the world would have become such a death-haunted place that no exclamation could be more purely *reverent* of life than the Neapolitan's "Health to ourselves!"? For they had suffered, starved, prospered, and en-

dured for nineteen centuries in the very shadow of that mountain that had laid an inexplicable and existential death upon
Pompeii. Their lot had always been squalor, conquest, calamity,
and deceit. Long ago they had earned a bitterness that should
have soured them to the very dregs of the spirit. But what they
cared about was sun, wine, the new day with its unknown possibilities for further riches, and all the passions—griefs as well
as joys—by which, alone, we become truly human. They knew
that the only real duty was to *survive* the past. Their faith was
in the unfolding of life, not in its close.

And now we had *all* lived beyond the time when mourning
did any good. Now there were too many corpses to be mourned,
and so often the mourners were only the murderers off-
duty—like those troubled G.I.'s who rebuilt schools, out of brick
and bad conscience, in the Mekong Delta. But everything in
Naples shouted, break the cycle! Let history (before whose altar
only fools or scoundrels kneel) insist that violence is inevitable,
that nothing can be done! Saigon will outlast those lies as Naples
has. Let the dead bury their dead, and bad dreams to them! But
let the living (among whom now I numbered myself) be done
with paralyzing memories, and proclaim instead a stubborn
"Health to those of us who are left!," in hopes of restoring to
human life that supreme value our century has held so cheap.

Shirley was fastening on a pair of Florentine earrings. She was
very handsome at that moment, and I thought to myself: "It's so
much harder for a pretty and fastidious woman to live out of
two suitcases for four months than it is for a man," and remembered a dozen nice things that I had failed to say to her in recent
weeks, and knew that back in America I was bound to get em-
broiled again, because I loved my country too much to remain
indifferent to the upheavals that were trying its soul, and, like it
or not, my final expatriation from its particular moment in history had yet to occur.

"We'll be home in three days," Shirley said, as if she had read my mind. "How do you feel about it?"

"I'm looking forward to it in a way. If we could have stayed a lot longer, I might feel differently, but this way—well, I'm ready to go back. Maybe something's changed."

"And how about Naples?"

"Oh, Naples—" I said, and laughed, "We'll *all* be Neapolitans one day. If we're lucky."

Epilogue

In effect, that was the end of our trip. I read my first copy of *Time* magazine in four months on the *Rapido* back to Rome the next day, noting the usual clutch of demonstrations, motiveless murders, and drug busts that seemed a grisly reflection of the village-burnings that were "winning hearts & minds" in the DMZ—all of it the same as it had been during the summer. Back to Rome and a dingy little *pensione* near the railway station where a scrawny Christmas tree sat under a niggardly light bulb in the foyer, and we braved showers to get an indifferent meal, and repacked the last of the bags on an oil-clothed table, then slept four hours, and somehow got out to Leonardo da Vinci on the bus through the ragged mists of dawn, to bolt a last *Negroni* as our flight was being called.

There was snow just north of Nice where we had had such carefree gustatory fun with George and Francesca ten years before, snow blanketing the valleys of central France, and snow melting into the featureless Atlantic as we climbed out of all visibility. I spent the nine hours listening to a couple of construction engineers, who had been posted for two years to Teheran, detail just how they were going to burn down Ft. Worth when they finally got there. Shirley nursed a drink for half an hour, and slept the rest of the time away.

Then, in late afternoon, the first glimpse of the mottled ocean from 34,000 feet, and the wide, pale southshore beaches, and the lights coming on around the Great Necks, and finally the long, perfect, twilight swoop down into the red runway markers of JFK, and we were home. We were not being met, and rushed to make the limousine to New Haven, and I felt odd, marvelling at how tangled and mysterious the land seemed, all wooded and houseless along the Connecticut Turnpike, and how deliciously seasonal the chilly snap in the air tasted as we stood under the marquee of the Park Plaza, haggling for a taxi to take us the last thirty-five miles to Old Saybrook, and how good it was to find that a degree of wit had come back into my conversation, talking American with the driver.

It was full dark as we turned into our street past the hedges that seemed to loom higher than we remembered. Cheerful lights were on in our commodious old house. My sister and her husband were there to greet us, the radio was turned to the news, the coffee-table piled with months of *Newsweeks* and *Village Voices,* and eerily nothing had changed. I tipped our taxi driver, and joined the others in the living room, discovering with the first bourbon just how really long a day it had been. Checking my wallet for our airline ticket receipts, I counted our assets. We had precisely $14.76 left, and we would have to start scrounging the very next day.

Now, all these years later, it seems marvelous to me that we had gone so far on so little, and that my late-summer burn-the-bridges impulse to go "no matter what" had proved prescient after all, though not for any of the reasons I could have imagined then. I got strong enough, and sensible enough, while I was gone to come home when it was all over, and take up my life again, and let the Old World (and the New) mend on its own. That bald and obvious fact was the soundest bit of wisdom that I had brought out of those perilously unwise times.

L.A. IN OUR SOULS

It was six-thirty
of a bland, midweek morning, and like millions of other people
in Los Angeles at that hour, I was indulging a fantasy. For years
back East, it had seemed to me that the quintessential Southern
California experience would be sitting behind the wheel of a
powerful American car, tooling out to Malibu on a morning that
smelled like a fresh-sliced cucumber to the strains of pop music
on the radio. And now here I was—the rented '71 Galaxie begging to be let loose to run its own race, James Taylor singing of

all the highways of America that inevitably end up in L.A. if you go down them far enough, the sun just gilding the shaggy fronds of the palms along Santa Monica Boulevard, and the last day of my trip—the first *superfluous* day—stretching ahead of me.

I had come to Los Angeles to get a firmer imaginative purchase on the milieu of a novel about southern California that was floundering. After months of dirty-dishrag winter days in Connecticut, during which I had tried to find images to cloak my feeling that whatever was going to happen in the America of the seventies was happening already in Los Angeles, I had given up and gotten on an airplane. Now, two weeks later, it was time to leave. After twelve days in a motel in West Hollywood, I was as poised and mindless as the seismographs out at CalTech that were daily registering the unsettling aftershocks of the big quake of two months before, and the more I absorbed from this point on, the less I would know for sure.

I had put seven hundred miles on the car and never left Los Angeles or its environs. Half a dozen times, I had driven up to the highest point on Mulholland Drive, and gotten out, and tried to contain the staggering size of the city in a single metaphor, able to come up with nothing more accurate than the image of a thirty-mile-broad Blue Plate, on the central ridge of which—the Santa Monica Mountains—I was standing at that moment. Far out there, vanishing towards an invisible horizon, the tasteless meat and potatoes of downtown L.A. steaming in the smog; just below me, the salad-greens of Bel Air, Beverly Hills, and the gardens of Brentwood; behind me, the bread and butter of the San Fernando Valley—a vast, ten-mile-wide bedroom where over a million people slept; and to the west, far off in the Pacific mists but little more than half an hour away by car, the beach-communities ringed like pieces of Baba au Rhum on the edge of the plate.

The conventional image of the nineteenth-century city—

concentric circles of suburb, borough, and neighborhood narrowing towards a hot center—had no application here, and so, drawn on by the plaguing suspicion that the special sense of L.A. that I was seeking was just another tankful of gas ahead, I had wandered the freeways and the canyons and the basin, increasingly aware that my own memories and premonitions about the place were sabotaging my objectivity.

* * *

As it happened, my personal version of the Great American Daydream of innocent, bucolic boyhood was centered around Los Angeles, and over the years since I had been here last, a certain kind of winter's-end morning had always aroused in me a powerful longing for California. The fugitive smells of orange grove and just-cut lawn would tease my nostrils, a taste of guava and avocado would come up into my mouth, and I would suddenly recall the five-year-old boy, who had once stood barefoot in the hot, dusty sunlight of Pasadena in 1931, watching the rain inexplicably falling just down the block, and experiencing the first amazed discovery of a world of which he was not the absolute, dreaming center. To that boy, California was the voluptuous, bottom-of-the-well odor of an over-lush patio down into which the sun rarely reached, and the hot breath of the Santa Anas strumming the afternoon nerves to an awful pitch. It was a milkshake too thick for a straw, and bungalowed boulevards shimmering off under skeletal phone-poles all the way to the fabled world of Hollywood. It was the hairy legs of a tarantula come upon in a kitchen cupboard, and butter dripping out of a rolled tortilla over the fingers, and all the first stirrings of a body newly become aware of its hungers and its ignorance. 1931 in

Pasadena was my first more-or-less continuous experience of myself, and part of my longing was a longing for the thrilling sensuousities and terrors of that buried past.

But in the decades since, another Los Angeles had been superimposed over this one: the Los Angeles of popular myth—a space-age Sodom, a dream-factory, a city that was the doom towards which all America was marching in lockstep; a sprawling, smog-stifled, freeway-bisected urban jungle that was as vulgar as a Hawaiian sportshirt worn outside the suitpants, as ecologically schizophrenic as an oil derrick in Eden, and about as cultured as an astronaut reading *Love Story*. In short, a civilization of such spiritless artifacts as mushroom burgers, Hula Hoops, the metaphysics of Charlie Manson, Forest Lawn and Doris Day; a city that was haunted, for me, by the hopeless pealing of Marilyn Monroe's telephone the night she took the overdose of pills, and by Scott Fitzgerald's humiliated reply to Joseph Mankiewicz, "Oh, Joe, can't producers ever be wrong? I'm a good writer—*honest*." For years, I had entertained the notion that Los Angeles was a glimpse of all our tomorrows, a drive-in Babylon where the end of the world would arrive on its ominous Harley-Davidson, accompanied by the maracas of a cocktail shaker at poolside.

Innocence and corruption, Paradise and Paradise Lost, memory and premonition ... I was as unprepared for the real Los Angeles as Voltaire for Judgment Day.

* * *

Now, the wide, palm-lined blocks of Beverly Hills opened out on the righthand side of Santa Monica Boulevard. Buried sprinklers played, like silvery maidenhair ferns, over the manicured lawns of palatial houses in the early sun. Chicano maids walked poodles as meticulously clipped as the tall hedges behind which you fancied you could hear the thwunk-pause-thwunk of pre-breakfast tennis games. If Buddy Ebsen and Irene Ryan had come rolling down these very streets in their outlandish Ozark truck, I wouldn't have been surprised, for Los Angeles only disappointed those who had no expectations about it, and after half a century of movies and TV that species was as nearly extinct as the American bald eagle.

Expectations. Two weeks ago, I had assumed myself to be free of them. None of the shallow gauds of movieland for me! I would begin my search for the special character of L.A. where I had begun similar searches for other cities in the past, in that district—part marketplace and part tenderloin—that is usually designated as *Downtown*. I would get a room somewhere off the night's mart of Pershing Square. I would prowl the Pueblo de Los Angeles where the city had been founded. I would take its pulse close to the heart. I would *walk*.

Two days later, I admitted my mistake. Downtown Los Angeles was as characterless as downtown Gary and, aside from noting that three out of five faces that you passed along scruffly Main Street were non-white, and that Filipinos could be distinguished from Hawaiians by their cheekbones, and that Chinese waitresses in L.A. were often fluent in Spanish, the only insight that I derived from my two downtown days was the not-very-pithy realization that Los Angeles was a Pacific city, more akin to Tokyo than to Chicago. Like center cities all over America, it was at once dying and coming to birth. Wherever people lived—the poor and powerless, the excluded-from-the-dream— it was as wretched as backstreet Mexico City. Wherever people worked, it had all the many-leveled, dwarfing complexities of an ant-city between Windexed-panes of glass. The veteran of ten years of tramping in New York, the walker of the length and breadth of a score of European cities, suspected for the first time that his usual *modus operandi* had scant meaning here. Los Angeles wasn't an Old World town centered on a river or a railhead or a harbor. Eighty years ago, it had had barely fifty thousand citizens, and now L.A. County numbered over seven million. It hadn't simply exfoliated, it had exploded, and its peculiar character, if there was one, had nothing whatever to do with such old-fashioned conceits as "downtown." At that moment, the Walker began his metamorphosis into the Driver.

Canon Drive was coming up, and I was off-duty at last. There was nothing more that *had* to be done, except to rent a dinner jacket (Henry Fonda was opening in a play that night, and I was scheduled to go to the party at the Hilton afterwards), so why hurry to the beach? Los Angeles was spatial after all, not temporal. I recalled the climax of my downtown stay: Charles Manson, accused of complicity in the deaths of eight Angelenos, and Lt. William Calley, accused of murdering at least twenty-two Asiatics, had been found guilty within hours of each other. I had gone to the Hall of Justice where members of Manson's "family" had vowed to immolate themselves with gasoline if he was convicted, and found dozens of cameras at the ready but not a single fire-extinguisher; I had stayed awake all that same night, listening to the outraged voices of Orange County (on a phone-in radio-show) demanding that Calley be awarded the Distinguished Service Cross, and I had sensed another Los Angeles out there—immense, contradictory, decentralized, and above all contemporary; a city that seemed to epitomize those violent extremes of mindless obedience to authority and senseless rebellion against it that Calley and Manson had revealed in the current American spirit. "California is an Early Warning System for the rest of the Country," Herbert Gold had written. How true was it?

On a whim, I turned into Beverly Drive. I'd go up into Ben-

edict Canyon where Sharon Tate and her friends had been murdered, and eventually take Mulholland to the ocean. Sunset Boulevard was broad, islanded, and verdant-as-a-park there in the
9000 block. A mile or so back, along the Strip, it would be
drifted in last night's Zig Zag papers and Orange Julius contain-
ers, and ten miles ahead it would come to an end on the beach
at Pacific Palisades. The Beverly Hills Hotel rose out of its palms
and rich plantings with all the pink-stucco hauteur of a Monaq-
esque palace, making the new hotels down around Wilshire look
as if they had been scissored out of plastic and polyethylene by
an architect who had since moved back to Miami Beach. The
soft morning air of California that always seems to promise you
the accomplishment of a dream that you will have forgotten by
twilight smelled deliciously of coffee and eucalyptus and money.

Even in this town of early-risers, Benedict Canyon, winding
up through the Hollywood Hills behind the hotel, wouldn't
wake up for half an hour. Its heated pools steamed with fairy-
mist among the bougainvillaea. Above English Tudor and
French Provincial, above banks of geranium and hibiscus, the
raw scrub-and-crumble of the canyonsides loomed precipitously,
scored by the concrete Vees of drainage ditches. To a New En-
glander, used to worn, inhospitable, rock-strewn hills, it seemed
shockingly new land, as humped and spineless and temporary as
the mountains that a child palms together in a sandbox. The
native California brush—chapparal—that rooted these unstable
hills in place was one of the most combustible varieties of flora
in the world, and if you weren't in a slide-area where the rain
washed the land out from under your house, you were in a fire-
area where you weren't supposed to light a cigarette even in your
own living room. Fire and water being treacherous elements
here, the canyonites had taken to the air, and their houses were
cantilevered out over empty space, like those precarious castles
that tease the imagination in the illustrations in children's books.

On the other side of Mulholland, there was a huge, metallic flying saucer hovering motionless over two hundred feet of nothing. Ten-room chateaus and twenty-room cottages clung, mirage-like, to the sides of slipping arroyos. There were swimming pools that had less purchase on solid ground than the normal bridge. Everywhere there was evidence of an attempt to repeal the Law of Gravity by the Los Angeles construction industry, and yet in few places on earth was that law more remorselessly operative. According to even the most conservative seismologists, Southern California had been overdue for a major earthquake since 1957, and probably every house up in the canyons was doomed to become rubble at the bottom.

"How's the old San Andreas today?" one native would joke over his shopping cart, heaped with health food, in the mammoth Hughes Supermarket on Van Nuys Boulevard.

"You know what they say," a second would reply. "Los Angeles is going to lose by default . . . Have yourself a good day."

The quake of two months before had killed sixty-four people and dumped Fisher's Furniture Store into the main street of San Fernando ten miles away, and only six days ago the latest of over two hundred aftershocks had injured half a dozen more, tumbled pink cement-block garden-walls all over Northridge, and shaken me awake in my motel-bed in West Hollywood. Aftershock or forewarning? It depended upon who was speaking. "What's the sense of worrying about it?" said a canyon-dweller on his sundeck up in Beverly Glen. He was wearing a pair of portable stereo-earphones, with ten-inch antennae, that made him look like a large nut-brown insect, tuned into the inaudible static of interstellar space. "You people back East are involved with tomorrow, with the mind. We're involved with the body, with today. Why prepare for an unknown possibility when you can go to the beach and work on your tan?" Manson's "family," on the contrary, squatting on the sidewalk outside the courthouse, their heads shaven like Buddhist monks, quietly mad with the certainty that the great quake-to-come would save Charlie from the gas chamber, intoned, "Go to the desert, lock your doors, protect your children. Because it's going to be *heavy*."

But then there was something in the very air in Los Angeles that aroused apocalyptic feelings. Sometimes torpor or violence seemed the only options in the long, windless afternoons. Girls in the sunny streets around Fairfax High handed you slips of paper that read, "Jesus is coming soon." A converted yellow bungalow on the Sunset Strip advertised *Timeless occult books and bell-bottom jeans*. On a bridge over a scummy canal out in Venice someone had written in spray paint, "The earth is not a stable place—it sucks!" Up in deepest Topanga Canyon, there was a more or less continual encounter-group cum nudist-camp cum orgy going on at a place called Sandstone. And the *L.A. Free Press* that very week had come up with the Swiftian proposal that Lt. William Calley execute Charles Manson in the Los Angeles Coliseum on closed-circuit TV, the proceeds to go to charity.

Driving farther up into the canyon, I could see how all this reckless expenditure of money to construct hanging gardens and floating houses in a subtropical never-never land might have encouraged Manson in his messianic reveries. "Why not?" he must have asked himself, echoing the words of countless Los Angeles contractors, who said: "You want a cantilevered swimming pool? Why not?" Because none of this would last. Its very attempt to imitate styles more rooted in time or tradition only served to emphasize some fatal ephemerality beneath the naïve zests of the canyon life. One day the poor or the desperate would simply burn it all down while the rich and hedonistic frittered away their afternoons, trying to make a perfect margarita. These houses would fall, these pools would burst, these gardens heave. And what was he, Charlie Manson (jailbird-prophet, scruffo-seer), but an advance-agent of those vast psychic and geologic forces that were inexorably building up towards the ultimate cataclysm? In the land of Aimee Semple Macpherson, where show-biz and evangelism had always shared the same bed, he thought to deliver his message in the religious epistle that most typified L.A.—the Rock lyric; and when no one would listen, he had initiated a dialogue with himself no less indigenous to this city of interchangeable identities than the gossipy back-biting of the cynical hopefuls in Schwab's Drugstore on the Strip: *Who am I?* I am the Stranger in possession of the truth. *But then who are they?* They are the ones to whom my truth is strange. *So what must I do?* By the logic of a Vietnamized America, I must bring them the truth even if it kills them. *Show me the flaw.*

If the bewildered and resentful voices of Orange County, justifying Calley's murders by turning him into a contemporary Dreyfus, produced the eerie suspicion that America had become morally schizophrenic at last, the justification for Manson's crimes that you heard on the lips of dozens of young, blue-eyed, law-abiding Southern Californians suggested that sympathy for the Devil—in one guise or another—was everywhere in L.A. just then.

I turned onto Mulholland Drive, and pulled over, and got out for a cigarette. Down there, the smog, which at street level lent a faintly leprous cast to everything (exactly as if the eye had been rinsed in linseed oil), hung in a dirty zone of grease smeared above the Civic Center complex that rose like a group of headstones almost ten miles away. A week before, leaning on the parapet of the Griffith Park Observatory, I had looked down onto the dirt path that wound up through mountain pine two hundred feet below (in this largest of all municipal parks in America) where Boy Scouts were hiking up through dappled sunlight, and I had seen—a level below them—a red fox scamper across the path, his bushy tail carried weightless and aloft behind him, and then looked up, and out, and seen, as well—in the blink of an eye—those same downtown buildings. The astringent smell of pine needles, the chilly plash of water somewhere far below, birdsong, a feeling of mountains; and in the same glance, the architectural cemeteries of bureaucracy rising out of the stews of the basin. There was no avoiding it: L.A. was as astoundingly horizontal as New York was vertical. But why had a city materialized on this unlikely spot? It was as if Manhattan had grown up out of the marshy wastes of North Jersey.

Except for the invention of the automobile, Los Angeles might have remained nothing but a second-class way-station off the mission-route to the north, instead of becoming the sixth largest city in the world, for a man without a car was an anachronism here, and L.A. had the highest ratio of automobiles to people of any major city anywhere. Mass transportation was all but non-existent, and you had to walk blocks, often miles, to get a bus, and it rarely took you anywhere near where you wanted to go. The old Pacific Electric trolley line that I had ridden from Pasadena to Los Angeles in 1942 had ceased to function years ago, and there were people in Watts who had never been to Glendale. But once behind the wheel of an automobile the Angeleno was liberated as few citizens of modern cities ever were. It was easier to get from Hollywood to Santa Monica than to taxi crosstown on 45th Street in New York, and I regularly drove the twelve miles to Hermosa Beach for breakfast.

Superhighways in other cities were predicated on the principle of *avoidance*; they were designed to move cars over or around the densities of the urban-center. But the idea behind the freeway-system here was *accessibility*—to provide high-speed arteries that could feed more cars *into* the city, and as a result every part of this horizon-wide metropolis was reachable in little more than half an hour from any other part, and when you got to your destination there was always a place to park. Here, where space was an abundance, a bank, a store, a restaurant, or a church without its own parking lot had small hope of custom, and contrary to the comic scare-stories of the Bob Hopes and Art Linkletters, driving on the freeways, except during rush hours, was not like being trapped on a hundred-foot-wide roller-coaster without tracks. It was merely the Connecticut Turnpike, doubled in width and flow, and L.A. drivers were generally savvy, quick-thinking and reliable in their reflexes, the automobile being as natural an extension of their nerves as the New Yorker's contortionist-agility in getting into a five-o'clock subway car. There was little or no cursing or honking in an L.A. traffic-jam, and people waited behind their wheels, each isolated in his own small, air-conditioned portion of space, patiently listening to the Top Forty or the Sig Alerts.

Probably what accounted for this was the curious psychological fragmentation, the disoriented time-sense, of this most mobile of all cities where the Bekins moving vans were continually transporting people, and their differing lifestyles, from one section of the town to another, and where no one took very much notice of anyone else, being too absorbed in his own house or pool or patio. The automobile had made L.A. an intensely private city, a city without a distinct sense of neighborhood, and no real nightlife. One's friends mostly lived ten miles away, and there was little of the public-conviviality provided elsewhere by bars. People got together in each other's houses, and a girl from Palos Verdes either slept over, drove herself home, or was designated G.U. (Geographically Undesirable) by her date in Westwood. Indeed, city-living in Los Angeles resembled nothing so much as living in the country, and the hippie-enclaves up in Laurel Canyon had little more to do with the garden-apartments-full of young marrieds on Fountain Avenue a few blocks south than upstate New York farmers have to do with the harried fatalists of Manhattan.

I got back in my car, and turned the key. The motor hummed with the quiet power that was the source of the feeling of limitless *availability* that always witched you, in Los Angeles, into the illusion that Time was only a spurious obsession with linearity, whereas Space was a Zen-like awareness of simultaneity; an idea that gave the average Angeleno the slightly distracted look of a man hesitating among too many pleasant choices. I pressed the gas-pedal, and turned towards the Pacific.

Down there on my right, the Valley floor stretched away like the enormous grid of a waffle-iron all the way to the Santa Susanas that were lavendar-tinged and indistinct in the morning. I rolled down my window, and smelled the elusive, herbal odors of L.A.'s fixation on foliage, remembering the summer I had spent alone out here in 1942, after which I had gone back East again, a sixteen-year-old rebel-against-puritanism convinced that he had seen a new civilization—a leisure-oriented civilization of drive-ins, supermarkets, private pools, and casual clothes—an informal, almost Mediterranean civilization that had come to him as a vision of Utopian proportions in the hard-nosed reality of wartime America.

Now, Mulholland Drive became a twisting, houseless, gravelled mountain road. I passed a family of motorcyclists—the mother and father on full-size machines, the kids on tot-size replicas—drag-racing on a level stretch. I slowed down for a loin-clothed youth, beaded headband securing shoulder-length hair, who was loping along bareback on a pinto. A sense of everyone beginning his private day, in accordance with his own private whim, possessed me. Yet I was tooling along well within the municipal limits of a world-city. *Was* it a new civilization as I had felt years ago? ("L.A. is only embarrassing when it tries to imitate other cities," the sundecker in Beverly Glen had said, "—mostly New York.") *Was* it the city of the future as both its knockers and its boosters were so fond of saying? ("New Yorkers are ulcerous—Angelenos orthopedic," a sociologist had concluded, ". . . the difference between brooders and act-outers, mullers and maniacs.") Or was it, above all, a city of Now, a city *without* tenses, on which the past exerted little or no drag, and the pull of the future might best be measured by a seismograph? Wasn't it the America of the seventies, plain as the self-carved X on Charlie Manson's forehead?

I thought of him racing along this very road in a carful of his girls ("These days in L.A., every profession has its groupies," a young man, drinking Sangria on the Strip, had said), freed to any and all distances by the internal combustion engine, which had eventually built a psychic equivalent of itself into his soul, at once the most pitiful pariah and the most pitiless judge of whatever America was coming, calmly thinking to himself (as he would hint in the courtroom later): "I am only a mirror of all this—the hamburger stands that look like hamburgers, the money that builds hills as well as the houses to put on them, the miniature rain-forests that arrive on truck-beds, and all the fantasies that are built on other fantasies in this land of lost distinctions. *What they see in me is only the madness they have made.*" But I was dissatisfied with the monologue. Like all conclusions about anything in L.A., it seemed facile, off the mark.

Far below me, and parallel to Mulholland, the neons of Ventura Boulevard (which Romain Gary had once called the most interesting street in the world) were just coming on, redundant in the morning sun. It had been early prototypes of such shopping strips that had seemed so Babylonian to me in 1942. But on this trip I had been mostly surprised by my *lack* of surprise, for in the twenty-five intervening years the peculiar lifestyle of Los Angeles had spread back across the mountains and the deserts and the prairies, and now Iowa City had its equivalent of the Sunset Strip, and there were supermarkets in all the Fayettevilles that rivalled those in Burbank, and my own town in Connecticut sported, proportionately, almost as many swimming pools as Inglewood. The Los Angelization of America had become complete, and people in Evanston and Shreveport one-stop-shopped to Mantovani, banked from the front seat of their cars, barbequed in their backyards, went soft in the leg in their split-levels, and eventually took on that faintly passive, vegetal, dreaming look that had once seemed so peculiarly Southern California.

When you lounged on a garden chaise outside a summer house on Cape Cod, with Burt Bacharach on the hi-fi and a steak on the charcoal, you were in Los Angeles. When you made drinks, built around fruit-juice, at your tufted, black-leather, mini-bar with the abstract painting from Sears on the wall behind it (as Calley had been photographed doing countless times), you were in Los Angeles. When anxiety, and the Kantian sense of personal responsibility to which it sometimes leads, seemed less urgent than the next fleeting pleasure, then too. All America was California dreamin'—as the song had said.

Perhaps only the inhabitants of the vast, decaying cities of the East, where the nerves sizzled and the feet burned, had escaped this process of Los Angelization, but probably those cities were doomed anyway. How could such places as New York survive in an era of proliferating population and pollution? They had nowhere to go but upwards into the poisoned air, whereas L.A., whose regulations concerning auto-emissions were already more rigorous than future national standards, had only to annex another community or two, link them to the city by a freeway, and build their own versions of Ventura Boulevard.

The most interesting street in the world? No, that was only a lefthanded, Gallic way of stating that an ultimate had been reached—like saying that Hiroshima was the most interesting ruin in the world. Still, Ventura Boulevard had achieved some kind of giddy zenith of the Shopping Center Vision. There was an air of finality about it, as if the science of arousing the acquisitive hunger had at last exhausted all the commercial possibilities of neon, poured concrete and plate glass. It stretched unbroken, arrow-straight, all the way from the Hollywood Freeway to Woodland Hills, tying together a string of such separate communities as Studio City, Sherman Oaks, Encino and Tarzana. *Ten miles of midway!* It resembled nothing so much as a light show, a Rock festival, the Indianapolis 500, and a Saturday afternoon carnival all rolled into one, and then tripled. For ten long miles, not one thing was calming to the nerves, tasteful to the imagination, or pleasing to the eye in any recognizable sense of these terms. And yet there was a stupifying fascination about it.

You could live out your entire life on Ventura Boulevard—be born, get married, die and be buried from it. You could eat in a Taco Belle, a hard-boozing Kansas City steak-house, or a chic French restaurant. You could furnish an apartment in Swedish modern or a mansion in fine antiques. You could learn Karate or how to swim. You could bowl, dance, ice-skate or ride a horse. You could buy, rent, wash or repair a car—or a motorcycle, or a camper, or a mobile home. You could go to movies, saddleries, nude entertainments, jazz-clubs, church or a lecture. It was the ultimate bazaar, and driving its length three days before—the temperature up in the high eighties, everything two blocks away unfocussed by a shimmer of heat and exhaust, the glare off cartops, chrome, neon and aluminum piercing even my polaroids—I had had one of those premonitory hallucinations that a man, who has been quits with cities for some years, occasionally experiences: Eventually this street would lengthen, store after store, mile after mile, state after state, all the way back to the other ocean—the vast sign-boards walling out the trees, the leveled concrete denying the contours of the land, the towering neons creating a perpetual, timeless hour that was, eerily, neither night nor day. At last, the continent would be conquered; its ability to disturb us, enlarge us, depress us, or arouse us, finally annulled. And the Valley that had given birth to this incredible street—the Valley that was over a hundred square miles of tract houses and subdivisions where *No Down Payment* and *Instant Financing* made the split-level paradise of leisure-living and wife-swapping available to all—the Valley would finally leap over the mountains that circumscribed it here, and *become* America. The meaner side of the democratic dream would be achieved at last: everything, in this land founded on the idea of diversity, would have become *one* thing.

Now, I looked out across the vast shimmer towards the mountains that were paling from lavendar to beige as the smog accumulated. Had a similar vision of an air-conditioned, middle-class prison, into which millions of Americans seemed to be so happily rushing, relieved Calley of any sense of personal complicity in his own actions? There were probably thousands of replicas of his black-leather bar down there in as many "recreation rooms," and certainly tens of thousands of Valleyites could see nothing wrong in what he had done. To them, Manson's assumption of nihilistic freedom was the real danger, and they glimpsed no similarity to it in Calley's appallingly literal enslavement to "orders"—no matter how inhuman they were. A feeling of the hopeless polarization of life in Los Angelized America swept over me. I felt as alien in it as a refugee from the novels of Henry James. Then I swung around a curve on that mountainroad, on either side of which this endless, flattened city sprawled, and started the gradual descent, and sensed the ocean like a hope.

Deciding to skip Malibu, I turned into Topanga Canyon Boulevard, wanting my last sight of the Pacific to come after those wild miles of gorge and thicket where the red tiles of Italianate villas baked in the sun atop precipices, and houseless roads wound up into hills where there was nothing but the omnipresent water-pipes of a city optimistically anticipating endless expansion. I wanted to get a quick sense of how this last, this greatest of oceans must have looked to the Spanish dons. Continent's end! Nowhere else to go. And there it was—blue-grey, milkily opaque, with a mild surf, and no horizon. Indeed, I had yet to see the Pacific horizon on this trip. There was always a strange fog-bank obscuring it half a mile out, and farther down the coast the evil exudations of the oil refineries filled the air with a visible murk.

The morning was sunny and cool and half-clear (a combination of conflicting attributes that perhaps only an Angeleno could comprehend), and I turned south on the Pacific Coast Highway, looking for breakfast. A firm wind blew in bland, sea-freshened gusts across my face. Early hitchhikers waited at the lights with transistors, sleeping bags, surfboards, even babies. The slopes of the massive headlands up towards Malibu were pale yellow with a profusion of tiny mustard flowers. The coast along there was raw, sandy, looming, misty, with that disturbing feel of new land about it that always arouses a powerful sense of the impermanence of things, a feeling that was somehow only intensified by the imitation, lathe-and-plaster Portofinos and Torremolinos that dotted it.

At Pacific Palisades, I gave a lift to two girls—all cascades of hair, fringed buckskin, beads and bare feet—who were taking a portable cassette-player to Hermosa Beach for the day. They got in the back, and on a whim I offered to drive them there. They seemed typical specimens of the perpetually-tanned, streaked-blonde, salt-burnished, pretty young Narcissist that the Southern California beachlife produces in such numbers out of sunshine and orange juice, and the tale I overhead in the next

226

half hour may not have been untypical either. They were both eighteen, and they had met only the day before in Lum's in Santa Monica. The taller one with the freckles had left her husband and three-month-old baby two weeks ago. "I'll never marry again," she said. "Every kiss is an obligation. Man, they figure they've got you. You're not free anymore." The plumper one with the bangs had been beaten up by her father last Tuesday after a week-long argument about getting her own apartment. "I managed to call the police, and he got so embarrassed—because of the neighbors—that I had a chance to cut," she said. She had just sold her Camaro, and would live with a friend in Ocean Park until June when she graduated from high school, and then pack it in and go to Vegas. Both of them suspected they were pregnant.

All of this came out in an easy, casual, chatty flow as we passed the algae-choked canals of Venice where dirty cats and uncombed dogs scavenged around the mudguards of 1964 Studebakers in front of run-down bungalows, behind the psychedelically-painted windows of which I imagined shaggy-faced young men, who carpentered for a living, having a second cup of tea with the blue-jeaned girls who cooked their macrobiotic rice. A scant two minutes later we were in Marina del Rey with its ten-story apartments, crenelated with balconies, its subterranean garages full of Porsches, and its enormous man-made harbor where six thousand pleasure craft were berthed—an instant-Brasilia risen full-grown out of a bog; and I was amazed again by the violent juxtapositions (the dropped-out and the upwardly-mobile living literally within sight of one another) that didn't seem to amaze the Angelenos at all.

"Oh, yes, I watched my afterbirth come out when I had Cheyenne," the taller one was reassuring the plumper one as we passed the massive, scum-green oil tanks beside the highway in El Segundo where gay borders of pansies had been planted along the chain-link fences, and the air stank of chemicals. "It's kind of groovy really—the whole having-a-baby number."

"This guy I'm with now is really beautiful," the plumper one replied, seeming not to notice the long pier in Manhattan Beach at the end of which the ominous tankers waited, or the sudden unearthly roar of the jets climbing out of L.A. International, leaving an ugly brown trail-stain behind them in the sea air."But I won't stay with him after June. He's into too many weird scenes . . . I think I may have the baby though," she added. "Don't you just *dig* babies?"

I drove them down to the public pier in Hermosa Beach where motels, tacoburritos joints and live-bait stores fronted a wide, absolutely pebbleless esplanade of soft sand. A few surfers were paddling out on their boards in shiny black wet-suits to the breaking point, and the sun was as wan as a moon in the white sky. "It'll work out for you," the taller one was saying, "just like it'll work out for me. It always works out . . . Say, you know, really though, Mister, thanks for the ride. It was real nice talking to you."

I watched them ankling off across the sand, their lives seemingly no heavier in their hands than the cassette that hummed with Melanie—off for a day at the beach to work on their tans. I drove on south of town to Cap'n Ahab's Coffee Shop on the marina, where the gun-stock beams were sleek with too much varnish, and the plank tables had been laminated with protective plastic, to be faced with one of those enormous California breakfasts—hash-browns, sausage patties the size of beer coasters, ranch eggs (never less than three), and grape jelly in an impenetrable little cube—that always make the Easterner feel vaguely stingy with his coffee and toasted English. I pondered the meanings of the beachlife, which burned the hours away like pools of sea-water evaporating under the sun. What else did it burn away? The surfers paddled out,waited, gauged the swell, missed it, and waited again—finally to be rewarded by fifteen pure seconds of the surrender of the Self to a tidal rhythm, the body energized by its brief moment on the wave's crest, rushing downwards—loosed, free—towards the brink of a state before consciousness, that primal state we had lost when water ceased to be our element. But was something more surrendered too?

I walked off my breakfast in seaside streets full of campers, their curtains still drawn, the occupants still asleep, reminded of the minor uproar that was going on just then over this use of the public thoroughfares as hotels. The kids of California seemed to have taken, en masse, to the VW buses, the Econolines, the delivery vans chromeless with age, and they were wandering up and down the coast, following the surf, the Rock festivals, or some elusive promise of better vibes elsewhere. It seemed gypsy-ish and good to me. Nothing in Los Angeles awakened that need for roots—for a roof and a hearth—which seasonal change necessitated back East. Life here was as undulant, and gravity-free, and crazy as making love on a waterbed. The fact that the ski-slopes of Mammoth Mountain were only a few hours away from this very beach narcotized the sense of having to earn an experience in advance. Had it, as well, so hypnotized my two passengers that the panic or despair about the fix they were in, which they might have felt in Boston's winter streets, simply hadn't materialized? I didn't think so. After all, the psyches of the young, who had all grown up in Los Angelized America, had been Los Angelized too, and the conceiving of a baby was no more a *consequence* (with all the moral and temporal hangups of that word) than an earthquake—which also happened while you weren't paying attention. It was simply an event, an occurrence among a myriad of other occurrences, to which it had little more direct relation than Manson to Calley, or Watts to Westwood.

"The riots?" a magazine writer had mused to me eight days

ago. "Well, I've never even been to Watts. I mean, it's twenty miles from here, and it's almost as hard to get into—because of the freeways—as it is to get out of." He seemed troubled by my pursed lip. "Well, what I'm trying to say is this—it wasn't happening *here,*" and any idea of the city as a single cohesive human unit, held together by a community-conscience, seemed unreal, even dishonest, in a town where out-of-work actors arrived in Bentleys to pick up their unemployment checks, and the Mayor regularly indulged in racial innuendo at election time.

All at once, I decided that I wouldn't go to Henry Fonda's party after all. These were my last hours in L.A.: why spend any of them with people I could just as well see in New York, Rome, London or Nassau? It didn't seem relevant to the trip somehow. Then I had to laugh, realizing that my two passengers would have considered partying with Henry Fonda very relevant indeed. After all, he was related to Peter and Jane, wasn't he?

* * *

It was after twelve when I eased the Galaxie into the pell-mell, four-lane flow of northgoing traffic on the San Diego Freeway, with a feeling that I was completing a great circle (the canyons, the Valley, the beaches) that had Hollywood as its terminal point. Sun-blistered boulevards of stuccoed-courts, where you imagined the Bogart of *In a Lonely Place* trying to open a can of Coors for his hangover, fanned out into the heat-haze on both sides of the highway, and I almost missed the exit for La Cienega Boulevard which arrowed through the barrens of the Baldwin Hills where dead oil derricks stood against the glassy sky like those gaunt skeletons that survive a forest fire, and working pumps seesawed up and down like genuflecting grasshoppers.

What other major city in the world would tolerate an oil field in its center? But then oil had created L.A., along with aviation, electronics, tourism and the movies—commodities as ephemeral as the next defense-budget and the passing taste in fantasy, and in Pasadena the $70,000 homes of thirty-four-year-old computer analysts were up for sale, and you saw their owners reading the want-ads in the *L.A. Times* over coffee in the House of Pancakes.

What other city, where power and water should have been elements as chancy as sun in winter London, would build a perpetual waterfall over a downtown freeway, or sport so many swimming pools that from the air its vast grid looked as if chips of turquoise formica had been scattered over it, or burn with so much candle-power at night that it all but put out the stars in the telescope of the Mt. Wilson Observatory twenty miles away?

What other city could boast that the richest source of Ice Age remains in the world (the La Brea tarpits) was a tourist attraction almost as magnetic as the richest source of Plastic Age imagery in America (CBS-TV City) that was barely ten blocks away? You felt the bones of extinct Mammoths under the bubbling macadam of the parking lots around the Farmers' Market nearby, and the tired husbands from Des Moines, in see-through nylon shirts, plodding on through mountainous displays of gift-wrapped fruit after their tireless wives, seemed no less bewildered and unadaptive than the enormous, sad beasts upon whose viscous graves they rested their open-work huaraches.

What other city suffered so publicly from an identity-crisis that feature-writers in its newspapers continually, obsessively anatomized the soul of the town, and comparisons to San Francisco came up in dinner-party chat like the paranoid fixations of Kafka writing to his father? If you said (as I had many times) that you much preferred L.A. to Frisco, Angelenos looked at you as if they were searching for an ulterior motive, and when they learned that you were from New York the waves of defensiveness made your psyche *beep-beep* like a radar-screen registering the entire Russian missile-force coming in over Seattle.

What other city expended such astonishing creativity on the decor of its restaurants, and then set afire every foodstuff that wouldn't actually be destroyed by flame? For Los Angeles was as infatuated by the idea of *flambé* as it was by the concept of the cantilevered-strut, and I had spent two weeks ducking the skewers that burned like torches in the pagan catacombs of L.A.'s singed cuisine.

Yet despite all this, I liked the place. Parts of it were as surrealistically ugly as if Luis Bunuel had designed them as sets for *Los Olvidados,* but parts of it were as impressionistically beautiful as an Italian hill-town reconstructed by the artisans of MGM in the 1930s. If someone had given an imaginative, impatient, pleasure-prone adolescent a billion dollars, and told him to build a city that would gratify all his divergent urges, he would have built something very much like Los Angeles, and the city had all the unselfconscious charm, vitality, and naîveté of *The Threepenny Opera* staged by Holden Caulfield in his girlfriend's garage.

I drove on towards the castellated hills that rose in a patchwork of sere-brown, tropic-green, and stucco-white over Hollywood. Now that I had no need of a dinner jacket, what was left to do? Pack up, retrieve some shirts from the cleaners, check my reservation on the morning-flight home, and make an eight o'clock curtain for *The Trial of A. Lincoln.* Suddenly, I missed my wife with a keenness that had nothing to do with the usual, nagging absences that a man discovers, one by one, after a few days in a motel. The trip was all but over, the "business" done, and I wished that she was there beside me in that car. She had never been to Los Angeles, and I imagined the pleasure of showing her—what? Hollywood Boulevard with its bronze stars (each bearing the name of a show-biz personality) embedded in the sidewalk? The Grand Central Market in downtown L.A. where you could buy Chinook salmon, calamyrna figs, cooked lamb's heads like Francis Bacon skulls, chili pasilla, sweet paprika, roasting rabbits, and all the other ingredients of the Oriental, Mexican, and Southern European cuisines that intermingled here? Acme Hardware on La Brea that would sell you a flowered-porcelain toilet bowl for $325? The chic shops along Wilshire? Universal Studios where the tourists gawked at "sets" that had been carefully built to resemble *real* sets? Disneyland? No. Turning onto Fountain with its stubby palms and peeling stucco, I wanted her to be there to sense what I sensed so strongly in the afternoons of Los Angeles: the ambivalent mood of a nation adrift among its conflicting desires—either to star in the next half century's all-time money-maker, or drop out of sight as completely as a hermit among the scorpions of Death Valley.

I parked, and went to pick up my laundry, and almost bumped into one of those apparitions that I had come to call "the ghost ladies of Hollywood." They were usually in their late sixties or early seventies, and there was an air of musty eccentricity about them—of over-sweet perfume and too much Coty face-powder; of diaphanous clothes saved in attic trunks and the time-shriven flesh of lonely women who have taken to gossiping querulously with themselves. They came drifting up the block under the palm trees with their 1920s pocketbooks, and their hectic shades of lip rouge, and their huge, haunted eyes—to buy a lamb chop, a container of cottage cheese, and a single can of beer. You always saw a face inside that ruined countenance that you fancied you recognized—Mary Miles Minter, Billie Dove, Barbara LaMarr—and in that face you glimpsed a vanished Hollywood of champagne corks, cocaine-eyes, Hispano-Suizas,

233

and tango-violins. These ladies took no notice of the girls in hip-huggers and Capezios getting out of Karmann-Ghias in front of garden-apartments with names like the Fountain Blu. Ghosts themselves, they seemed to be conversing silently with ghosts. They were always on foot (a fact unusual enough in this town without pedestrians), and for a moment the rueful, twilight sadness beneath Hollywood's flamboyance came over you. All of its cheap dreams had come cruelly true in the faces of these wraith-like "Norma Desmonds," and the brevity of glamor, the attritions of a lifetime devoted to the phantasmal, and time's inexorable passage no matter what, were as graphic there as the lines no powder puff would ever expunge again.

I put the shirts in my car, and locked it up, and walked. Dyan Cannon, fur-coated despite the temperature, taller than she appeared on the screen, her caramel-tinted hair in need of a rinse, strode into Schwab's as if nothing could ever ruin the moment of celebrity she was enjoying. The spindly Washingtonia palms lining Hollywood Boulevard, like so many Ray Bolgers in fright-wigs, leaned towards their lengthening shadows. A young man with an Elliot Gould moustache, pausing at a stoplight, craned out of the window of his Volvo, and called, "Hey, New Yorker!" having identified me by my walk. Buses of tourist-faces went by, wondering if I was "anybody."

Hollywood! My earliest ambition (rather than to act or write or make a fortune) had been to direct movies, and in snow-drifted New Hampshire milltowns in the late thirties, I had survived puberty's first awareness of estrangement on a diet of two films a week, and dreamed of Sunset Boulevard as feverishly as other boys dreamed of the Boule Miche. But the dream, even then, had never been a dream of the Hollywood of glamorous parties, glittering premieres, or jasmine-scented girls whose bodies were the stuff of masturbatory myth, and when I arrived here

234

in 1942—all of sixteen—I found that something in the B-films that had been shot in these very streets (something connected to that hallucinatory sense of milieu that movies deliver in a flash) had prepared me for the other Hollywood—the Hollywood of mouldy side-street bungalows where whirring table-fans moved used air through stifling bedrooms; the Hollywood of ugly trolley tracks under a webbing of power lines; the Hollywood of the 1937 version of *A Star Is Born* where, for every Janet Gaynor who succeeded in wooing the gods of fame, there was a Fredric March who walked into the Pacific as a suitor who had failed; the seedy, anonymous, dream-shattered Hollywood of Nathanael West—a Hollywood to which I was still drawn, because, with age, you come to have a certain distant fondness for your illusions. They are your last connection to your earliest self.

Just the day before, at dawn, I had made an ironical pilgrimage down to the old Paramount Studios on Melrose where I had hung around through sweltering summer afternoons almost thirty years before in hopes of seeing Cecil B. De Mille, or at least his automobile, passing through the famous wrought-iron Spanish gates. The neighborhood was rundown now—dingy stucco courts advertising rooms for singles, an early-morning smell of pinto beans and sour coffee, Western Costume rising like a mausoleum out of the Mexican cafés, and the not-unpleasant air of an abandoned 1930s airplane hangar about the Studio itself. The billboards on its sand-brown, windowless walls touted three TV series for every film, and just inside those fabled gates on Marathon the stanchions stacked with the bicycles of extras on an early call were visible evidence that—as the leaders of a floundering industry had told President Nixon two days before in San Clemente—seventy-six percent of the members of the Screen Actors' Guild had made less than $3,000 last year, a sum that was considered below the poverty level.

Plainly, the action and the money had moved elsewhere—to Cinecitta, or Shepperton, or Timbuktu.

Hollywood, which had been the dream-factory of the twenties and thirties when America's aspirations were as innocent and hopeful as a youth planning to marry Jean Arthur and thinking of bedding Jean Harlow, had become at once an Assembly-line of Sop, in the form of dozens of hours of inane situation-comedy ground out for TV like sausage meat each week, and the Capital of Raunch where, along Santa Monica Boulevard alone, you could paint a girl's nude flesh for a few dollars an hour, or study her crotch in full-color close-ups in movies made on the outskirts of Burbank, or have her "service" you in any one of two dozen massage parlors, or purchase glossy-paper picture-magazines of her eating or being eaten—by men and women and assorted animals. *Green Acres* or *Lust Girl*? Calley or Manson? Was there an honest choice between them? Sometimes it seemed that it was to such antitheses of unreality that America's secret life had come down. Yet perhaps it was as important to resist the simplicities of this Either/Or as it was for those of us, who could, to continue to remember and to hope—particularly in this city of the present tense.

I walked to La Brea, went down to Sunset, and started back to the car. A golden, late-afternoon glow burnished everything with that warm light that always seems to foretell a languid, yellow moon that will hang—like some over-ripe, nocturnal grapefruit—in the palm trees later. The air wafted against the skin with the softly phantom caress of long-since-bulldozed orange groves. I felt that elusive lift that comes to even the most skeptical of men in places that are still unfinished, still enamored of the day, still inventing themselves, and with some amazement I realized that perhaps this city was the only city in America in which it might be challenging to live again—at least for a while.

* * *

There was no moon when I parked just east of Sunset and Vine some hours later, but the long fingers of searchlights were playing on the upper stories of darkened office buildings, and *No Left Turn* signs had been set up in most of the intersections. Jesus! (I thought) do they still indulge in all that hyping-up of false excitement? In 1971? For a *play*? The crossings were thronged with kids in gypsy-garb. There were a lot of policemen on the sidewalks, trying to look like tolerant Dutch-uncles. The metronomic thumping of a bass-drum and the steely whang of over-amplified guitars filled the night with their blurred reverberations.

Then I saw that the searchlights weren't in front of the Huntington Hartford Theater two blocks away, but just outside a parking lot on El Centro, across from which some sort of carnival lofted its canopy of light and noise out of a canvas enclosure. The green and yellow struts of a Ferris wheel turned leisurely, out of rhythm to the music, and I realized that all the panoply was for the 10th Annual Los Angeles Teen-Age Fair, and not for *A. Lincoln,* after all. The Rolling Stones wailed against Hollywood and all that it had once meant, but then, of course, *they* had commandeered the searchlights now, they were the objects of the false excitement, and if there was an Establishment anymore—an in-group whose money, fame, and influence would make a difference to tomorrow—they certainly cut more of the mustard than the likes of Henry Fonda.

But Fonda had a searchlight too (though it was smaller and older than the others), and three-quarters of an hour before curtaintime there were all of ten or fifteen people in front of the theater. A TV camera-man was filming the fans who were filming him filming them, and the bronze star in the sidewalk under the marquee bore the name of Theodore Kosloff, a Paramount feature-player from the early twenties. Fonda's own star was in the sidewalk in front of the parking lot just down the block, and it was streaked with tire-marks.

I took up a position in the lobby across from the ticket-window as more people began to gather—people who all had that indescribable look of the out-of-towner that a certain kind of middle-aged Angeleno never loses—the look of a vacationing dentist from Wichita. They took pictures of the billboards with their Instamatics, and studied each other surreptitiously as if Dennis Weaver or Edgar Buchanan might be hiding behind that plaid shirt, those sagging Bermudas.

George Montgomery arrived, and smiled, and was photographed. Van Heflin came, shaggy-looking, tired, and smiled, and signed autographs. As a star, he was a bigger draw than Montgomery, and so he joked with the news photographers who, when he had gone into the theater, said, "Well, who else is going to turn up?"

"The ushers, that's who," someone cracked.

"Listen," another said, "This is all routine ... Last week, I caught Shirley and Jack and *David* Cassidy outside the Ambassador."

James Garner arrived in a tuxedo (obviously he was going to the party at the Hilton afterwards), and he was bigger than either Montgomery or Heflin, because he was a TV star, and he smiled his bland, apologetic smile as the flashbulbs exploded in his face.

The crowd was thickening now. Two tall, disdainful Blacks, with a Diana Ross look-alike between them, swept into the theater in ankle-length black-vinyl coats with epaulettes of ostrich feathers. The play was about the arraignment of "A. Lincoln" before a kangaroo court of angry Blacks, and they had the look of critics who had already written their reviews. Lee J. Cobb came in tweeds and an expensive English cap, and he was bigger than Garner, being a *current* TV star.

The searchlight-tractor coughed and roared. Faces, as famished by fantasies as by a diet of chow mein, hungered for more under the unreality of the lights. Then one of the news photographers, looking down the street, called out: "Hold it right there, Liz—for a good one," and a deep, expiring gasp—somewhere between Cheyne Stokes and orgasm—swept the crowd forward as if on cue. But it wasn't Liz Taylor. It was—oh, you know, you know—whatzername! It was Elizabeth Ashley and George Peppard, and *they* had been invited to the party too, and looked cool and dressed-up and married, as the autograph books were thrust into their faces, and the newsmen begged for "just one more."

The lobby was filling now. Industry-men—producers with fishy, dead, Sanpaku eyes; agents with swept-back, greying pompadours stiff with lacquer—stood around with their chic, fortyish wives, who winced under the lights, and pulled the collars of brocaded opera capes over the telltale wrinkles on their tanned throats. These people knew the dangerous emotions that the proximity, in the flesh, of the symbols of magic could unleash in this crowd—"But he's—he's *short!*" or, "It's her—it's really her!"—and their faces were pinched, weary, emptied, *scared.* They knew what was under the rock, they knew the jungle of vanities behind the jewelled screen, they were the diamond-merchants who had trafficked all their lives in expensive glass, and to me, at that moment, there was a certain old-whore bravery about them, because of all the squalid secrets they kept. They were like aging Tammany ward-heelers. Their world was over. The as-if, on which their lives had been constructed, had about as much relevance as the snout of an Edsel, and yet they "showed the flag," they came. There was the sadness of long-unexamined compromise about them, of a cynicism that had become sentimental, of the dinosaur's bewildered roamings in the first icy twilights that foretold his doom.

Then I noticed that Martha Scott was talking to the man right next to me. Unrecognized in that crowd of TV-addicts, she seemed as at ease as the hostess of a successful dinner party once the brandy has been poured. I stared into her lovely, animated eyes—the peculiar vulnerability and poignance that had made her performance in *Our Town* so memorable years ago still there, elusively matured—and all at once she looked at me, at the expression of recognition that must have melted my public-face, and seemed a little flustered, and smiled, and nodded, and said: "It's so nice to see you again," cocking her head a little, and faking it, as if saying to herself: "Martha, you're *forgetting*. Now, who *is* he?" For an instant, the peculiar false intimacy that shared-fantasies encourage held us together, as if we were twenty-years-ago lovers who had forgotten each other's names. I smiled, and she smiled back, and neither of us knew how to acknowledge, much less explain, the flash of counterfeit-sympathy that seemed to flow between us. "It's good to see you *too*," I said. "You look marvelous." Her smile was as modest and pleased as the smile of the girl in *Our Town,* and then she was swept away by the press of people trying to get closer to Fernando Lamas and Esther Williams.

Ricardo Montalban arrived, and the lobby cracked with flash-bulbs. There was the gathering tension of boredom in the crowd—more, more! They wanted to touch the hem of glamor, and having touched it, they wanted to touch the sleeve of magic, and having touched that, they wanted—what? Immortality! Anthony Quinn! But having touched him, they wanted him to write down his name on their postcards and souvenir-programs as proof that they had actually been close enough to see through the image to a homelier reality: "Oh, yes, Mabel, Tony's only five-eleven, and a regular guy ... Sure, we talked for a minute, and he's not so special really." I stood there, and realized that it was precisely as if these people had read Nathanael West, and were willingly, even gleefully playing characters out of *The Day of the Locust,* and that I wasn't really so different from them—my Martha Scott for their Anthony Quinn.

What was it in American life that had starved us so grotesquely? I had met enough movie-actors to know that most of them were sad and mixed-up Orphan Annies trapped in the bodies of the Dragon Lady or Smilin' Jack. Was it the film medium itself that gave them such a compelling power over our imaginations? Was the fantasy the only refuge for a people without a sustaining past? Or had the fragmentation of modern cities, the process of Los Angelization, aroused some last vestige of hunger for a life of proportion, coherence, wonder, meaning? A hunger that could only be assuaged these days in the pathetic make-believe of the most vicarious of dreams?

Anthony Quinn smiled the empty smile of a man named George who had been caught in a conversation in which he is repeatedly addressed as Bill, and the lobby-lights flicked off-and-on to announce the curtain. Suddenly, I didn't want to see a play, I didn't want to see Lincoln tried for his sins of omission, I was sick of the lust to expiate ourselves by judging others that had made us strangers to each other—Manson to Sharon Tate, Calley to the villagers of My Lai, and all of us to *them.* I craved the luxury of my own thoughts, and left my ticket, unclaimed, at the box office, and walked back to the car. On a so-far-unengraved star in the sidewalk on Vine Street, one Duane Broder had written his name with a Marks-A-Lot. *I'm here, it's me, I exist!* The gesture seemed so emblematic of Southern California—the Southern California now proliferating in the

American heart—that I wrote the name down in my notebook. Duane Broder, a celebrity in Hollywood, and Richard Nixon, from nearby Whittier, the president of the Republic.

* * *

The trip was over, but I had no sense of completion, and as I drove down Hollywood Boulevard towards my motel, I succumbed one last time to the urge—to get up into the hills, to search out a taller building, to take to a helicopter, anything to get *above* the city—that testified to how L.A. frustrated the visitor's eye by its smog-blurred, amorphous distances. I took a turn into Laurel Canyon, and on a whim veered onto the white curve of concrete that ascended into a new and expensive housing development, called Mount Olympus, that had been carved out of a small mountain on the right-hand side of the canyon. Eight-foot cypresses and spectral Grecian fountains appeared fleetingly in the swerve of my headlights as I climbed Venus Drive past scores of empty, leveled building-lots where exposed water pipes already snaked in right angles across the dry, crumbly earth on which, overnight, those pleasure gardens that money can always buy in Southern California would miraculously blossom.

"But you can't put cisterns, roads, houses, pools, tennis courts—*anything*—a quarter of a mile in the air, up circuitous inclines hardly a car wide, on precipitous ledges on the sides of hills that *walk*!" I would have said. "You simply *can't*!"

"Why not?" all of Los Angeles replied to my eye.

I pulled onto the highest lot of all, drove to the very edge, killed the headlights, and got out. As yet, there was nothing there but the soft, parched dirt under my shoes, and a few clumps of chapparal, and the distant plash of a fountain playing on and on through the night with no one but me to hear. Yet just across the narrow canyon the opposite hill was verdant, mysterious, dark, a-wink with life, *peopled,* and down there, spread out before me in vivid bands of red, yellow and blue light, the thousand glittering boulevards of Los Angeles stretched away towards some lost point of convergence on the horizon itself. The sight was awesome, appalling, and spectacularly beautiful. A city that had engulfed every square mile that could be seen from that height under the blanket of a million blazing lights. An underwater city laved in phosphorus. An endless city. Perhaps the last.

The ghosts of the five-year-old boy and the sixteen-year-old youth stirred up in me again. The heavy, sweetish odor of nighttime orange groves was long gone now, and these days the splendid white beaches were fouled with gobbets of oil and the carcasses of poisoned terns. Off those sparkling boulevards, violence and despair ripped the silken dark with the angry scream of police sirens. And yet those ghosts longed to contain Los Angeles enough to justify their stubborn fondness for it—its energy, its gaucherie, its honeyed-nights and salad-dawns, its very size that was commensurate with something untrammeled in the enormous continent itself—just as the forty-four-year-old man longed to love again the tragic, bedeviled, violent, and idealistic nation that stretched back three thousand miles from here, bafflingly, under the unjudging night.

For what had built this most American of cities was nothing less than the unfettered and impatient national genius that often seemed to be foundering in bitterness and confusion back East, and L.A. might turn out to be the last place where Americans had taken a stand and created a mirror-image of their peculiarly complex souls. It was all our dreams—the meanest and the most audacious—made astoundingly visible.

Suddenly I realized that I was loathe to leave it, and that the reason for this was that it had maddeningly eluded me, and that I hadn't experienced that most American of emotions in a long time. *What's over the next ridge? What's it like there? There's bound to be more!* After all, weren't the habits of limitlessness and horizon-chasing, in themselves, our oldest tradition, our uniquely sustaining past? What else could have gotten us through the Nebraska grass, and Colorado snows, and desert alkali to build this final city on the margin of the last ocean?

I remembered a friend of mine, a director from New York, who had phoned me one night from Beverly Hills, after spending six fruitless months here, to say: "Listen, everything you've ever heard about L.A.—good and bad, pro and con, everything—it's *all* true!"

The fantasy-starved crowds at the theater, the reality-numbed girls on their way to Hermosa Beach, Ventura Boulevard, the canyons, Manson and Calley: *all this was a reflection of the madness we had made.* But wasn't it just possible that we could assume the human responsibilities of our own audaciousness?

Something—perhaps a waft of far-off Pacific salts in the warm night-air—whispered: "Why not?"

THE HUCKLEBERRY PARTY

A Search for the American Character
1976–1986

Of all historical problems, the nature of a national character is the most difficult and the most important.
  —*Henry Adams*

In 1976, the Bicentennial Year, a lot of Americans refused to come to the birthday party. After the traumas of Vietnam and Watergate, they wondered what it was we had to celebrate. Our streets were violent, our air was polluted, our government seemed either apathetic or a captive of the corporations, and our spirits were as soured as they had been in the two hundred years since the founding of the Republic. The radical young referred to the country as "Amerika," revisionist historians ransacked our past in search of avarice, cupidity, deceit or bad faith, and the American Dream (as it used to be called) appeared to have been a squalid nightmare all along.

Just ten years later, in 1986, the nation's mood had swung 180 degrees in the opposite direction. Patriotism of the most jingoistic stripe was fashionable even on Madison Avenue. Bruce Springsteen's anthem, "Born in the U.S.A.," quavered over the air waves everywhere, expressing with defiant pride what once would have seemed an embarrassing chauvinism. We celebrated the 100th Anniversary of the Statue of Liberty in a four-day orgy of self-congratulation that would have stirred anyone but Benedict Arnold to cheers. The air was heavy with the emotional fireworks usually associated with wartime.

Polar extremes such as these have characterized the relationship between Americans and their country since 1787. The patriotic idealism of both sides in the Civil War was followed by the cynical materialism of the Gilded Age. The restlessness and expatriation of the Roaring Twenties led to a rediscovery of American values, and of the land itself, in the Depression Thirties. Sinclair Lewis satirized the country with a corrosive bitterness fully as simplistic as the lyricism with which Thomas Wolfe rhapsodized it a few years later, but few writers and not many social observers have managed to strike a temperate note of appreciation to which a literate and intelligent man might repair.

As a consequence, I have always found myself unable to join either the knockers or the boosters. I don't believe in H. L. Mencken's America any more than I believe in Ronald Reagan's, and a simple, nagging fact remains. Even after two hundred years, *Americans don't know who they are*—a condition as unsettling in a nation as in an individual.

Some years ago, I became disturbed by this national identity crisis . . . What was America? I couldn't find it. All I found was a chimera, a fiction, an idea. Who were Americans? I found I didn't know, and I began a search for them, vowing to confine myself to the small, the private, and the subjective. What follows is an account of that search.

Like many young would-be writers, I took as one proof of my evolvement during college a conviction that my country was uncultured, vulgar, complacent, and materialistic. I thought myself quite clever for stating that the railroad depot in Terre Haute represented the zenith of the American imagination. I was fond of intoning Ezra Pound's bitter line about "artists broken against her, astray, lost in the villages." I took my country's material plenty as a sign of spiritual poverty, and thought her as barren of tradition, suspicious of ideals, and impervious to beauty, as a developer selling building lots in the Okeefenokee on TV.

After college, when I began to seriously write and think, I looked to Europe with the curious longing of the American youth, the longing of an *exile*—albeit for a home he has never seen. I went to French movies, and Italian restaurants, and even the most anemic new novel from England found, in me, an attentive reader. I dutifully repeated the same old clichés Americans have been muttering since Fenimore Cooper's time, each generation discovering them anew: they name boulevards after writers in France, and listen to their opinions; men of the mind are buried in Westminster Abbey, and their words can be read in bronze along the Mall; *their* literature, music, painting, philosophy, and politics have a long and respected history; *ours* are imitative, shallow, demagogic, and money-corrupted. I did not realize that all these half-baked notions have always been a tradition among Americans—a kind of intellectual puberty through which we all seem to pass.

But, nevertheless, something in a man yearns to be reconciled with his past, his memories, his images. He feels a need for a larger pride than his own personal pride, and that need works in him. It worked in me too, as I think it works in all Americans (a people who know less about themselves than any other in the world, and, possessing practically everything else, still lack the one essential thing: a national image), and finally I began to map out grounds on which a reconciliation might occur—that age-old reconciliation between America ("Old Bitch America," as Sinclair Lewis called her) and one of her faithless sons.

In true native fashion, it began with baseball—a fact which amuses me now, because I am anything but a fan, and used to think that the American's seasonal obsession with the horsehide was the most maddening symptom of our national frivolity. Nevertheless, one day I found myself reading an article on Dizzy Dean, and when I came to an account of how he had walked the first three batters to face him in one of his initial major league games and then proceeded to throw out the next three on ten pitched balls, I found myself laughing against my will, and saying to myself: "Good God! Who but a crazy American would do a thing like that?"

What impressed me was not so much Dean's skill as a pitcher, as the fact that he had loaded the odds (as well as the bases) against himself before demonstrating it. A European might have thrown out the first three men to come to the plate, but no European would have jeopardized the whole game simply for a display of such gratuitous self-belief. But clearly Dean's drive was to triumph over the game itself, over the sheer mathematics of it, over chance and probability, even over common sense. Something in the action struck me as quintessentially American in its goofy audacity, its incredible expense of spirit on an abso-lutely trivial matter. But I couldn't for the life of me say why I felt this, so I simply filed it away in my head—the first item in a collection of instances of our national character.

National character? Then, I would have scoffed at the very idea. Wasn't America, after all, nothing but a melting pot of adulterated European traditions, which grew weaker and less distinct in every generation until they were all but lost in a general savorless stew? Didn't the American lack any single trait as idiosyncratic as the Frenchman's subtlety, the Englishman's perseverance, the Italian's volatility? Was there, in fact, any such *thing* as an American trait—other than raucousness and bad manners? My answer was an easy "No," and yet I had felt in the unbounded, good-natured conceit of a rookie ballplayer something to which I could give no other name.

In the months that followed, I decided that though Americans might lack more profound traits, they were "crazy" all right, for I found Dizzy Dean's wild brand of self-assertion in a lot of unlikely places. I found it in Louis Armstrong's Twain-like familiarity with King George the Fifth, who had come incognito to one of Satchmo's London performances in the thirties: "This one is for *you*, Rex." I found it in the long-rifle soldier of the Revolution, who up and disappeared each spring, to straggle back home, and do the planting, and see his wife, and probably get drunk—only to turn up again sometime later, and lose another indecisive battle, but somehow, maddeningly, win the war. I also found it reflected in Emerson's exasperated appraisal of Thoreau: "Instead of engineering for all America, he was the Captain of a huckleberry-party."

Americans were crazy, unaccountable, full of juice, and for the first time I enjoyed that in them, seeing that it had a deeper source than I had imagined. But Emerson's remark troubled me, because though the Concord handyman struck me as being immeasurably more native than the Concord philosopher, the judgment made good sense. Why was Thoreau's cantankerous refusal to do anything "serious" so much more to the point somehow than Emerson's scold?

I was still puzzling on this when I hiked up to the Berkshires one August and discovered D. H. Lawrence's little book, *Studies in Classic American Literature,* in the Lenox Library, and in it, these provocative lines: "The old American art-speech contains an alien quality, which belongs to the American continent and to nowhere else . . . The world has declined to hear it . . . out of fear [because] the world fears a new experience more than it fears anything." Walking in the long summer evenings amid the soughing of great trees, up there in the wild and isolated hills, still somehow awesome and remote though men had raised their hand-hewn rooftrees there two hundred years before, I thought about this, and became, for the first time, aware of the tremendous, untamed impact of America, still unfenced and untidy behind the billboards and the superhighways. I suddenly saw how the raw continent itself (even that settled New England corner of it) could make a man as sagacious as Thoreau experience a truer reality in captaining a huckleberry party than engineering for a nation—and I remembered his approval of an English traveler's feeling that "the heavens of America appear infinitely higher, the sky is bluer, the air is fresher, the cold is intenser, the moon looks larger, the stars are brighter" here than anywhere else. It need only be added that these days the smog is thicker, the water dirtier, the food more tasteless, and the wounds to the land more grave—*and* the outcry about all of this louder, angrier, and more effective here than anywhere else.

But if there *is* an American character, it probably began to form in the new experience that men encountered here; and the source of the experience was the land itself. I began to look closer, and to search farther back. "A hideous and desolate wilderness," William Bradford of Massachusetts had called it in the very beginning; and, for a moment, one can glimpse the whole grim-mouthed origin of New England Puritanism in that stark image—meeting-house, bundling-board, and witch-tree—for the very land must have seemed pagan and amoral to those first colonists, like the world before Original Sin. Beyond their hearthsides, their frowning God and His Salvation ended; just beyond their rocky clearings pressed the whole huge weight of a trackless, savage Eden, so distracting in its stark beauty and immensity that they had to grapple for their souls, as well as for their lives.

Over a hundred years later, Daniel Boone used almost the same words as Bradford to describe virgin Kentucky, but with an enigmatic difference: "Thus situated many hundred miles from our families, in a howling wilderness," he wrote, "I believe few would have equally enjoyed the happiness we experienced." *Happiness?* What had happened in those hundred years? Nothing less than the beginnings of an American character. For Boone was subtly different from the original colonizing Europeans, already something else, something native to this place. The very breadth of the land aroused in him a like breadth of soul, and drew him, and others, continually beyond the last settlements, as if they were pining for a purity of contact with nature which towns distracted.

Distraction—that was it. Distraction from the concerns, and issues, and habits of thought that we had brought with us from Europe; distraction, also, from the old European conception of man as the prisoner of a given social structure, unchangeable and foreordained; the distraction of civilized man, able to think, yet faced with a landscape that was not saturated in thought, and had never been subdued and transformed by the mind. The American continent called to a deeper, broader man than Europe had produced, whispering to the will and the imagination, so that the only people who lasted here were those who consented to become new men.

I began to see that these "new men," able to think of the wild land as a home rather than an exile, and nourished by it in more than body, could think new thoughts as well. I discovered little by little that Americans, far from being materialistic, were incurably lured by the Ideal, as if they had actually sensed from the beginning that new men, in a new land, might make a new start. But before I realized this, and began rummaging back through our history to see if it was so, I began to discover American types that were as indigenous to this country as Dickens' Pickwick or Balzac's Lucien were to theirs, and my list of native traits lengthened.

First, there was W. C. Fields. They were reviving *You Can't Cheat an Honest Man* and *Never Give a Sucker an Even Break* just then, and I went to see them because I had loved Fields as a boy, and I wondered whether he was really as funny as I remembered. I discovered that he was more than merely funny: he was, in fact, one of the most recent examples of an authentic native type, which I took to calling The Great American Windbag.

Most American humor, most American myth, has been created by, or deals with, the Great Windbag—who is really only everybody's disreputable uncle or wandering father in disguise. He is the con-man, card-sharp, or carnie-barker, whose outlandish pretensions to gentility (as signified by Fields' omnipresent gloves and frock coat) are a sardonic contrast to his perpetually "out-of-funds" condition. He is the lineal descendent of such Homeric talkers as keel-boatman Mike Fink (who could outshoot and outbrag any man on the Mississippi), and Davy Crockett, and Twain's Duke and Dauphin, and those itinerant journalists, Orpheus C. Kerr and Petroleum V. Nasby—and how much like Fields' fanciful pseudonym, Cuthbert J. Twillie, these last are.

The essence of the Great American Windbag is talk, and the essence of the talk is exaggeration. There is more than a little of him in the inflated rhetoric of such political spellbinders as William Jennings Bryan and the late Sam Ervin, such hypnotic evangelists as Billy Sunday and Billy Graham. The Windbag loves to talk, he loves to tell stories, and Mark Twain was certainly referring to his style when he wrote that "the humorous story is American, the comic story is English ... (for) the humorous story depends for its effect upon the *manner* of the telling; the comic story ... upon the *matter*." The Windbag loves words; he invariably uses long words rather than simple ones; and most often *two* words where one would suffice—as if the thing he is attempting to describe is much too big for the tools at hand.

Looked at in this light, there is something of the Windbag in all the most typical American writers—Melville, Whitman, Twain, Dreiser, Wolfe, Faulkner, and Kerouac, for example. They are fabulists, rhetoricians, exaggerators all. America, its landscape and its experience, seems to have driven them into a creative frenzy of loquaciousness, as if the only way to subdue the emotions that are generated here is to snare them in a net of language, and, if this fails, to expand the point of reference out of all proportion to the thing itself—as Washington Irving did when he began his history of New York City with the creation of the world; and as Melville did when he saw in Moby Dick not just the fluked object of a mad vendetta, but all"the intangible malignity which has been from the beginning."

It is this touch of inner-Windbagism that has made our most native writers, almost without exception, sloppy craftsmen and superb stylists—a perfect reflection of the feeling of limitlessness (which begins with what the eye can see, and leads directly to what the mind can imagine) that is the essential American perspective.

Limitlessness—that was the key; the limitlessness for which W. C. Fields' recurrent and mysterious line, "I'm off to the Grampian Hills," was a kind of comic embodiment; and the intellectual limitlessness I found a little later in the American type I had always thought to be the cause, as well as the epitome, of our national materialism: the inventor, the machine-shop tinkerer. Or, as I came to refer to him after more searching: The Inspired Crank.

I first encountered him in the letters and memoranda of the Wright Brothers. As I read along, I became awed by a simple and astonishing fact, which the rapid development of the airplane since Kitty Hawk has obscured for most people: namely, that two Midwestern boys, with no scientific background; without even a college education between them; who knew nothing about man's attempts to fly except what was contained in government pamphlets anyone could obtain by writing; who financed their hobby with the proceeds from a small-time bicycle shop; and, in defiance of all the experts and accepted theories, and the ceaseless experimentation of decades, nevertheless solved the obdurate problem of wing-curvature simply by fiddling with a cardboard box, and then discovered the inaccuracy of the tables of air-pressure (on which the construction of all flying machines up to that time had been based) by building a ramshackle wind-tunnel out of an old starch carton, finally made the first man-carrying, powered flight in the history of the world, wearing (as Orville put it) "stiff white starched collar(s) and . . . neckties . . . as usual!"

I found myself wondering if the Wright Brothers in 1901 (fully two years before they succeeded in flying; when they were unknown anywhere but in Dayton, Ohio—and known there only as "those crazy Wright boys") had had any idea that they already knew more about aeronautics than anyone else in the world. Probably not. They were awed by the experts, like Chanute, who gradually became aware of them; they felt nervous about being "mechanics" and not "scientists"; and yet they didn't see why a man couldn't fly if he simply used his head, and, troubled by their audacity in questioning accepted scientific data, went right ahead and did it anyway.

Just as Henry Ford did in 1914 when, wanting to give a wage raise, he kept adding quarters to the maximum, "sensible" figure suggested by his experts, until he hit a nice round sum of five dollars a day for *every* worker in his plant—which amounted to a revolution in the world's economy far more radical than anything proposed by Marx. It was a "crazy" idea, running counter to all economic theory. And what was the reason for it? The reason was the bitter and angry look on a worker's face when Ford and his son came through the shop one day—and Ford's frowning desire to make "that fellow . . . glad to see us when we come along." It was crankish, and it was inspired. As was Ralph Nader's David-like assault, some decades later, on the very Goliath Henry Ford had created. Nader didn't see why one outraged citizen couldn't take on a multi-billion dollar industry, and so he went ahead and did it.

It was this same inspired crankishness that caused an American portrait painter to invent the telegraph, and an American landscape architect to create the Steamboat, and such Founding Fathers as Jefferson and Adams to resemble no other men alive in their time, in the spaciousness of their minds, the breadth of their interests, and the incredible diversity of their accomplishments in everything from horticulture to Latin translation—almost as if to prove the proposition that a man could venture as far as his imagination could take him, and if he had a good notion it didn't matter whether he had letters after his name, or figures in his pocket, to back it up. For here a man is no more bound by a given profession than he is by a social class, and Americans seem to have realized from the beginning that the mind has no boundaries. How else account for Thomas Edison, Buckminster Fuller, and Frank Lloyd Wright?

Materialism? Europeans always take our refrigerators, dishwashers, ice water, central heating, and television as symbols of the squalid little machine-shops they believe Americans have for souls, but I think D. H. Lawrence hewed closer to the truth of it when he wrote: "The most idealist nations invent the most machines. America simply teems with mechanical inventions, because nobody in America wants to do anything. They are idealists. Let a machine do the doing." For centuries the world has been saying, "Why?," but the essential American question has always been, "Why *not?*"

I turned over a shelf of books pursuing this American "Why not?," and came to realize that the question could unleash energies in a man, other than the imaginative and the inventive, for I encountered the Fallen Hero, and, through him, what might be called the Dark Night of the American Soul.

I first glimpsed it in Sam Houston, Indian fighter, Congressman, General of the Army, Governor of Tennessee, and President of Texas. I glimpsed it, not in any of these sizable accomplishments, but in a mysterious three-month period that separated the Tennessee and the Texas phases of his life: the three-month period of his marriage to the daughter of one of the most influential men in the state; a period over which so impenetrable a veil was thrown that it suggests a secret that even the dueling, drinking, double-standard morality of the frontier in those days could not countenance; a period which, when it was over, found the girl back with her parents in a state of nervous prostration from which she never fully recovered, and Houston's brilliant career in ruins. He resigned as Governor, left Tennessee for good, and disappeared into Indian territory to live with the Cherokees, and eventually push on for Texas and a new start.

Questions are unavoidable. What happened during that disastrous three-month honeymoon? What dark side of himself had this attractive and ambitious young man (riding a wave of popularity that might have led him to the White House) been moved to show his young bride, that would cause even her outraged kinsmen to remain forever silent about it? What scabrous acts had he asked her to perform? What damning quirk had he exposed? The mind produces a variety of intriguing answers, but we will probably never know for sure. Certainly, however, it was something that gentlemen of his time never revealed to their wives; and certainly it was something that was indicative of a belief that if a man could climb as high as Will would take him, he could also sink as low as Whim would let him—and another aspect of our national limitlessness glimmers close to the surface here.

It is the same dark aspect that I later found in U. S. Grant's buried, pre-Civil War years as a drunken and disreputable wood dealer in St. Louis, considered by everyone to be a failure beyond redemption. It hints at the same curious taint that emerged in Captain Joshua Slocum, who had been born, as he said, "In a cold spot, on coldest North Mountain, on a cold February 20," but who found enough warmth in him after sailing a thirty-six-foot sloop (built with his own hands) all alone around the world, to be arrested at the very height of his notoriety for molesting a teenage girl. It illustrates the same surrender to murky and questionable urges that is in Melville's disorderly months as a beachcomber in Honolulu, about which the missionaries later raised such an outcry; and in Eugene O'Neill's years as a near-alcoholic derelict, prior to the writing of his plays; and in the enigmatic period in New Orlean's French Quarter that changed Walter Whitman into Walt, but about which he would never speak.

In every case, this "dark night" immediately preceded the brightest achievement, and I found myself pushed to the conclusion that without these appalling private depths we might never have had the astonishing public heights for which these men are known. It was as if they could only discover, in the acknowledgement of weakness, the peculiar strengths that were to make them exceptional. For certainly they came back from these experiences broader, harder, purer than they had been before.

This curious inversion of the classic tragic cycle—the hero *created* by his weakness, rather than destroyed by it—seemed more and more characteristic of this country as I read on—for, though they may have had their quirks, it is unthinkable that Houston's or Grant's counterpart in Britain or France would ever have let themselves *go* so completely in public; or, if they had, it probably would have *followed,* rather than preceded, their best-known exploits. Almost everywhere but in America, a man's slate is written in indelible ink.

Countless contemporary autobiographies by reformed drug addicts, drunks, lechers, and whores leave little doubt about it: Americans simply love the Comeback Story, and (all charges of narrow-minded morality to the contrary) it doesn't seem to matter to us what terrible extremes of degradation people experience, if only they can say, in the face of all indications that they will never rehabilitate themselves, "Why not? Why not?"

I found this same "Why not?" in an austere New England lawyer and a California hermit-naturalist, and in the simple thing they had in common—what I call the American Poetic Moment. The lawyer was Edward Dickinson of Amherst, the hermit John Muir of Yosemite, and neither, to my knowledge, ever wrote a line of poetry in their lives (though Dickinson, it is true, had an eccentric recluse of a daughter who wrote some). But beneath the veneer of business in Dickinson's case, and science in Muir's, there existed a receptiveness to the unlanguaged poetry of life that sometimes erupted in actions typical (it seemed to me) of the American character.

For here was a grim Calvinist lawyer, who had once been a member of Congress, wildly ringing the Amherst church-bell one evening, as if to alert the village to an actual (or at the very least, theological) conflagration. But when the whole town assembled in alarm, it was only to be told to please observe the incomparable sunset that was gilding the western hills that evening. And here was a gentle, misanthropic botanizer suddenly scrambling up a towering Douglas spruce during a mountain storm, to ride for hours, a hundred feet high, in the very vortex of the gale's unearthly music, almost losing consciousness from ecstasy. The eye of the one could sometimes lift from his briefs, and the eye of the other from his specimens, and the elusive thing both must have glimpsed was certainly the object of what Hart Crane was later to call "the seal's wide spindrift gaze toward paradise." You can find it hinted at, as well, in Thoreau's journals, and Frost's poetry, and Ryder's painting, and in the strange, trembling thrill of sad awe that most Americans feel when they hear, "Oh Shenandoah, I hear you calling . . . across the wide Missouri . . ." It is a suspicion that if we can only penetrate reality to its core, experience it without philosophical preconception, we will know a final truth. It is why, from the beginning, Americans have been drawn towards Eastern modes of thought.

Searching on, I began to find the most outrageous idealism wherever I looked. Every eccentric prophet of every hairbrained Utopia from communal marriage to pastoral communism could find a horde of eager disciples here, willing to follow him into the wilderness, or the law court, or even the jail house. Highfalutin' notions of ideal societies, which had lain unnoticed around Europe for decades, were actually put into practice here with utmost seriousness, though often with hilarious results, and the communes of some years ago were anything but radical or new to the American scene. The cautious, state-by-state ratification of our Constitution probably remains the most widespread public debate on abstract principles in the history of the world, and most Europeans were baffled when, during the Impeachment Hearings in 1974, the House Judiciary Committee spent weeks of philosophical rumination before beginning the procedures that would result in the removal of President Nixon.

Yet, we accuse ourselves of cynicism. Cynicism? On the contrary. Our mistreatment of the Indians, for example, far from simply being written off as the necessary ruthlessness with which civilization has always justified its dealings with native races, has given the Americans the collective bad conscience that has been the major cause of decades of Western films, which, if they viewed the Indian as a primitive, invariably saw him as a Noble Savage too, who had been victimized and corrupted by renegade white men. Imagine the English making a popular hero of Jomo Kenyatta as we have made one of Chief Joseph or Cochise, and you will see the difference.

Demagoguery? Sometimes. But then, animated and acrimonious disputes about "the decline of democracy" and "the dangers to our freedoms" began almost before the ink was dry on the Constitution, and have continued unabated ever since, so that for every abuse of liberty in our history there have been at least two committees of alarmed citizenry immediately organized to protest it. For every Joe McCarthy, there is a Joseph Welch; for every Nixon, there is a Barbara Jordan.

Complacency? Never for long. Every distressed or persecuted minority has a group asking, and getting, voluntary contributions for their relief, and having run out of victims here at home we have tirelessly adopted any we could find overseas, to the extent that a day rarely passes (as Jacques Barzun has pointed out) without a plea for the sick, the destitute, or the oppressed arriving in the morning mail. On top of this, Americans are their own most ruthless critics, and one characteristic of the American is that when he hates America he hates it worse, and deeper, and more intelligently than any outsider ever could. Indeed, our national obsession with the Ideal is nowhere better evidenced than by the very fact that someone is always loudly proclaiming that the country, the state, the individual, or the human race, is on its last legs.

No, the hubbub of American life, about which Europeans so often complain, is as much in our souls as in our streets, and the almost-mystic idealism that is crudely clothed in such popular catch-phrases as "manifest destiny" and "the winning of the West" is precisely the same sort of thing that stands behind Washington's feeling that "with our fate will the destiny of un-born millions be involved," and Lincoln's vision of the Union as "the last best hope of earth." This messianism is almost solely responsible for the murkier chapters in our history—from the Mexican to the Vietnam War; from our abuse of the Indians to our fanatical anti-Communism. But the motive, often to the de-spair of the rest of the world, has always been a conviction of our unique mission as democratic men with "God on our side," rather than merely a chance to turn a profit. Adolescent and dangerous, perhaps. But neither mercenary nor totalitarian.

Idealism? Yes, from the beginning. For the most interesting thing about our Revolution was not the effrontery of a gang of colonials daring to oppose their mother country, nor the eco-nomic and political conditions that caused them to do it, but the fact that in setting up a new republic they paused to justify it with a new philosophical perception into the relationship be-tween man and society; and having decided that "all men are created equal . . . endowed by their Creator with certain inalien-able rights," proceeded to work out in the most careful detail a governmental structure that translated this contention into prac-tical realities. They could have simply separated from England because it was in their interest to do so; there was no need to brood upon the nature of man. It was simply limitlessness again, the American "Why not?," new men able to think new thoughts; and the only crucial difference between our Revolu-tion and the French Revolution (almost contemporaneous with it) was the recognition that man is more than merely a free *citizen*, a kind of tame animal in a cage so constructed as to need no bars: at the bottom, he is a free *soul*, as well. We built a society based on the principle that man's rights and freedoms are endowed *in* him by God; the French built one on the principle that they are bestowed *on* him by the State. And it was precisely this abstract difference that proved to be the concrete difference between success and failure.

Mysticism? That too. For, as Edmund Wilson saw, the single idea that motivated Lincoln during the Civil War, and without which his actions often seem contradictory, was a transcendental belief in the inviolability of the Union. It is certain that he had little intention of abolishing the institution of slavery by edict when he came to the presidency in 1861—he was no John Brown, no William Lloyd Garrison. His decision to go to war after the South seceded was based primarily on what was to him a more abstract, yet more important, conviction: namely, that free men having entered freely into a contract with one another—a contract whose primary purpose was the establishment and protection of freedom—were, nevertheless, *not* free to nullify that contract unilaterally. He saw (almost alone in those days of extreme opinions) that the one thing which would destroy our constitutional republic was the treasonable lawlessness of secession, rather than the evil injustice of slavery.

It was something which neither the Abolitionists in the North nor the Secessionists in the South could really understand, for in effect he was saying: regardless of the relative merits of this particular dispute, regardless of the question of slavery or the question of States' Rights, the Union offers the only hope by which *any* dispute can be equitably solved, and therefore no one has the right to destroy it—whether for self-interest or for principle. For when men freely establish a government of law, they agree that that law must be beyond the reach of men. "Order is the price of liberty," as Constitutional historian Clinton Rossiter wrote.

It was a visionary idea, arising from an almost-religious belief in the Federal Union. It was also an answer to the single most important question left unanswered by the Constitution. It made one nation of us at last, sealing that unity in grief and in blood—and, incidentally, providing the painful precedent to which the world may one day repair when it finally decides that it must unite in a strong Federation of States. As Whitman wrote in his journal on the day of Lincoln's death (attesting to how well the president had educated his countrymen): "Death does its work, obliterates a hundred, a thousand—President, general, captain, private—but the Nation is immortal."

Yet often it appears that we have made a mess of the vaulting hopes of Lincoln and the Founding Fathers. Big business seems to wield the heftiest clout right now, and acts exactly like the cartoons of the fat-cat Capitalist that used to appear in the *Daily Worker*. Our awesomely beautiful continent lies supine and ravaged under the bulldozers, the strip-miners, and the sub-dividers. The FBI and the CIA intrude their grubby, bureaucratic fingers into the *sanctum sanctorum* of the original American social contract—the individual's right to grow mushrooms, dress up like Marie Antoinette, or mimeograph seditious pamphlets in his basement. And only recently have we become aware how close we came to losing the legacy of 1776 to the machinations of a new kind of American—rootless, humorless, resentful, the kind of scary contemporary man whose dead eyes, numbness to language, and general poverty of spirit are nevertheless more typical of this century than of this country. Still, between the press, the Congress, and the people, we managed to save the nation from such zealots.

For myself, I accept being an American with equanimity, if not always joy. Prodigious energy has always troubled the air here, and I see little diminution of that energy in these befuddling times. I see a black man from South Carolina speaking his way into national leadership. I see consumer groups keeping tabs on everything from aerosol cans to the Alaska pipeline. I see the federal government belatedly paying for the land it stole from the Seminoles over a century ago. I see conformity, apathy, corruption, and greed, but I also see tremendous concern about them—some of it silly, some of it selfish—but all of it evidencing the age-old American conviction that—damn it!—something can be *done.*

The cynics, in our Bicentennial Year, morosely prophesied that the promise of two hundred years ago had been soiled beyond cleansing. They spoke of rewriting the Constitution in terms that made one wonder whether they had ever read it. Ten years later, the boosters talked nostalgically about a small-town America that existed only in the paintings of Norman Rockwell. What neither could accept was the diversity and uproar that have always characterized our attempts to build some sort of workable society here. But the plain fact of the matter is that every American has an ideal America in his head, which some other American is continually threatening.

In defense of my own "America," I'll confess an unpopular sentiment: I have an outrageous love for my country and my countrymen. The extravagance and the moodiness, the inventiveness and the chicanery, the humor and the dead-serious craziness, even the blunders and the excesses—there's some stubborn hope in it all, it seems to me. In what other country could one be treated to the dubious spectacle of Abby *and* Julius Hoffman, Patty *and* William Randolph Hearst? Though we are not one race, though we came from many backgrounds and out of many traditions, and, but for the Indians, are all immigrants (and even *they* came from Siberia), nevertheless by some mysterious process of amalgamation that holds out hope for a world

266

that must become *one* world or perish, we have, often gracelessly, become one people, and this may be the only country in the world that has failed to become a nation in the traditional sense—that is, a *Father-* or *Mother-land,* but has achieved the attributes of nationhood anyway.

What do we have to remember? The distance we have come since the terrified colonists first felt the power and the challenge of this all-but-manless continent. What do we have to celebrate? *Ourselves.* "The better angels of our nature," as our most complex president once said.

That's a peculiarly American idea, assuming (as it does) human perfectability, and the limitlessness of life. And it's an idea about man and society that we've never really abandoned in these two hundred plus years. We step on the moon in the name of mankind. We inconvenience our children in the cause of justice long-delayed. We go on disputing with one another day and night, year in, year out, and yet the Republic stands.

So let's blow out the candles and make a wish. That we will come to understand our uniqueness at last. That we will listen to the Shenandoah calling us beyond the wide Missouris that lie ahead of us as a people. That we will be braver, wiser captains of the huckleberry party.